Fruit from a Poisonous Tree

Fruit from a Poisonous Tree

Mel Stamper

iUniverse, Inc.
New York Bloomington

Fruit from a Poisonous Tree

iUniverse books may be ordered through booksellers or by contacting:

iUniverse
1663 Liberty Drive
Bloomington, IN 47403
www.iuniverse.com
1-800-Authors (1-800-288-4677)

ISBN: 978-0-595-52496-9 (pbk)
ISBN: 978-0-595-62549-9 (ebk)

Printed in the United States of America

But of the tree of the knowledge of good and evil, thou shalt not eat of it: for in the day that thou eatest thereof thou shalt surely die.

(Genesis 2:17)

WHAT OTHERS ARE SAYING

"This book is a veritable powerhouse that shatters, in one instant, the wall of lies and deceit that took decades to build upon our impressionable minds. Stamper's ability to explain complex legal and political information in a comprehensive yet concise manner is without equal. Like a master sculptor he has chipped away the 'Words of Art and Deception' to reveal the inescapable and undeniable Truth. This book has single-handedly bared Adam and Eve's shame in the Garden, the cleverly crafted schemes ('Fruits from a Poisonous Tree') of a Power-lusting Elite ('The Serpent' and his minions)."

~ Paul Nash, DC, ND, CCN, ACU, Holistic Medicine, Minneapolis

"If only a portion of what this researcher has discovered is verifiable, we as a nation of free people must hang our heads in shame. The future generations will not forgive us or forget the terrible injustice we have let befall them."

~ Fred Diaulas, Professor of Ethics, University of North Florida

"As a young Marine officer, I believed without question that my government was infallible and most assuredly on the side of the Angels. Now I know how wrong I was, and I'm angry at myself for not questioning its policies or the continued restrictions on the liberties of its citizens. It took another Marine to uncover it."

~ William P. Negron, Lt. Col., U.S. Marine Corp, retired

"In 1954 I began my legal practice as an assistant district attorney in the city of Miami. We switched from common law pleading to statutory pleading and no one asked the question, Why? Now I know the answer to the unasked question, and it depresses me to no end."

~ Ralph G. Mitchell, JD, Attorney at Law, St. Augustine, Florida

Contents

FOREWORD

Melvin Stamper has experienced a remarkable life journey few of us will ever experience. His background in law and criminal investigation has enabled him to uncover facts of the crime of the millennium, exposing the motive along with the conspirators. The subtle and not so subtle threats from the government agencies that he was investigating merely served as a motivating force and conformation of his investigation. Experience is the one factor we must all use in determining credibility of another, and Stamper's experience in law, analytical thinking and detection rivals that of any other in the investigation of a crime involving government subterfuge and cover-up.

This author served his country as a U.S. Marine in Southeast Asia, a police chief, railroad special agent, CIA intelligence source, industrial engineer, pilot, law professor, legal researcher, private investigator, and an ombudsman with the Department of Defense; his analytical skills were honed by all of his experience and education for the investigation of his life – the United States government.

My personal relationship with the author has spanned two decades, and he never stops amazing me with the information he uncovers.

Get comfortable and hold on to your hat!

J. Randolph Appleby, Municipal Judge, retired,
Newark, New Jersey

FRUIT FROM A POISONOUS TREE

INTRODUCTION

Several months prior to the writing of this book, I began questioning my motivation for doing so. I had a comfortable lifestyle with no real bone to pick with anyone, especially the government. I had achieved a comfortable financial position – well educated, firmly established in the legal profession and most importantly of all, I had a loving, caring family. What then motivated me to take on both the state and federal governments, the proverbial biggest bullies on the block?

The answer is that I had discovered that both the state and federal governments have been lying to and stealing from We the People. Of all criminals, the ones that are personally repugnant to me are liars and thieves. These species of criminal I cannot abide in any manner, from any source, especially the government. Ergo, the years of research uncovering the story you are about to read. The government and the international Global Elite have systematically stolen our wealth and our birthright as Americans. The title of this book, *FRUIT FROM A POISONOUS TREE*, explains the theft of our wealth and identity, and the book tells what we can do about it.

This story is not about high drama, but it has that. It is not a story about insatiable greed; it has that also. This story is about the planned, deliberate destruction of the United States of America by the archenemies of this nation who have been around since its inception – the Global Elite, whose identity you will discover.

During my investigation I became so overwhelmed by the government's deceit and unabashed arrogance that I went back to the history books trying to identify the point at which our republic swerved onto the destructive path towards democracy – where our creation, the government, servant of the people, became the master and we became the servant – where the nonproductive, who are consumers of the public treasury, elect politicians who promise them even more government benefits at the expense of the majority of productive, wealth-producing Americans. That is the democracy we live in today and our founding fathers' worst nightmare.

This change from a republican form of government to our present democracy was silent and insidious. There are many contributors to this metamorphosis who we might fault, both inside and outside of government, such as teachers, clergy, judges and politicians, but laying blame would solve nothing. Ultimately "We the People" are to blame; we are responsible. We have permitted both state our and federal governments to have control over our children's education, which has resulted in the dumbing down of generations so that most of us cannot detect the slow perversion of our freedom.

Thomas Jefferson cautioned us that *"freedom is not free; the price you must pay for freedom is eternal vigilance."*

As a people we have for many years been apathetic to the Congress, the President and the Judiciary, so much so that we never noticed the subtle, diminishing changes that were occurring to our freedom, right in plain sight. We have not been vigilant.

Somewhere along the way this plan for a republic went dreadfully wrong. Without any constitutional authority, the republic was transformed into a democracy. Now the President makes law by Executive Order, again without constitutional authority. The Congress is powerless because of fierce partisanship and the constant pursuit of money from the international corporations needed to perpetuate their political lives. The result is that they do nothing to check and balance the other runaway branches of our government. The agencies that were created by Congress to make and enforce regulations and administer the draconian laws of the Congress and the Executive branch now answer only to the diseased, corrupted body of the Executive branch, which answers to no one but the international cartel of bankers, philanthropists and senior level policy wonks.

These incomprehensible laws of Congress, especially the taxing statutes, are patently unconstitutional in their application to the citizens of the fifty states. But this seizure of the productive people's wealth for the benefit of the non-producing minority and the imprisonment of those who resist this theft have been ratified by a corrupted federal judiciary and Supreme Court. That briefly sums up our present day democracy and the state of the union.

Where did it all go wrong? You are about to find out, and you are not going to like it one bit.

I truly believe that many of the problems we have with government and the judiciary today stem from the deliberate bastardization of the English language by those in government.

The laws of English grammar are totally inflexible. It is absolutely impossible for any English-speaking nation that prides itself on the assertion that it is a nation of law and not of men, without adhering to a strict discipline in the use of the English language and grammar, to be anything other than a nation of men without law. Proper English is essential in the drafting of those national laws; otherwise tyranny will always be the end result.

The Supreme Court has pontificated that the Constitution is a living, breathing document, and that, as such, it must evolve with the changing society that it governs – that they, this majestic body of legal intellectuals, in this process of an ever-evolving society, must interpret the organic Constitution for us, the ignorant masses.

Preposterous!

The Constitution is written in plain English so that anyone with a fifth grade education can understand its simple meaning. It isn't written in Russian or Chinese and doesn't need interpretation. Does the Constitution get cold or hot, sick or diseased? Does it get old and senile?

The Constitution is not a living, breathing document. It's a dead tree! – a dead tree that was processed into paper so that eternal ideas and heavenly concepts of men governing themselves could be preserved for future generations. It was written by noble visionaries that we call our founding fathers. That is what the Constitution is, period!

The visions and concepts immortalized in the Constitution cannot evolve with our society, because man by the very nature of being man rarely rises to a higher level of nobility. We as a species usually evolve to a lower base of decadence – immorality – one notch above a slug; that's the nature of man and it has been so since the Garden of Eden.

The United States Constitution – this document that the learned justices say must evolve to keep up with our society – is why we were the only nation in the entire existence of the human race to ever promise life, liberty and the pursuit of happiness to all of its citizenry and then deliver on that promise. Look around and determine for yourself if we are a moral society that must have an evolving Constitution to keep up with us.

Our government has taken from us our common law and the protections it afforded us and replaced common law with government-made vulgar law, called statutory law, that strips us of our freedom by creating legal fictions and compelling performance from those legal fictions which common law did not.

As a nation we have more citizens in prison than any country in the world – over two million – and ninety percent of the crimes of which they are accused are victimless crimes. The law they violated most likely was paid for by corporations to protect them from us.

We, however, are the problem, because we operate like the tool of the new king and we do his bidding without questioning whether the law is a good law or a bad one. It is our responsibility as jurors to ask those questions, but we have let the prosecutor and the judge tell us what the law means instead of using God's gift of intelligence to discern for ourselves. We are responsible for determining not only the facts but also the law. If that were not true, then we would still have legal slavery and be prosecuting people for helping slaves escape under the Fugitive Slave Act. That law was interpreted and upheld by the courts of the time. Decent jurors who did not agree exercised their right of jury nullification, the most cherished right we as Americans possess.

We now have replaced morality with abortion on demand, and if we do not kill our children in the womb, we tax them to death the moment they are born. Does it not seem immoral to permit a Congress to spend money that it does not have so that every future generation will be obligated to pay, from their labor and property for their entire life, on a debt that is sixty or eighty years old? The moment your child is born, she has a debt to the Federal Reserve Bank, Inc., of $22,000 and rising. It is not only immoral; it is the thing of which violent revolutions are made. If we do not stop this insanity here and now, our grandchildren will, and it will not be pleasant. Waco, Texas, is the example of what the New King wanted us to see, because that is our future if we do not comply with the King's demands.

We permitted our government to negotiate and pass the NAFTA and GATT treaties, which guaranteed that this nation will never again be an industrial or technological world power, assuring that our people are doomed to a third-world agrarian life within the next fifty years.

As I write this introduction, my book is finished and I have reviewed its contents. Because of my knowledge of government corruption, I am becoming incensed while organizing my thoughts for this introduction. My antagonism was so great while I was researching that I expatriated my citizenship from the corporate UNITED STATES. That expatriation document is in the first chapter of this book and sets the tempo for the remainder. I hope that if nothing else you will come away from this reading experience a wiser and more determined citizen of your state, with a passion for recovering what was ours and what was stolen from us.

Melvin Stamper. JD. Sui Juris

CHAPTER ONE

CITIZENSHIP EXPATRIATION

Not like the brazen giant of Greek fame
With conquering limbs astride from land to land;
Here at our sea-washed, sunset gates shall stand
A mighty woman with a torch, whose flame
Is the imprisoned lightning, and her name
Mother of Exiles. From her beacon-hand
Glows world-wide welcome; her mild eyes command
The air-bridged harbor that twin cities frame,
"Keep, ancient lands, your storied pomp!" cries she
With silent lips. "Give me your tired, your poor,
Your huddled masses yearning to breathe free,
The wretched refuse of your teeming shore,
Send these, the homeless, tempest-tossed to me,
I lift my lamp beside the golden door!"

by Emma Lazarus, New York City, 1883

CITIZENSHIP IN MODERN AMERICA

In 1798, Thomas Jefferson instructed that "Congress has not unlimited power to provide for the general welfare, but only those specifically enumerated."

Wilson Nicholas, a delegate to the Virginia convention that ratified the Constitution, said, "Congress has power to define and punish for counterfeiting, and felonies committed on the high seas, and offenses against the laws of nations; but they can not define or prescribe the punishment for other crimes whatsoever without violating the Constitution."

Chief Justice Marshall said: "The police power unquestionably remains, and ought to remain, with the States."

Until this past century, federal courts upheld the view that the federal government could deal only with crimes specifically mentioned in the Constitution. In 1911 the Supreme Court said:

"Among the powers of the State not surrendered – which powers therefore remain with the State – is the power to so regulate the relative rights and duties of all within its jurisdiction as to guard the public morals, the public safety, and the public health, as well as to promote the public convenience and the common good."

At the founding of this Republic, there were only four federal crimes: treason, counterfeiting, piracy, and crimes against the law of nations. Now there are three thousand federal crimes, three hundred thousand federal administrative regulations, many of which are punishable as crimes, and about eighty-five thousand local governments with five hundred thirteen thousand elected officials, or one in every five hundred people. We have an estimated forty-five million laws – state, federal and local. God, the Creator of the universe, gave us only ten laws with which to live our lives, and although I fail often, I try to conduct my life by those Ten Commandments. It would be impossible, however, to obey forty-five million laws.

Those millions of laws and the government enforcers are destroying our Republic.

In 1900, one in every fifteen dollars went for government use; in the year 2000 it is nearly one in every two. We must contend with sixty-five times more laws than our grandfathers did at the turn of the 20th Century, the most cruel and unjust of those being the tax laws.

Every federal program takes on a life of its own, so it will be extremely difficult to transfer power from the federal government to the states. It is difficult to change, much less kill or transfer a federal program once it has been established, even after it has outlived its usefulness. The New Deal view of an all-powerful central government must be replaced with a firm separation of powers if this republic is to survive.

Increasingly in the last hundred years, powerful corporate interests have deliberately subverted the intent of the Founders by financing the appointment of judges who would enhance corporate and federal power and weaken the constitutional system of checks and balances.

While many today attack the New Deal as representing the demise of constitutional government in America, the assaults actually began in the late 1800s, when federal courts led by the Supreme Court started chipping away at state sovereignty. This allowed the federal government to assume numerous duties and responsibilities that under the constitution had been reserved to the states or the people.

Recalcitrant southern states did not turn to the Supreme Court to leave the Union before the Civil War, partly because the Constitution does not grant the federal courts the right to control state sovereignty. The Constitution did not create a judicial supremacy, and there is extensive evidence that the Founders never granted the Supreme Court the power to rule over the President, Congress, or the states.

Every July 4th we honor the signing of the Declaration of Independence. By signing that document, the founding fathers, many of whom were Deists, pledged their lives, fortunes, and sacred honor to the premise that all men are created equal, endowed by their Creator with unalienable rights, to be secured by a government that was subject to and inferior to the consent of the governed.

The British pursued them as traitors to the king. Of the fifty-six original signers, nine did not live to see freedom, five were imprisoned, and seventeen lost everything they had. Their sacrifice for the Constitution of the United States has guided this nation through a continuing effort to bring liberty and justice for all. Can any of us do less?

The courage of America's founders was based on their belief in God's Providence. George Washington called America's liberties "the object of Divine protection." James Madison, President and signer of the Constitution, affirmed their beliefs, saying, "Before any man can be considered as a member of civil society, he must be considered as a subject of the Governor of the Universe."

At the Constitutional Convention, Benjamin Franklin began the tradition of prayers in Congress, saying, "In the beginning of the contest with Great Britain, when we were sensible of danger, we had daily prayer in this room for Divine protection. Our prayers, sir, were heard, and they were graciously answered. I have lived, sir, a long time, and the longer I live, the more convincing proofs I see of this truth – that God governs in the affairs of men. And if a sparrow cannot fall to the ground without His notice, is it probable that an empire can rise without His aid?"

If our liberty and nation were still under God's protection, none of us would be reading this book; we would be in full measure out in pursuit of our happiness. By rejecting God's plan for our future, we have chosen to adopt man's temporal plan, and we must suffer the consequences of that choice.

Many years of legal research has led me down many paths in pursuit of truth. I didn't receive Truth in law school or at any time during my formal education, with the exception of a one-room schoolhouse in Kentucky. That school didn't receive any federal funds for education, so the subject matter the teacher taught was not restricted. Our teacher had a remarkable understanding of the national and state Constitution and the framers' intent, along with Thomas Jefferson's negotiations with the State legislature documented in the Kentucky Resolutions – fascinating reading then; visionary in the present day.

In later years far removed from that one-room schoolhouse, what I received at public schools supported by federal grant money was revisionist history and omission of the truth in everything other than the sciences. After all, I had an education controlled by the federal government's money. I was taught what the federal and state governments wanted me to learn – nothing more, and certainly not the truth.

The old axiom that "truth is the first casualty of war" is as close to any truth that you will ever find in your investigation of the federal government. That being the case, we have been lied to by our government and have been at war with our national government for a very long time, and I believe that is the truth.

As I write, for each of us within this country, our liberty is perishing – that liberty crushed beneath the constant growth of state and federal government power. More than ever before, the federal, state, and local governments are confiscating citizens' property, trampling rights, and decimating opportunities for any prosperous future you may have hoped for. Since 1933, a concentrated effort has been made to impoverish the people of America. Our wealth has been systematically stripped from us by rapacious taxation and outright theft in the form of usury (interest) and fractional reserve banking policy.

Federal agencies publish an average of over two hundred pages of new rulings, regulations, and proposals in the Federal Register each business day. The expansion of the federal code is one of the most obvious measures of the increase of administrative control over the citizen. The politicians' effort to socially engineer society by an endless multiplication of penalties, prohibitions, taxes and prison sentences, is a dismal failure. What has been lost in their effort is our freedom.

The attack on the individual's rights has reached a point in our lives where a citizen has no right to the use of his own land if the bureaucracy determines it to be a wetland, no right to the money in his pocket or bank account if an IRS agent determines he has taxes owed, and no right to his property if a duck, flying south for the winter, lands in a puddle in his backyard. A man's home is his castle, except when a politician wants the land the house is built on for a low cost housing project.

In America today, a citizen's use of his own property is presumed illegal until approved by multiple zoning and planning commissions. Since 1985, federal, state, and local governments have seized the property of over two hundred thousand Americans under asset forfeiture laws, often with no more evidence of wrongdoing than an unsubstantiated assertion made by an anonymous government informant.

Government officials now exert vast arbitrary power over citizens' daily lives, from Equal Employment Opportunity Commission bureaucrats that can levy a $145,000 fine on a St. Louis small businessman because he did not have 8.45 minorities on his payroll ... to the Minnesota and Wisconsin departments of natural resources, which regulate property so that you may not use the lake or swamp contained on your land because an endangered mouse species lives nearby.

Federal agricultural bureaucrats can prohibit Arizona farmers from selling fifty-eight percent of their fresh lemons to other Americans.

Customs Service inspectors can destroy import shipments without compensating the owners.

Federal bank regulators are officially empowered to seize the assets of any citizen for allegedly violating written or unwritten banking regulations.

Federal regulations dictate what price milk must sell for, what size California nectarines can be sold, what crops a person may grow on his own land, what apparel items a woman may sew in her own home, and how old a person must be to buy a beer, even though he is old enough to die for his country.

The Internal Revenue Service is carrying out a massive campaign against the self-employed that seeks to force over half of America's independent contractors to abandon their own businesses.

NAFTA and GATT agreements are forcing small industries into bankruptcy because their customers have moved to Mexico or Indonesia.

Government agencies are more out of control than ever before, and the Supreme Court, the supposed bastion and protector of the Bill of Rights, has ratified the power of these federal employees.

Privacy is vanishing beneath the rising floodtide of government power. Government officials have asserted a de facto right to search anybody, any time, on the pretext of "terrorism."

The average American now has no freedom from having government agents strip-search his children, rummage through his luggage, ransack his house, sift through his bank records, and trespass in his fields. Today, a citizen's constitutional right to privacy can be nullified by the sniff of a dog.

Federal officials have given rewards to hundreds of airline ticket clerks for reporting the names of individuals who paid for their tickets in cash, thereby allowing police to confiscate the rest of people's money on mere suspicion of illegal behavior.

Local police are conducting programs in two hundred thousand classrooms that sometimes result in young children informing police on parents who violate drug laws.

The number of federally authorized wiretaps has almost quadrupled since 1980 (except the ones intended to catch spies of our nuclear secrets), and the Federal Bureau of Investigation is trying to prohibit development of new types of phones that would be more difficult to wiretap. The demagogues in Congress are rabid with the intent of taking away our right to carry and bear arms. Could this description of events occurring in the United States today have applied to pre-war Nazi Germany?

Freedom of speech and freedom of the press are increasingly under assault. The proliferation of vague federal regulations have had a severe chilling effect on the free speech of millions of businessmen who cannot criticize federal agencies without risking reprisal that could destroy them. Thanks to a 1992 federal appeals court decision and a late 1993 congressional uproar, even pictures of clothed children can now be considered pornographic, thus greatly increasing the number of Americans who can be prosecuted for violating obscenity laws by taking pictures of their own children.

The government is manufacturing more criminals now than ever before. It is increasingly choosing the citizen-target, creating the crime, and then vigorously prosecuting the violator. During the past fifteen years, law enforcement officials have set up thousands of elaborate schemes to entrap people for "crimes" such as buying plant supplies, asking for a job, or shooting deer. Hundreds of private accountants have become double agents, receiving government kickbacks for betraying their clients to the IRS.

Total federal spending has increased from under $100 billion in 1963 to over $3 trillion in 2002, and as spending has grown, so has bureaucratic control and political power. Since 1960, the federal government has created over a thousand new subsidy programs for everything from medical care to housing, from culture to transportation. Subsidies are the twentieth century's method of human conquest: slow political *coups d'etat* over one sector of the economy and society after another. Government subsidies have become a major factor in squeezing out unsubsidized developers, unsubsidized schools, unsubsidized theater producers, and unsubsidized farmers. The money is extorted out of the lifeblood of the citizen by rapacious and unlawful taxes while the subsidies slowly smother his freedom. A government powerful enough to give you everything is powerful enough to take everything away.

Former President Clinton set aside 1.7 million acres of Utah to be protected by the federal government. That sounds warm and fuzzy until you understand that the land federalized was the nation's largest reserve of soft coal. The electric utilities must now buy their coal for electrical generation from Indonesia – soft coal owned by the Lipo group, the same organization that donated millions to Clinton's election campaign.

Beggaring the taxpayer has become the main achievement of the welfare state. The federal tax system is turning individuals into sharecroppers of their own lives. The private economy has become an agent of the federal government. At least fifty percent of the total productive resources of our nation are now being organized through the political market in the form of taxes. In that very important sense, we are more than half socialist. The average American now works over half of each year simply to pay the cost of government tax and regulation.

High taxes have created a moral inversion in the relationship between the citizen and the state. Before the income tax, the government existed to serve the people at least in some vague nominal sense; now the people exist to provide financial grain for the state's mill. Federal court decisions have often bent over backward to stress that citizens' rights are nearly null and void in conflicts with the Internal Revenue Service. IRS seizures of private property have increased by six hundred percent since 1980 and now hit over three million Americans each year.

Not only do we have more laws and regulations than ever before, but the laws themselves are becoming less clear, consistent, or coherent. An example is the tax code. In 1913, a debate was held on the Senate floor regarding the first income tax act under the 16th Amendment. Senator Elihu Root commented about the complexity of that first law. His comment was humorous then; it is hilarious now:

"I guess you will have to go to jail. If that is the result of not understanding the Income Tax Law, I shall meet you there. We shall have a merry, merry time, for all of our friends will be there. It will be an intellectual center, for no one understands the Income Tax Law except persons who have not sufficient intelligence to understand the questions that arise under it."

All the confusion over an eighty-page Act then is exponentially compounded now by the current ten thousand-plus page Internal Revenue Code 26 USC, along with more than thirty thousand pages of implementing Internal Revenue regulations – 26 CFR and some borrowed from 27 CFR. It is now practically impossible for citizens to keep track of government's latest edicts.

Today the law has become a tool with which to force people to behave in ways politicians approve, which is politically correct, rather than a clear line that citizens can respect in order to live their lives in privacy and peace.

With the proliferation of retroactive regulations, government agencies now have the right to change the rules of the game at any time, even after the game is over.

The "Rule of John Ashcroft," whereby federal officials on a whim create new rules to bind and penalize private citizens, has replaced the Rule of Law – the classical concept endorsed by the Massachusetts Constitution of 1780 as a restraint on government power.

Each night we are deluged with "cop" shows that reveal how far out of its box the beast of government has crawled. Government agents dressed like military commandos wearing black jumpsuits, bulletproof vests and armament that would give a seasoned military force pause to reflect, wear full head masks to conceal their identity. No one busy doing the constitutional work of the Republic needs to wear ski masks concealing their identity. Criminals and outlaws wear masks, not constitutional officers. They bash in doors and throw the inhabitants to the floor, screaming children watching in horror as their parents are manacled and dragged off to prison.

The government is supposed to set the example that we the citizens are required to emulate. When the government breaks the law, then there exists no law. We have anarchy. That, I am afraid, is the state of the union as of today.

In the famous Supreme Court case of Elkins Et Al v. United States, 364 U.S. 206, the Court, reinforcing judicial integrity, stated:

"In a government of laws, existence of the government will be imperiled if it fails to observe the law scrupulously. Our government is the potent, the omnipresent teacher. For good or ill, it teaches the whole people by its example. Crime is contagious. If the government becomes a lawbreaker, it breeds contempt for law, it invites every man to become a law unto himself, and it invites anarchy."

The time in which Justice Brandeis spoke was a simpler time, and the government had not broken the chains with which the Constitution bound it down. Unfortunately, the federal judiciary has opted out of the Separation of Powers doctrine of the Constitution, and now has become self-regulating.

The courts do not maintain their independence as a judiciary. Without constitutional authority, the system elevates judges above the law. The courts are no longer our courts of justice or a bastion of freedom. With the passage of the War Powers Act of 1933, they have become the Executive's tool. The judges are little more than organized crime families. They have invaded the people's court and now only impersonate and give lip service to justice by exchanging obfuscation and sophistry in place of a justice system, void of any form of judicial integrity.

Enforcing judicial standards on judges under this system is impossible. Even though the court has rules, the judges make up their own rules as they go or break the rules with impunity whenever it is convenient for them to do so.

How can you take a judge to court when the judges control the court and have granted themselves immunity from prosecution? How do you call the police when it is the police who are breaking the law? The judges' dishonesty is contagious, and the government as teacher has sewn the seeds of discontent and anarchy.

The LORD God Almighty has granted a judge immense power to judge His creation, we the people. But along with that power comes immense responsibility in that the LORD on the Day of Judgment will hold each judge to a higher standard of judgment.

The people have learned their lessons well. They follow by example, and the example of the courts and the criminal justice system has led the people to behave criminally, just as Justice Brandeis predicted.

Government now appears more concerned with dictating personal behavior and political correctness than with protecting citizens from the private violence of murderers, muggers, and rapists. In 1990, for the first time in history, the number of people sentenced to prison for drug violations exceeded the number of people sentenced for violent crime. The number of people incarcerated in federal and state prisons in 2001 was almost four times the number incarcerated in 1980, and America now has a higher percentage of its population in prison than any other country in the world – two million people. If those on probation and parole are taken into account, the number controlled by the justice system is over six million. So much for "the land of the free and home of the brave," which is now just another oxymoron akin to "military intelligence."

Unfortunately, the more that government has tried to manage people's behavior, the more unmanageable American society has become. Gangs have replaced families, resulting in a greater proliferation of drugs and illegal weapons. Our babies are becoming parents with no jobs or education, spiraling an entire generation of children into grinding poverty and third world expectations of life.

We have lost our moral compass as a people and have embraced a secular view of morality rather than God's. This observable fact, as America has entered the new millennium, is the circumstance of the New World Order, as envisioned and planned for a very long time by the International Banking cartel and the United Nations.

Oppression has become more refined and more insidious in recent decades. We frequently see scenes like IRS agents dragging Amish tax resisters out of their scanty homes or the Los Angeles police beating a suspect. We can expect to see the frequency of similar scenarios escalate as we are pushed forward into a global government and the New World Order.

The fact that only a minimum number of people physically resist government agents is not confirmation that the state is violating fewer people's rights. The level of tyranny imposed by government agencies is less evident today primarily because the vast majority of citizens capitulate to government demands before the government resorts to enforcement. America is ripe for a cataclysmic revolution. The lack of an armed uprising is not evidence of a lack of discontent and hostility. Six corporations presently control all forms of media (newspaper, TV, radio, etc.) in the United States, and they have been diligent accomplices in a massive cover-up of federal crimes and oppression of the people.

Many Americans apparently believe politicians and policy experts have been wise enough to create a government that does not crush the people it was created to protect and serve. The question of individual liberty is now often marketed as a question of a ruler's intentions toward the citizen. But lasting institutions are far more important than transient intentions.

The last seventy-five years have seen the sapping of most constitutional restraints on capricious government power. American political assessment suffers from a predisposition to appraise government by exalted ideals rather than by insipid and shocking reality. We have a romantic tendency to judge politicians by their dictum rather than by their day-to-day actions and a tendency to view the growth of government power by its promise rather than by its results.

The decline of liberty is not primarily from specific acts of government, but from the collective force of hundreds of thousands of decrees, hundreds of taxes, and thousands of officials with unrestricted power over other Americans.

Our political leaders say they have tried to improve the quality of life by multiplying the amount of intimidation, by militarizing police power, by giving one group of people the power of invention over others as to how they must conduct their affairs.

The power accumulating in a central government is not put on display at the Smithsonian Institute; it is exercised in day-to-day life. The larger it becomes, the more oppressive it will become, regardless of the intentions of those who advocate larger government.

The average American's understanding of liberty and the threat to its survival has declined sharply since the nation's birth. The Massachusetts colonists rebelled after the British agents received "writs of assistance" that allowed them to search any colonist's property.

Modern Americans submit passively to law enforcement sweep searches of buses, schools, and housing projects without valid search warrants. Virginia revolted in part because King George imposed a two-pence tax on the sale of a pound of tea. Americans today are complacent while Congress imposes billions of dollars in taxes, increasing the projected federal debt into double digit trillions.

Federal agencies have the power to act as prosecutor, judge, and jury in suits against private citizens. Maine revolted primarily because the British Parliament issued a decree confiscating every white pine tree in the colony; modern Americans are largely complacent when local regulatory agencies impose almost unlimited restrictions on individuals' rights to use their own property.

The initial battles of the Revolution occurred after British troops tried to seize the colonists' private weapons; today, residents in Chicago, Washington, D.C., and other cities submit to de facto prohibition on handgun ownership imposed by the same government that grossly fails to protect the citizen from private violence.

The 1775 Revolution was largely a revolt against growing arbitrary power. Nowadays, seemingly the only principle is to have *no* political principle: to judge each act of government in a vacuum – to assume that each expansion of government power and nullification of individual rights will have no future impact. The Founding Fathers looked with horror at the liberties that they were losing, while modern Americans focus myopically on the freedoms that they still retain.

America needs fewer laws, not more prisons. The Founding Fathers realized that some amount of government was necessary in order to prevent a "war of all against all." By trying to seize far more power than is necessary or granted by the Constitution over American citizens, the federal government is destroying its own legitimacy. We face a choice not of anarchy or fascism, but a choice of limited or unlimited government. Because it is a necessary evil, it is necessary to vigilantly limit government's disruption of citizens' lives.

We the people delegated to ourselves the responsibility as the ultimate protector of the Constitution. We the People are the ultimate court. When our government is unwilling or refuses to abide by the constitutional mandates we required, it is our sacred duty to stand up against that government and to either alter or abolish it.

But oppression remains an evil that must be minimized in a free society. The ideal is not to abolish all government, but to structure it so as to achieve the greatest respect for citizens' rights and the least violation of their liberty.

The question is not whether Americans have lost all their liberties, but whether the average American is becoming less free with each passing year – with each session of Congress – with each new shelf row of Federal Register Publications.

American liberty can still be rescued from the encroachments of government. The first step to saving our liberty is to realize how much we have already lost, how we lost it, and how we will continue to lose our liberties unless fundamental political changes occur.

I would propose that the Constitution be amended to require that the entire House of Representatives be composed only of females and the Senate be composed only of males. That would be a natural balance of power. It works in families; why not Congress and the American family?

The most recent example of congressional action and loss of liberty can be found in the new PATRIOT Act (short for "Uniting and Strengthening America by Providing Appropriate Tools Required to Intercept and Obstruct Terrorism").

This act of Congress primarily expands existing law, giving federal law enforcement agencies greater intelligence-gathering power, and has the effect of curtailing or eroding constitutional protections for citizens. In the wake of September 11th, most of us believed that the law might be reasonable in granting enforcement agencies these expanded powers. But the facts as have been revealed by Congress do not support that contention. That tragedy occurred not because of inadequate anti-terrorism law, but because of the federal intelligence agencies' own internal procedural failure.

The PATRIOT Act does not, therefore, help us to fight terrorism better. What it does do is:

1. It upsets the balance of power in our government, putting unnecessary power in the hands of the Executive, and brings us one step closer to what Chancellor Hitler achieved in pre-war Germany.

2. Increases the administrative burden on presently overburdened intelligence agencies; making terrorism more difficult for them to fight.

3. Destroys many of our hard-won unalienable rights and liberties for which so many of our ancestors and our own generation fought and died.

The Patriot Act is a complicated law. I have assembled for this Chapter the sections which I feel are most troubling. Specifically, the Patriot Act:

1. Permits agents of law enforcement to enter and search your home, in secret, without ever informing you. The U.S. Constitution requires not only probable cause to search, but that you are notified of the search. Section 213 of the Patriot Act disembowels the notice requirement of the 4th Amendment.

2. Section 216 of the act permits agents of the government to tap your phone or computer without probable cause having been established. Under this section, a judge MUST authorize a warrant as long as law enforcement agents certify that the surveillance is "relevant to an ongoing criminal investigation." No probable cause of criminal activity is required to issue the warrant, and the criminal activity does not have to have anything to do with terrorism. This violates the probable cause provision of the 4th Amendment. So for all intents and purposes, the 4th Amendment is a dead letter.

3. In addition, Section 218 permits the government agent to carry out secret searches and wiretaps without showing probable cause merely by certifying that there is a "significant" foreign intelligence purpose. This also evades the 4th Amendment protection.

4. Section 411, in tandem with section 802, expands the power of government to designate a group as a "foreign terrorist organization." Any group which endorses so-called "terrorist activity" which under 802 may be otherwise a lawful protest activity, can be designated as a terrorist organization. This would enable government to designate such groups as the California Tree Huggers, Protestors in Puerto Rico objecting to bombing of their land, or those Protestors against the World Trade Organization, as terrorists, such as in Seattle, New York, Chicago and Washington. Good-bye, 1st Amendment.

5. Section 411 also allows the government to indict anyone who provides material support or assistance to a terrorist organization. It is now possible for the federal government to determine that a domestic organization is in fact a terrorist group, i.e. the Michigan Militia, or Save a Patriot, American Rights Litigators, or any group who may disagree with government policy. One man makes the determination of terrorist – the President. No evidence is necessary and no court can stop that designation. No more 5th Amendment!

6. Section 412 of the PATRIOT Act permits the government to arrest and detain immigrants indefinitely for nothing more than a visa violation. In fact, of the one thousand, two hundred known immigrant detentions since 9/11, the ACLU determined that only about five had been detained on terrorism-related charges.

7. Section 802 creates the crime of "domestic terrorism." This criminalizes any acts of any member of the public that merely appear to the government's determination to be intended to "influence the policy of the government by intimidation or coercion" or to "intimidate or coerce a civilian population." This section would make just about any act of civil disobedience in protest against government policy into an act of domestic terrorism. Anyone who responds in writing to the IRS by objecting to one of its decisions could and probably will be labeled a domestic terrorist. There goes the 5th Amendment.

Our Congress, at the urging of the President and the Attorney General, has enacted criminal, unconstitutional legislation. As an example of its new application, we now see what is planned for the rest of us.

Attorney General John Ashcroft said, "If you don't agree with the government, YOU are a terrorist."

Attorney General Ashcroft pushed the U.S. Patriot Act through an overwhelmingly dim-witted Congress soon after September 11th. He has subverted more elements of the Bill of Rights than any Attorney General in American history. This is the same man who was beaten by a dead man in his bid for the Senate.

Under the Justice Department's new definition of "enemy combatant" (which won the enthusiastic approval of the President and Defense Secretary Donald Rumsfeld) anyone can be defined as an "enemy combatant," very much including American citizens, and they can be held indefinitely by the government, without charges, a hearing, or a lawyer – in short, incommunicado. Good-bye the entire Bill of Rights.

Now more Americans are also going to be dispossessed of every fundamental legal right in our system of justice and put into camps.

Ashcroft's terrorism FBI guidelines:

"The nature of the conduct engaged in by a [terrorist] enterprise will justify an inference that the standard [for opening a criminal justice investigation] is satisfied, even if there are no known statements by participants that advocate or indicate planning for violence or other prohibited acts."

That conduct can be simply "intimidating" the government, according to the USA Patriot Act. This book would qualify under those guidelines.

The following words of Thomas Jefferson from the Kentucky Resolutions sound as though they were written yesterday in describing the Patriot Act.

"That if the acts before specified should stand, these conclusions would flow from them; that the general government may place any act they think proper on the list of crimes, and punish it themselves whether enumerated or not enumerated by the constitution as cognizable by them: that they may transfer its cognizance to the President, or any other person, who may himself be the accuser, counsel, judge and jury, whose suspicions may be the evidence, his order the sentence, his officer the executioner, and his breast the sole record of the transaction: that a very numerous and valuable description of the inhabitants of these States being, by this precedent, reduced, as outlaws, to the absolute dominion of one man, and the barrier of the Constitution thus swept away from us all, no rampart now remains against the passions and the powers of a majority in Congress to protect from a like exportation, or other more grievous punishment, the minority of the same body, the legislatures, judges, governors and counselors of the States, nor their other peaceable inhabitants, who may venture to reclaim the constitutional rights and liberties of the States and the people, or who for other causes, good or bad, may be obnoxious to the views, or marked by the suspicions of the President, or be thought dangerous to his or their election, or other interests, public or personal…"

Jefferson's statement is as valid in 2003 as it was in 1798. It lends a chilling historical prospective to the present "Patriot Act" and our present condition compared to events in America in 1798 brought on by the Alien and Sedition Act (Whiskey Rebellion).

Congress and the other branches of the federal government are not a party to the Constitution; they are products of it. The Constitution vests Congress with certain delegated authorities under Article I; nothing more. Within its own borders, state authority is antecedent to that of the United States, and as parties to the Constitution, the several states have both the right and responsibility to correct their agent, the United States, when ambition seeks to abuse or expand powers which have been delegated.

Of more immediate importance where the instant matter is concerned, those who exceed the law, whether of the State or the United States, are accountable to the law of the land and, ultimately, to the People of the land within the several States. Operation under color of law is outlaw, criminal, and accountability must be in law. Judges, magistrates, attorneys for the Department of Justice, and enforcement people do not have immunity when they exceed the law as it is written.

This War on Terrorism is not a war at all. Congress is the only constitutional body that can declare war. It is a convenient tool being used by the President to expand power and control over each of us Citizens – nothing more. The government will not be happy until the last vestiges of our Constitution are torn from us, leaving no protection from the servitude expected from us all.

The federal government has never kept its word in either the conduct of internal policy (Constitution), in treaties with the Indians or in international policy.

The course of conduct being displayed by the government is merely ensuring that new generations of "terrorists" are being created at home as well as abroad.

The Constitution was written and the federal government created in order to insure that all of our liberties were protected even during times of war. They have failed miserably in that task. Ashcroft now says that "we will protect you, but some of your liberty must be surrendered to enable us to protect you." Rubbish!!!

It is time that all Americans with courage say to the federal government, "Go to Hell!" There can be no higher expression of patriotism than opposing your government when you believe they are wrong. That should be the responsibility of our state governments, but they have bought into the federal agenda because it expands their power and control over us and they are no better than the federal fascists that they emulate.

Freedom is a word not often reflected on by us. Thomas Jefferson said, "Freedom is not free; the price we must pay for freedom is eternal vigilance." Collectively we have not been vigilant, and now we can see the result of our apathy.

It is not too late to correct our agent, the federal and state governments. Individually we are not a threat to the vested interests of the new king, but collectively we can still control if we wake up and smell the dead rotting corpse of this once great republic. Together we must demand that they cease and desist in their plan for world domination and control over us before the United States of America crashes, smoking and burning, upon the scrap pile of history.

When I left the battlefield of Southeast Asia, I vowed that I would never again take up arms against another human being, and I never will. But as long as I have a breath in my body and a right of freedom of expression, I will educate, agitate, and indoctrinate as many of my fellow Americans as possible in order to stop or delay this march into madness that we are now on.

The Administration forced a vote on the Patriot Act before many legislators even had a chance to read it. That is the way the world elite always slip in legislation that destroys our freedom. That is the way the War Powers Act of 1933, the Federal Reserve Act, and the 16th and 17th Amendments to the Constitution all were passed into law. Then, NAFTA, GATT and countless other laws were shoved down our throat because Congress has no backbone or are co-conspirators in treason. The Patriot Act passed by a majority of 337 to 79.

We must prevent these changes from becoming malignant and spreading to the body politic. Insist that the Congress require these anti-terrorism laws be re-examined in a few years before they become permanent. This is your only chance to protest what may end up being the most significant event in our nation's history – events that your grandchildren will not forgive you for if you do nothing.

Some people argue that we live in a "lenient" society that has more than enough liberty – that we can afford to lose some. Others have argued that only those people who are criminals or buying and selling drugs or gun owners have concern about the Bill of Rights.

Some might think my perception is too negative; they are probably correct. But being a sentinel for freedom is my responsibility and yours as well if we wish to remain a great nation. On my way to Hawaii three weeks after the New York tragedy, I was sitting next to a young woman who worked for the World Bank in Washington. She maintained those sentiments. As I excused myself and moved to another seat, I told her that I was not going to spend the next seven hours listening to an idiot mouth concepts about which she had absolutely no understanding of the gravity of her conclusions.

In my opinion, most of the general population who espouse those beliefs do not have the brains God gave a goose. They don't realize that once the freedom is given away, it will never be returned, and the rights which are used by criminals to evade incarceration are the same rights which protect each of us. If one is denied that right, so too will all be denied that right.

In undergraduate school, I took several American history courses, as that subject has been of interest to me for the last thirty years and it is an excellent foundation for law. But I discovered that what was written in the history books was not the same as what was written in the settled case law of that same time period. The law is where the true history of a nation is found, not in a revisionist history book.

This nation's history is composed of many great dreams and ambitions which were sacrificed upon the altar of "pragmatism," "necessity," "circumstance" and "thousands of dead heroes." Our constitutional rights are like that.

The government has never simultaneously observed all the first Ten Amendments to the Constitution for the United States of America as they are actually written. The government, all three branches, has always been quick to say, "That's not what they meant," as if we are too stupid to read the simple language of that compact and understand the founders' intent; and that's in good times.

In dreadful times, when things get difficult and Americans are concerned, distressed, or angry, things get suddenly worse. This has been true from the very start of our nation.

Here are some examples of American history that we were not taught in school.

The second President, John Adams, a founding father (a forefather of Yours Truly), someone who should have known better, got the Alien and Sedition Acts passed. That law allowed the deportation of any non-citizen who was judged to be dangerous to the United States even if the country was not actually at war. No trial was required. The Sedition Act made criticizing the government a prison offense. These laws were passed and used to silence the public's opposition to Adam's foreign policy, especially used to imprison newspaper publishers of the opposing political party (Thomas Jefferson's Democratic Republicans). A long time ago, right? That may be so, but it was the beginning of a tradition within our body politic.

In the twentieth century, there was the infamous Sedition Act in World War I. It was used to jail social reformers, activists, and other people with whom the government disagreed and, if they were non-citizens, to expel them. Specifically, it made speaking out against war a prison offense. Prominent journalists and civil libertarians were jailed for merely reading from the Constitution. Oliver Wendell Holmes, the famous "liberal" Supreme Court justice, voted to uphold this curtailment of the First Amendment with his now famous statement comparing the activism for peace during war to "shouting fire in a crowded theater." I have often believed that a judge is a lawyer with a 50 I.Q. – nothing more.

The next shameful event in our history which still plagues us to this day was the "War Powers Act of 1933." This Act permitted President Roosevelt to make law in the form of Executive Order, bypass Congress and create his socialist state. We (citizens of this country) were ever after to be considered enemies of the United States who must be licensed to engage in any commercial activity. With the aid of the Federal Reserve (the same people who created the Depression), the President confiscated our gold and silver coin and replaced it with worthless pieces of paper and a debt system that will eventually destroy this great country. Our land and our labor were pledged to the Federal Reserve Bank, Inc., as collateral for a debt system that could never be paid. How can this most important event in our history not be taught in school?

Everyone knows about the imprisonment of Japanese Americans during the Second World War. All people of Japanese descent, even natural-born Americans, were subject to detention in prison camps. The federal government jailed 120,000 men, women, and children for three years for the crime of being Japanese. The Supreme Court upheld the capture, internment, and the effective seizure of their property. That fact alone confirms my theory that they all have IQs of 50 or lower.

The Smith Act, also passed during this period – in 1940, before America's entry into WWII – mandated the fingerprinting and registration of all aliens in the United States. To be an unregistered alien was against the law. This law also outlawed all organizations that advocated the overthrow of the government, perhaps a reasonable measure in war, but this law was passed during peacetime. The Smith Act was abused to jail labor leaders, socialists and communists who were opposed to the ways of the robber-baron capitalists, the very ones who created the conditions for the Great Depression.

The Red scare of the 30s and the communist witch-hunt, of the 40s and 50s ruined many American lives. Their only crime was to know the "wrong people," or to hold liberal opinions, or to have such opinions in their youth and the gall to stand up to demagogues and others who used anti-Communism as the key to increasing their own power.

The 1950 Internal Security Act, passed by a super-majority to override Truman's veto, required registration of people and groups who were communists or who had beliefs similar to communists. It created detention centers around the country, which would be filled with FBI-identified subversives if the President declared an emergency. Those detention centers are still in existence and new ones have been built all over this country to hold us. There are over forty-three of them at present under the direct control of the Federal Emergency Management Agency (FEMA).

More recently, many are familiar with the history of the civil rights and anti-Vietnam War movement. Did you also know that the FBI's operation Co-intelligence Program (CointelPro), approved at the highest levels of government, had as its object the suppression of those who worked to change the system? It was used to intimidate the membership, discredit leadership, and even put into jail those who fought for freedom and peace, in a manner that was not only grossly immoral but also completely illegal. That was only thirty years ago.

And there is Watergate and Nixon's inches-thick list of enemies. He used the power of the IRS, FBI, Customs, and other federal agencies to harass or eliminate his political opponents and everyone he suspected of disloyalty or political opposition. That took place only twenty-five years ago.

And now, after twenty-five years of drug war and a drug-war friendly Supreme Court, we've seen our protections under the 4th and 5th Amendments eroded to nothing. All of these deprivations of liberty are always under the pretext of some alleged war.

We're at a watershed point in our nation's history. Not everyone who cries, "We must fight terrorism!" is really a friend of the Republic and freedom. Some people think that we should live in a society with a lot fewer "civil rights." They believe that some opinions should be illegal, some activism should be forbidden. It is this type of individual that permeates the Congress and the federal judiciary.

Will these new laws affect you?

Maybe not at first, perhaps. They'll be used to stop people with whose opinions you disagree – to jail civilian militiamen from Montana and Michigan; to put a stop to the KKK, ACLU, Operation Rescue, or Green Peace. Depending on your political beliefs, that's a good thing, right?

But the way of judging such a law is not how it operates today, but how it will operate when your most feared enemy is in control. Who is your most feared enemy? If no one you know now qualifies for that position, imagine what use these new laws could be put to by Hitler, Stalin, Osama bin Laden, or even George Bush, Jr.

How would you safeguard your freedom and those of your friends and family when *your opinions* are labeled as terrorist?

My point is this: freedom walks a very narrow road. On one side of that road stands conformity, censorship of ideas, and the use of force to compel people in their role as citizen or antagonist. On the other side stands social engineering and political dissent. The only thing in the middle of the road is dead skunks and ignorant people.

That narrow road is supported by the Bill of Rights and the settled case law which support our rights. There's nothing magical about the Constitution; it's a dead tree ground into paper so those immortal, heavenly concepts of freedom and self-government could be memorialized. It's a document written by people for people and interpreted by other people. It can be followed or it can be ignored. If it's followed, there are a few precious, fundamental restrictions on government actions against the individual.

There is in the Constitution, for instance, a guarantee of due process of law before life, liberty, or property is taken from you. This isn't a guarantee that you won't be wrongly prosecuted, or that you won't be investigated or even punished for your beliefs. It's only a guarantee of exposure to other people, your fellow peers and the press, including some judges, who will be watching to see that the rules are being followed.

Sometimes that exposure is enough to make the difference; sometimes it's not. The judges are there only to make sure that the rules were followed. Justice does not reside in the courtroom. If you want justice, go to church: that's in God's hands. All the judiciary cares about is if the rules were followed; nothing more. The same Congress that has legislated our freedoms away writes the rules.

But when by our apathy we set aside those few guarantees contained in the Constitution – when we allow searches made in secret, the seizure of property without trial, the detention of people without proof of a crime or opportunity to defend themselves – then that form of democracy becomes a paradigm for disaster. Our silence is freedom's death knell.

People suffer because those who have and exercise power are imperfect people. They always make mistakes. They get eager in protecting us and, in so doing, forget that the actions of the over-eager bureaucracy are the clear and present danger to the people. Some of them have a desire to exercise and abuse their power, to silence their antagonists, to persecute those who are different from them, to make others bow to their demands. Those types of individuals make great prison guards, politicians and judges.

A strongly respected constitution helps keep a restraint on all that. Nothing but God can stop a government that is resolute to ignore its Constitution. The War Powers Act, Alien and Sedition Acts, Red scare, Watergate, CointelPro and now the Patriot Act, are examples in our shameful history that illustrate a government completely out of control.

But the Constitution was drafted in order to make things safer by introducing safeguards. Competing interests and the Separation of Powers doctrine between the three branches of government, each jealously protecting its own power, are the instruments by which our freedoms are enforced or should be.

When they are not, then you'd better watch your ass if your opinions are unpopular, unpalatable, or even dangerous to the status quo. The first rule of "Watching Your Ass" is making sure that you don't look or sound like an Enemy of the State. It's called the "Ostrich strategy." Self-censorship is always the first step in the loss of freedom, lest you draw attention and the power of those who might do you harm for speaking your opinion.

Self-censorship makes it easier for further more draconian steps to be taken, as no one says: "Stop! This is unconstitutional." We fear that if we said that, we might be singled out for government reprisal.

"When Hitler attacked the Jews, I was not a Jew, therefore I was not concerned. And when Hitler attacked the Catholics, I was not a Catholic, and therefore, I was not concerned. And when Hitler attacked the unions and the industrialists, I was not a member of the unions and I was not concerned. Then they attacked me and the Protestant church - and there was nobody left to be concerned."

This quote is from a pastor who opposed Nazism in Hitler's Germany. He was speaking for the reaction, or lack thereof, of all people of good will in Germany to the events that transpired there. It's the silence of people of good will that allows manifest evil and fascism to entrench its self. "Evil can flourish only when men of good will do nothing" is an ancient maxim that has profound meaning in our time.

I am not saying that the U.S. government is filled with Nazis. God willing, that specific species of human lunacy will never return. But the lessons learned in the fight against fascism should always live within us like a festering boil on the surface of our consciousness. Don't be silent, and don't censor yourself. Speak out against those in power and let them know you disagree and that you are watching their every move.

This is the responsibility of citizens in a Republic. I believe a Republic's strength does not result from voting. In our country, half don't vote because there isn't much in the way of a choice: There is Daryl, my brother Daryl and my other brother Daryl – not a penny difference between them. But we still have a strong country because people have a right and feel safe in expressing dissatisfaction. This operates as a relief valve for our frustrations and criticisms of those in power.

There's a partition between our leaders and us that has grown larger with each passing year and each new shelf row of Federal Register publications. Many of our representatives are hearing only the call from the President and Attorney General to give them more power in order to make us safe from terrorism, no matter the cost, no matter the loss of precious freedom. Absolute safety can be achieved only in a police state, and then it is the state that is the source of all terrorism. This has been the story of human societies from time immemorial.

Few of these new laws are made for the prosecution of a war on foreign terrorists. We already have every legal tool needed to do this. The purpose of most of these changes is for the collection of more information about Americans, without the regulation of a judge and the restrictions imposed by the Constitution. The law already allows intelligence and investigative agencies to spy on foreigners without any serious obstacle. These laws can be only for the monitoring and imprisonment of those living in the US who have differing opinions of what makes for a fair and just society, citizen or foreigner. The government's opinion may be diametrically opposed to your own.

Our war right now is against terrorists in the Middle East. The first people targeted in this country will be Arabs and Moslems. Since I'm not Arab or Moslem, it is none my concern. Next will be the civilian state militias. Since I am not a member of the militia, it is none my concern. Next will be the Christians with their belief in a power higher than the government.

Will there be anyone left to object?

We as the unified voice of We the People must, when the first of us is targeted, shout out from the highest hill…

Go to Hell!

CITIZENSHIP REPUDIATION

By Melvin Stamper, J.D., sui juris

To: Madeleine Albright
As: The SECRETARY OF STATE OF THE UNITED STATES
Washington, District of Columbia

AFFIDAVIT / ASSERTORY OATH AND REVOCATION OF CITIZENSHIP

This is to certify that I; Melvin Stamper, was born January 7th, 1940, in the Sovereign Republic State of Kentucky. I presently live upon the land of the Sovereign Republic State of Florida. I am not a Resident or Citizen of the UNITED STATES Government (Corporation), whose situs is Washington, the District of Columbia. My relationship to that Federal entity as far as jurisdiction is that of a non-resident alien to the Corporate United States Government.

I am a free and natural human man, described by the Lord God as a Living Soul, living under the common law and the fear of God. I have assumed among the Powers of the Earth, granted by the Lord God Almighty, the Separate and Equal Station to which the Laws of Nature and Nature's God entitle me. Therefore, in order to secure the Blessing of Liberty to my posterity and myself, to re-acquire my Birthright as a member of the Sovereign Body of "We the People," I hereby Asseverate and Revoke my Citizenship, if any ever existed, with the Legal fiction known as the UNITED STATES Government (Corporation).

I further rescind any and all feudal contracts with that Federal government, its agencies and with the State of Florida and its agencies. I have rescinded the Social Security number, fraudulently issued me by the government at the tender age of 13, as I was legally incompetent to enter into a legal contract with the government. The government by misinformation led me to believe at that time that I was required to secure a Social Security Account number in order to gain employment, which is simply not true. The government agent who obligated me to the Social Security System knew or should have known that there existed serious liabilities to anyone who accepted a Social Security Number. That Agent had a fiduciary responsibility to inform me of the true nature of the Social Security Trust Account and the obligations and liabilities that the Trust involved. By the government's silence on the matter, the government established, by fraud, a Constructive Trust Agreement with me which must be vitiated. Since receiving that Account, I have through my religious instruction come to the belief that the Social Security number may be what is referred to in the Holy Bible, Book of Revelation 13:16-18 and 14:9-10, as the mark of the beast or at the least its precursor. For me to participate in that program and continue to use that number may place my eternal soul in jeopardy. This I will not and cannot do.

The money which I have paid into that Socialist system for over forty years, including the monies paid by my employers' demand, is hereby made for full reimbursement to me. I do not wish, nor am I permitted by God, to make myself a ward of the State, as would be the case if I accepted the Social Security benefits. I demand the same treatment that was given to the people of the Philippines who were participants in the Social Security Trust and choose Citizenship of the Philippines over that of the United States. As the Social Security program is not a feudal contract, in that Congress gave no property rights to a Social Security Trust Account, I demand the contract be voided and all monies returned, as would be the case for any fraudulent contract or Constructive Trust Agreement. The United States Government Corporation should not enrich its self from the Fruits of a Poisonous Tree.

I emphatically deny that I have ever filed for bankruptcy protection. Nor have I ever given my Power of Attorney to anyone or to the State of Florida or any of the union states or the UNITED STATES (Corporation) government for the purpose of instituting a bankruptcy action in my name. Nor granting that my Labor and or my Property of whatever kind, or wherever situated, be held as collateral in any bankruptcy proceeding of the State or Federal governments. Nor any scheme, using my labor and property as collateral, to support or fund a fiat money scheme of the Federal Reserve Bank, Inc. and/or the State of Florida and/or Federal UNITED STATES Government.

Three generations of a proud and patriotic family will suffer the anxiety of their spirit as a result of my having chosen to recognize the malignant and treasonous misconduct of this government and speak out against it. Some of my reasons for repudiating that Citizenship status are defined in the following Articles and by the totality of this document, are made a part hereof.

I have lived a productive and eventful life, now in anticipation of the end and God's mercy. Undoubtedly the singularly most horrific moment of that life was the conviction to repudiate my Citizenship of the UNITED STATES. Those words, "REPUDIATE MY CITIZENSHIP," crushed the very soul within me. I stand now beneath that flag I served with pride for nearly forty years. The memories of our brave young men, my comrades in arms, who defended the Constitution, who never had a life, flood before me. They sacrificed all of their tomorrows so that I might have mine. Those memories will always remain with me and be remembered with humble honor and gratitude.

The awful knowledge and horror of betrayal by my own government of which I was once so proud, is an unbearable sorrow that I must now carry to my grave; but I shall do so a free man. Perhaps the American people are like the frog that is heated slowly to a boil in a pot of water. If we had detected the heat sooner, we could have jumped out, saving the Republic and ourselves.

But, alas, our grandfathers were asleep at the helm and not as vigilant as they were instructed to be by Thomas Jefferson. Americans are now awakening to the cataclysmic reality of a Fascist, one-world government, having replaced our intended Constitutional Republican Government.

ARTICLE I

The Declaration of Independence for the united States of America clearly outlined the necessary course each citizen must take when his government became insufferable. Over the past sixty years, nearly all of our unalienable rights have been stripped from us through the sophistry and obfuscation of the Courts and blood lust of the Congress for spending debt-based money borne on the back of the American people. What they have done is egregious, but as the Declaration of Independence points out, "... all experience hath shown that Mankind are more disposed to suffer, while Evils are sufferable, than to right themselves by abolishing the Forms to which they are accustomed." By sufferable, I believe they meant survivable.

That same Declaration also declared: "We hold these Truths to be self evident, that all Men are created equal, that they are endowed by their Creator with certain unalienable Rights, that among these are Life, Liberty, and the Pursuit of Happiness – That to secure these Rights, Governments are instituted among Men, deriving their just Powers from the Consent of the Governed, that whenever any Form of Government becomes destructive of these Ends, it is the Right of the People to alter or abolish it..."

Since 1933, beginning with the confiscation of our Gold and Allodial property, rather than "secure" our Right to Life, Liberty and the Pursuit of Happiness, our government has persistently and systematically reduced our standard of living. But this Evil seemed survivable, so we just suffered and let it pass, letting the water get a little hotter.

Since 1933, our government has refused to "secure" our Right to Life, Land or Liberty by persistently increasing our burden by Regulations, prohibitions, legalized abortion and unlawful taxes. They have bastardized our Judicial System with Statutory Law, replacing the Common Law and the protections which it afforded us with the severe and brutal Equity/Admiralty jurisdictions, where the Constitution is of no protection. They have lied and withheld the truth about the jury's power to judge the law as well as the facts, all but turning the jury system into a prosecutor's tool and not our protection from over-zealous prosecutors that it was intended to be.

They have increased our Prison population to nearly one and a half million inmates, the largest imprisonment of its own citizens of any country in the world. They now prepare plans for new prison construction for the new millennium, projecting twenty years in advance and building cells for our as yet unborn children, as though all or most of our offspring will be criminals. This reality alone reduces the expression, "The home of the brave and Land of the Free" to mere illusion and an oxymoron. But these evils were/are also sufferable, and we let the water get hotter.

ARTICLE II

Now, the United States government not only refuses to "secure" our Right to Life, it is openly seeking to diminish or even eliminate that Right in order that a foreign people we neither know nor see might survive. Thanks to the UN (New World Order), NAFTA, GATT, and every whore, coward and traitor elected or appointed to American public office that voted in favor of those dastardly Treaties, our very survival as a people is now at stake. Our government's Evils are no longer sufferable.

The La Paz portion of the NAFTA agreement provides for the forfeiture of a thirty-mile wide strip of American soil to a foreign power (the UN) across the entire 1,935 miles of border between Mexico and the U.S.A. Roughly sixty thousand square miles of American soil is being surrendered without a single shot being fired. That's more land than is contained in Rhode Island, Delaware, Connecticut, New Jersey, New Hampshire, Vermont, Massachusetts, and Hawaii combined, constituting the single greatest act of treachery in the history of this nation. Even more land is being surrendered as National Parks are converted to UN Biospheres. Thank the Lord that the legislature of Kentucky flat out refused to go along with the surrender of any of their land to a UN Biosphere.

There is no provision in the Constitution for Congress, the President, or the Courts to surrender any portion of our national sovereignty to any foreign government.

I am positive that there's no provision in any State constitution for those States along the Mexican border to surrender any portion of their State sovereignty to a foreign power. Those legislators who swore to uphold the national Constitution have violated their oath to God and the American people's trust. Our incumbent politicians are guilty of treason and should so be accused and tried.

The justification for surrendering our sovereignty to the UN (New World Order) is found in their ecological argument. "The Earth is overpopulated and its resources are inadequate to support our species. The human population must be reduced by at least half if our species are to survive."

If that argument is accurate, then there is not enough food or resources to sustain all currently living human life. In any other time throughout the history of human society, such shortages as described by the ecological pundits would precipitate violence and unimagined wars, as individuals, families and entire nations struggled for scarce resources in their survival against other human competitors. Such has been true since time immemorial. Under such extreme circumstances, where a foreign power or population might threaten your survival and mine, we would inevitably deduce that foreign power or population was our mortal "enemy." After all, for them to survive, we must die or at least condemn our children and ourselves to a diminished life span.

According to Article 3, Section 3, Clause 1, of the U.S. Constitution, "Treason against the United States shall consist only in levying war against them, or in adhering to their enemies, giving them aid and comfort."

If the world is on the threshold of a life-or-death Malthusian battle over scarce resources, what more "aid and comfort" could this government possibly provide to a foreign people or power than to voluntarily surrender our nuclear technology to China for political campaign contributions – the surrender of our land and sovereignty to the UN, as well as our very lives, so that some foreign competitors, our mortal enemies, might survive.

Will the American People just sit back like the frog and let the water boil, letting this government sacrifice their children's lives and futures to benefit some foreign slaves or aborigines? I don't think so, and I for one, in the capacity of a Citizen, want no part of this moronic agenda with that insane policy.

ARTICLE III

The United States Constitution is a Contract between the Federal government and the States of the Union. Its fundamental and guiding principle is the idea that the State is always a potential source of corruptive power and ultimate tyranny.

Originally the Federal government's responsibilities were confined to a few enumerated powers, involving mainly national security and public safety. In the realm of domestic affairs, the Founders sought to guarantee that federal interference in the daily lives of citizens would be strictly limited. They also wanted to make sure government would have a minimal role in the domestic economy and that it would be financed and delivered at the state and local levels, not by an evil and pestilential Central Banking System, as is the Federal Reserve Bank, Inc.

In Article I, Section 8, of the Constitution, the enumerated powers of the federal government to spend money are defined.

These powers include the right to "establish Post Offices and post roads; raise and support Armies; provide and maintain a Navy; declare War..." and to conduct a few other activities related mostly to national defense. No matter how long one may search, it is impossible to find in the Constitution any language that authorizes at least ninety percent of the civilian programs that Congress crams into the federal budget everyday.

The federal government has no authority to pay money to farmers, run the health care industry; impose wage and price controls, give welfare to the poor and unemployed. They have no authority to provide job training, subsidize electricity and telephone service, lend money to businesses and foreign governments, or build parking garages, tennis courts, and swimming pools. But they do. The Founders did not create a Department of Commerce, a Department of Education, or a Department of Housing and Urban Development. This was no oversight: they did not believe that government was authorized to establish such agencies. They were correct; Congress is forbidden by the Constitution to establish any such agencies.

The Tenth Amendment to the Constitution states clearly and unambiguously:

"The powers not delegated to the United States by the Constitution ... are reserved to the States respectively, or to the people."

In other words, if the Constitution doesn't specifically permit the federal government to do something, then it doesn't have the right to do it. May God have mercy on your soul for bankrupting and enslaving our people.

ARTICLE IV

The Bill of Rights clearly defines the most often "government" abused individual liberties. It forbids the Federal Government to violate any of these unalienable rights of the people and reserves all other rights of a sovereign not delegated to the United States, to the States: the States' authority and sovereign rights would be determined by the people in their individual state Constitutions. All sovereign rights not delegated to the Federal or State Governments by the people remains with the people.

On April 19th, 1993, at Waco, Texas, the United States (Corporation) showed its utter contempt for the unalienable Rights of its Citizens and the Sovereigns of its creation. Eighty-six men, women and children were murdered by Agents of the FBI and BATF, with the sanction of the Executive Branch of that government. An internal investigation by the Department of Justice (the fox asked to investigate the fox in the hen house), determined that the agents of the government perpetrated no criminal acts. The majority of this nation's population knows it was murder and will never forgive nor forget this manifestly evil work. I can no longer abide in this government's unlawful conduct and moral bankruptcy, because as a citizen, by proxy, I am guilty also.

This is one of the many reasons, I must sever my relationship with the UNITED STATES (Corporation) government, to ease the heavy burden on my soul these foul deeds have laden it with. The water has gotten too hot for me.

ARTICLE V

I am not anti-government, anti-military, or anti-American. For twelve years I served in the United States Marine Corps in both active and inactive duty all over the world. I served an additional nine years as a Police Officer, always defending the Constitution of the United States of America, always in harm's way. Veterans like me joined the military because of our love of Country and our constitutional obligation. At all times I have defended our Constitution against enemies, foreign and domestic. When I volunteered, I never imagined there were any real "domestic enemies." Today I know otherwise. The following is a partial example of the activities of those "domestic enemies."

In 1997, the Pittsburgh Post Gazette exposed the "Tuskeegee Experiment." It was conducted for forty years, from 1932 to 1972. According to the Associated Press, "The government withheld treatment from 399 black men with syphilis so they could study how it spreads and kills."

That's not an "experiment;" that's genocide. Whether it happens to one Black man or ten Eskimos or three Hispanics, it is wrong and violates everything this country stands for. President Clinton publicly apologized on behalf of this government to the aging male survivors. But it wasn't just the 399 men who were damaged. Their spouses also got the disease, causing their children to be born deformed. All told, 6,000 Americans were sickened, deformed or killed as a result of The UNITED STATES Government's "Tuskeegee experiment" to study how syphilis kills. President Clinton didn't bother to acknowledge their suffering.

In 1977 during the Senatorial Select Committee on Intelligence hearings (reported in "Project MK-Ultra; the CIA's Program of Research in Behavior Modification"), the CIA revealed that over forty universities and institutions were involved in extensive testing and experimentation using covert drugs on unwitting citizens at all social levels. In 1977, the University of Maryland newspaper reported that during the 1950s and 1960s, forty-four colleges, fifteen research foundations, twelve hospitals, and three prisons knowingly participated in MK Ultra experiments, but people that were experimented upon were never informed or asked to consent to be "guinea pigs."

Project MK Ultra was one of the biggest military experiments (there were one hundred forty-nine sub-projects) and lasted for years. It included human drug and biological testing by the Department of Defense (DOD) under the direction of the CIA over entire American communities. The Bureau of Narcotics and even the IRS participated in MK Ultra. When you see these government documents, they are more frightening than the rumors because our government actually admits to participating in these experiments.

In 1950, the UNITED STATES government released bacteria – "serratia marcesens" – that cause pneumonia and urinary tract infections into the San Francisco Bay. The bacteria were "aerosolized" by the surf and blown inland to study how effective an offensive biological weapon would be against the people of San Francisco. According to the report, it blew fifty miles inland. People died as a result of that experiment. Incidentally, the amount of "serratia marcesens" still remaining in San Francisco is three times the national average. It follows that we can legitimately ask how much of the syphilis that we have in the South today is a direct result of conducting the Tuskeegee experiment for forty years when they could have stopped it? How much of today's other diseases are a result of government "experiments"? Is it possible, as some have published, that AIDS is a product of one of these government experiments?

At the U.S. Army Biological Weapons Research facility at Fort Dietrich, Maryland, "weaponized" mosquitoes were developed. They actually grew viruses inside mosquitoes, placed the mosquitoes in balloons, released the balloons from aircraft over American communities and infected people. They had to infect people to tell how far the disease went and how far it would spread. How many of today's diseases are direct results of those experiments?

Tuskeegee was not a one-time anecdote; it's just the tip of an iceberg that indicates they're still doing experiments on the American people.

Another experiment was done in 1966 at Kessler Air Force Base. In 1966, 12,000 recruits at Kessler received the "micro plasma vaccine." Obviously another experiment.

"MK Ultra" considered various means of controlling human behavior; it was literally a mind control project.

"MK Action" was funded with CIA money through the Geschicter Foundation at Georgetown University. In the 1977 congressional hearing, Dr. Geschicter testified that during the Vietnamese War, the CIA didn't know if various Vietnamese nationals were double agents. Therefore, the CIA included a material in the anti-cholera vaccine given to pro-American Vietnamese, which made them glow when they were exposed to an ultraviolet light and helped identify those who rejoined the Viet Cong. This may be a clever wartime strategy, but it illustrates that as early as the 1960s, our government used vaccinations for purposes other than the prevention of disease.

The 1977 Senate Hearing report (Biological Testing Involving Human Subjects by the Department of Defense) actually says that unwitting American people were involved in open air testing. For example, it says, "The Army was using live organisms which we know can infect human beings." The Food and Drug Administration allowed it; entire cities were involved in the testing of these biological agents.

Our government even placed biological warfare agents in the New York City subway to see how many people would be infected. They did the same thing in Pennsylvania's Kittatinny and Tuscarora turnpike tunnels. You would drive through and receive aerosolized bacteriological agents.

"MK Naomi" – a biological project from the 1950s through 1969 which exposed six entire towns (including Ft. McClellan, Alabama; San Francisco, California; Ft. Wayne, Indiana; Minneapolis, Minnesota; and St. Louis, Missouri) to biological warfare agents dropped out of aircraft to see how many people would become ill. They say MK Naomi ended in 1969. Why should I believe them?

On page 160 of the 1977 "Human Drug Testing by the CIA" Senate report (S. 1893), they discussed "EA3167" – a compound they could rub up against you and it would absorb into your skin and kill you. They tested it in Pennsylvania and Kentucky prisons. It was applied to the skin through some type of adhesive tape. They also did this on military and civilian people without telling them what they were exposed to or getting their informed consent. As if anyone would volunteer!

The primary excuse for nearly going to war again with Iraq in February, 1998, was the suspicion that Iraq had been conducting biological experiments on its own prisoners. If those experiments are evil for Iraq, how then can they be legal, moral or ethical, in the United States of America? Have you clones of hydrocarbon base gone completely insane?

In 1997 Congressional hearings, the Army admitted conducting these experiments but argued, "We just didn't tell you about it because nobody was hurt and there was no problem." No problem?

I have a serious problem with this outrageous conduct. Title 50, Chapter 32, Section 1520, permits the government to experiment on us with biological and chemical agents. Thanks to a treacherous Congress, it is now legal for the DOD or their contractors to experiment with biological and chemical agents on the American people.

The only proviso Congress imposes on them is that at least two unspecified local officials be notified within the subject community, and they could be the garbage collector or the water meter reader. Once that major communication event occurs, the test can begin within 30 days. But we are not told; our children aren't told. No problem?

"And after these things I saw another angel come down from heaven, having great power; and the earth was lightened with his glory. And he cried mightily with a strong voice, saying, 'Babylon the great is fallen, is fallen, and is become the habitation of devils, and the hold of every foul spirit, and a cage of every unclean and hateful bird. For all nations have drunk of the wine of the wrath of her fornication, and the kings of the earth have committed fornication with her, and the merchants of the earth are waxed rich through the abundance of her delicacies.' And I heard another voice from heaven, saying, 'Come out of her, my people, that ye be not partakers of her sins, and that ye receive not her plagues. For her sins have reached unto heaven, and God hath remembered her iniquities.'" – Revelation 18: 1-5

As one of God's people, I must now also leave Babylon the Great and not partake of her sins any longer lest I receive her plagues, for her sins have reached unto Heaven, and God will remember her iniquities. May God have mercy on the United States!

Conclusion

On every front, with blinding speed and inexhaustible power, the evil forces of darkness of the New World Order are closing a Ring of Fire on freedom. In every domain and field of human endeavor, the choking, suffocating idolatry permeates all fields of human thought, corrupting our language, destroying truth and justice, demolishing integrity and virtue, enacting totalitarian legislation and controlling education and communications. Above all, the vilest evil is the destruction of our unborn children – a thing so horribly vile that even maggots in filth do not do. Then the attack on our faith and its foundations of Biblical thought and experience, demonizing God's followers as religious right-wing zealots to be held in ill repute, ever rapidly expanding its deviancy of evil, closing the parameters on the just, as the UNITED STATES collapses inextricably into Babylon.

What malevolent force of darkness captains the ship of State for Columbia, the Gem of the Ocean? God save me, but the UNITED STATES government is no longer sufferable. I can tolerate its pernicious and predatory conduct no longer as a citizen of the UNITED STATES (Corporate) fiction.

I hereby repudiate, rescind, renounce and disavow any CITIZENSHIP status with the UNITED STATES GOVERNMENT that I may have inadvertently acquired, by any scheme, for the reasons detailed in the foregoing Articles. My birthright now being re-secured as a member of the Sovereign Body of freemen and women known as Americans, I hereby pledge my allegiance. America demands no less from me in that freedom has never been free. My love for the united States of America has never been stronger.

So help me GOD; Lord Jesus come quickly.

Dated this 2nd day of September in the Year of Our Lord Nineteen Hundred Ninety-eight.

Melvin, Stamper, J.D., sui juris

SUPPORTING STATUTES – TITLE 25 USC § 1999

"Whereas the right of expatriation is a natural and inherent right of all people, indispensable to the enjoyment of the rights of Life, Liberty, and the pursuit of happiness; and whereas in the recognition received emigrants from all nations and vested them with the rights of citizenship; and whereas it is claimed that such American citizens, with their descendants, are subjects of foreign states, owing allegiance to the governments thereof; and whereas it is necessary to the maintenance of the public peace that this claim of foreign allegiance should be promptly and finally disavowed: Therefore, any declaration, instruction, opinion, order, or decision of an officer of the United States which denies, restricts, impairs, or question the right of expatriation, is declared inconsistent with the fundamental principles of the Republic."

The above statute reads like it was meant for foreigners who come to this country from all over the world. Definitions are all important in the reading of any legal writing. The definition most important in the above statute is the words "foreign states," so let's look at some other statutes, Supreme Court decisions and dictionary definitions that shed more light on those words.

The Constitution was made for States, not territories," wrote Daniel Webster. "[T]he Constitution of the United States as such does not under it extend beyond the limits of the States which are united by and under it," wrote author Langdell in "The Status of Our New Territories," 12 Harvard Law Review 365, 371.

Judicial note should be taken that the United States Constitution always denoted "Citizen" and "Person" in capital letters prior to the 14th Amendment; thereafter, "citizen" and "person" were not capitalized. The distinction between "citizens of the United States" and "Union States Citizens" has been fully recognized by the Congress and the Courts as follows:

"We have in our political system a government of the United States and a government of each of the several States. Each one of these governments is distinct from the others, and each has citizens of its own who owe it allegiance, and whose rights, within its jurisdiction, it must protect." [a] [Emphasis added]

The Federal Government is a "state". [b]

Foreign State. A foreign country or nation. The several United States are considered "foreign" to each other except as regards their relations as common members of the Union. (*Black's Law Dictionary*, Sixth Edition, page 1407)

Congress identifies these citizens of the "District" as "individuals" or citizens who reside in the "United States" and who are subject to the direct control of Congress in its local taxing and other municipal laws. Asking one question can clear up the distinction between the two types of Citizen:

Are both classes of Citizenship the same and, if not, what is the difference?

Citizens of the Union States have the right of suffrage (right to vote); District citizens have no such right.

If you are not a United States citizen of Washington, D.C., or the territories and possessions, then what are you in relation to the federal government?

NON-RESIDENT ALIEN

At first that term does not seem to describe your relationship to the federal government, but Federal Income Tax Law and the Supreme Court enlighten greater understanding of the term. The revenue laws do not use the term "sovereign citizen." Those laws refer to United States Persons, Resident Aliens and Nonresident Aliens. U.S. persons are defined to include, among other things, citizens and residents (i.e.: resident aliens) of the United States.

Treasury Decision (TD) 2313

The Supreme Court decision on a tax case determined the issue. *Brushaber v. Union Pacific Railroad Co. Inc.* (240 U.S. 1) 1916 is often cited by the IRS as demonstrating its authority to collect income tax and that the income tax is constitutional (limited application). What the IRS fails to mention, and what is not apparent from looking at the court's ruling in the case, is that the case concerned income from within the United States accruing to a nonresident alien, which is subject to the federal income tax because he was involved in a trade or business with a federally-chartered corporation.

Treasury Decision 2313 in elaborating on the case makes this apparent:

"Under the decision of the Supreme Court of the United States in the case of *Brushaber v. Union Pacific Railway Co.*, decided January 24, 1916, it is hereby held that income accruing to nonresident aliens in the form of interest from the bonds and dividends on the stock of domestic corporations is subject to the income tax imposed by the act of October 3, 1913." (Treasury Decision 2313)

It is based upon the decision of the Supreme Court in a lawsuit brought by a citizen of New York, living in Brooklyn, against the Union Pacific Railway Co., a federally-chartered corporation. The purpose of the suit was to prevent the railway company from withholding the 1% tax from the dividends payable to the New Yorker. The state citizen lost that case. In reliance upon that decision, the Treasury Department referred to the New Yorker as a nonresident alien who, as such, was not exempt from the withholding of taxes from dividends payable by a domestic corporation (i.e., chartered by the federal government)! The fact that TD 2313 called Mr. Brushaber a nonresident alien seems proof enough that citizens of states are nonresident aliens for all purposes of the Code, and if this is true, then a corporation chartered in a state is foreign, while only federally-chartered corporations can be domestic. So, anything done in a state is done without the United States.

The Treasury Department actually confirmed their understanding by their analysis of the Brushaber case on the status of a sovereign citizen as being a nonresident alien for revenue purposes.

A nonresident alien is anyone who is neither a citizen nor a resident (alien) of the United States. Since the sovereign citizen is not a "citizen of the United States" under the Code (by virtue of the definition in the regulations), and since he does not fit the definition of a resident alien, by elimination, he must be a nonresident alien!

The term "alien" must apply to the sovereign citizen, because he is alien to the status of subject citizen, and he does not fit the special definition of resident found in the 14th Amendment. It may also be said that, since the sovereign person does not live within the political jurisdiction of the United States, he is nonresident thereto. Thus, he can be nonresident to the place, as well as nonresident and alien to the status of subject citizen.

Under the language of the Code, as interpreted by the tax regulations, the sovereign citizen may be liable for the tax applicable to the nonresident alien. The Code subjects nonresident aliens to taxes upon income which is received either from a trade or business "effectively connected with the United States," or from a source "within" the United States. Do not assume that this means some place as foreign as France or Japan. It appears to refer to the fifty states, just as clearly as did TD 2313.

As to taxability of nonresident alien income, in order for such income of the nonresident alien to be taxable, it will have to emanate from sources within sovereign federal areas or from an activity that is effectively connected with the political jurisdiction of the United States by reason of the ATF laws, patents, copyrights, federally-created entities, etc. If it emanates from any of the fifty states and is not "connected" with those federally-controlled activities, such income is not taxable to the sovereign citizen. Once again, the problem is to find a court that will apply this truth. To do this, one must show to the court that an activity in one of the fifty states is "without" the United States.

To do this, it is suggested that a standard form subpoena, as issued by the clerk of any United States District Court, be marked as an exhibit.

Point to the return of service which states that it is signed "under penalties of perjury pursuant to the laws of the United States of America." Then attach it to a motion which cites 28 USC §1746(1). This statute defines that form of verification is applicable only "without" the United States! Also cite 28 USC §297, showing that the fifty "freely associated compact states" are referred to as "countries."

Combined with the Brushaber case and TD 2313, one would make it hard for the court to deny that income from within the fifty states is without the United States.

Since you have always been a non-resident alien of the United States, it seems absurd that you would be required to prove it with rebuttal evidence, but that is exactly what you have to do. The government and the courts are not going to let you easily out of the system that it took them so long to put in place to fund their criminal activity.

Through its regulations, the government has made it difficult to expatriate, as they require that you leave the country and do the deed at a Consulate or Embassy. However, President Bush may have made the task a little easier since he has Declared War against Terrorists as (6) formally renouncing U.S. citizenship within the U.S. (but only "in time of war") (Sec. 349 (a) (6) INA); Simply address the Document to the Attorney General per the regulation.

There exist mountains of supporting evidence and court decisions regarding your true status, and it seems absolutely preposterous to require you to jump over obstacles in order to expatriate, but if it were made easy, then everyone would be doing it. Again, this is one of the most important decisions of your life, so do not approach it in a cavalier manner. Study as much as you can, and ask the good Lord for direction before making that decision. The preceding is an example of one individual's Expatriation Document. Do not copy it word for word, as you can see it was a heartfelt effort and of a personal nature, as yours should be. Notice that taxes were not even a consideration, as having taxes as one's motivating reason makes the attempt a failure.

CHAPTER TWO

MAGICIANS

The people who walked in darkness have seen a great light. They lived in a land of shadows, and now the light is shining on them. (Isaiah 9:2)

NEVER WATCH THE HAND BEHIND MY BACK

While researching my first book, *High Priests of Treason*, I discovered some of the most fascinating information anyone could ever hope to uncover about money, finance and government. I will share it with you so that you have a better understanding of the issues you will be reading about and possibly facing in the near future. This knowledge could not be obtained without years of research; I have saved you the trouble of traveling that same forty miles of bad road. I do, however, advise any that wish to challenge this evil empire as I have to verify cites and information that I supply. Get educated on the facts before you act, and then act.

My investigation concentrated on the Judiciary; Internal Revenue Service; Federal Reserve Bank, Inc.; Bureau of Alcohol, Tobacco and Firearms; offices of the Secretary of the Treasury and State; as well as the President and the Congress. That investigation has disclosed, in my mind, a broad, premeditated conspiracy by the International Bankers and their agents in the United States government to defraud and enslave the Citizens of the united States of America since 1900.

Examination into the Statutes at Large, United States Code, Code of Federal Regulations, Congressional Record, Federal Register, the Internal Revenue manuals, and other sources too numerous to mention, reveal a conspiracy of such magnitude that I do not have the words to adequately describe that betrayal to the American people. This is why I repudiated my citizenship with the corporate government of the United States, its demonic masters and their tool on earth, the United Nations, controlled by the International Banking families. These families would slit their children's throat for a dollar, and they dearly love their children.

What I uncovered has clearly been designed to circumvent the intent and restrictions of the Constitution for the united States of America by the de facto government in operation today. I'm convinced that their purpose was to implement the Communist Manifesto within the fifty States and enslave us all. If you take the time to read that "Manifesto," you will discover that its principles are enshrined in our federal and state statutes. Engles and Marx espoused that to create a classless society, a "graduated income tax" should be used as the weapon to destroy the middle class of a country. Such a system is in place, managed by the US version of the KGB, the ever-benevolent Internal Revenue Service, which is not even a part of the government. For the proof, refer to *Diversified Metal Products v. T-Bow Trust Co., IRS and Steve Morgan*, within the United States' Answer and Claim at paragraph 4: "Denies that the Internal Revenue Service is an agency of the United States Government, etc.," signed by Richard R. Ward, US Dept. of Justice (US District Court, District of Idaho; Civil No. 93-405-E-EJL).

Illusion

Deception, quick hands, sophistry and obfuscation all constitute the art of magic. Those who practice in illusion are called magicians or, in the less poetic sense, "politicians" – "now you see me; now you don't." The Congress and the IRS are full of magicians who have created their web of deceit and illusion in the tax laws, not by quick hands but by illusory language. Have you ever questioned why your Christian name is spelled in all capital letters, when we all know that English grammar requires the spelling of all proper nouns in upper and lower case letters? I can assure you that it is not for clarity. Does the word "person" in statutory law mean the same as in everyday language usage? You are about to discover the answer to both of those questions.

In the beginning of the Twentieth Century, when the courts still had truly honorable judges, they ruled some of those early tax laws unconstitutional or unlawful. The IRS immediately removed themselves outside the jurisdiction and venue of the courts, to the Philippines and Puerto Rico. By deceiving and coercing the population, beginning with the War Tax Act of 1942, the Congress and the IRS continued their unconstitutional and criminal activity to this day. These criminal magicians have convinced the American population that citizens of this nation are of a status that they are not – that they are subjects of the federal government, which they are not not collective sovereigns. They led us to believe that we must do things that are not required to be done or go to jail. Through the clever use of "IRS-speak" and the Congress' "word art," the Executive Branch promotes the fraud, the Congress turns a blind eye to their misconduct (but they have hearings that they hope will demonstrate their outrage to the voters), and then their dishonorable courts ratify the alleged criminal misconduct by rubber-stamping the convictions of innocent Citizens.

To illustrate my point on the complicity of the court in this immoral scheme, I refer to a recent case before the Supreme Court, the case of *United States v. Sandra L. Craft*, Case No. 00-1831, in hearing on January 14, 2002. The Assistant Solicitor General, Mr. Kent L. Jones, was asked a question from the court:

Q. "… some penalties for failing to file a return?"

A. "There are some penalties, but the penalties, like taxes, have to be enforced against the property of the taxpayer, and if the taxpayer is allowed to exempt all of its property in this fashion, then there's literally no way that the taxes can be enforced through civil procedures."

Q. "What about criminal procedures? Are there any criminal procedures for – failure, continued failure to file – ?"

A. "Of course if you file a return, then you're not exposing yourself to any criminal obligations, and if you don't file a return, it would be – I'm not familiar with a statute that makes that a crime by itself. Now, it may be that it's a crime in connection with some intent to conceal, but just the fact that you didn't file – I'm not – even though I come before the Court on tax cases, I'm not an expert on criminal tax matters, but it's my impression that that would not by itself be a crime."

Q. "We'd better not let the word get out. I thought it was a crime, but I'll check." (Followed by laughter)

Over three thousand Americans each year are sent to federal prison for not filing a tax return, and the Assistant Solicitor General, Mr. Kent L. Jones, admits to the Supreme Court that it is not illegal to not file a tax return. The Supreme Court advises him, "We'd better not let the word get out." That supposed bastion in the protection of our freedom wants to keep it a dirty little secret among the privileged few and to continue to permit the imprisonment of thousands of innocent people and the resultant destruction of their lives. That is something to laugh about?

This is a perfect point in the book to educate you on your proper status as a Citizen of one of the Republic States of the Union. What you were taught in public school was exactly what the federal and state government wanted you to be taught. The most powerful tool of control of any population by the government is ignorance of its subjects.

"A sovereign is one in whom supreme power is vested. He may delegate whatever of his total authority he wishes. He can consent to whatever outside authority he may choose or none at all. However, he cannot be "subject" to outside authority; this would be in contradiction to sovereignty." (*Black's Law Dictionary*, 6th Ed.)

The creation of the enumerated powers in the United States Constitution was done by delegation of authority. The power of the sovereign people remained with the people. The federal government may exercise its enumerated power only on their behalf. This relationship was well-stated by the Supreme Court as follows:

"Sovereignty itself is, of course, not subject to law, for it is the author and source of law; but in our system, while sovereign powers are delegated to the agencies of government, sovereignty itself remains with the people, by whom and for whom all government exists and acts." (*Yick Wo v. Hopkins*, 118 US 353)

Are you a citizen of the United States?

Are you a Sovereign?

Those two questions and their answers hold the secret of our present day condition of servitude to the de facto federal and state governments. There have been massive fraudulent practices of the Congress and state legislatures in the creation of legislation (statutes) that has regulated our lives and commerce for over sixty years. Without a thorough understanding of your correct relationship to these legal fictions and the statutes they have created, you are doomed to a lifetime of servitude, which can be avoided.

I pray for more understanding and knowledge, as I do not as yet know the impact or total paradigm of this deception. What I do know is shocking but enlightening. I will attempt to explain as much as is possible with that limited knowledge of the methods used to obfuscate the law and your citizenship status, effectively placing you in a feudal relationship with government forces.

In order for you to take cognizance of the full context of this conspiracy, you need to understand the meaning of words of art used by the various legislative bodies to entrap you. The words used in statutory law do not have the normal, everyday, street meaning. By diagramming the statute, it is possible to understand the intent of the law and its application. Get out your old 10th Grade English Grammar Book and learn how to diagram sentences; it will save you a world of grief.

PREAMBLE TO THE UNITED STATES CONSTITUTION

"We the People of the United States, in Order to form a more perfect Union, establish Justice, insure domestic Tranquility, provide for the common defense, promote the general Welfare, and secure the Blessings of Liberty to ourselves and our Posterity, do ordain and establish this Constitution for the United States of America."

It appears that "We the People" of the United States, acting through our representatives, were sovereign, because we are doing the creating of this constitutional compact. But does that mean that you individually are a sovereign?

If King Juan Carlos of Spain were to submit to a kidney transplant and the recipient was a farmer from Ohio, would the farmer become a sovereign king of Spain the moment the kidney was stitched into his body? Of course not!

To be King Juan Carlos of Spain, you must be the whole person; you must be a living soul; you must wear a mask of your status. King Carlos would still be a king regardless if he had the two kidneys or one. What makes him a king and sovereign is that he was born with the title of sovereign (ruler's mask); nothing more. If he renounced that title, he would not be a sovereign but would revert to a different class (common man's mask) or subject of a higher authority – that which would replace him. So being a sovereign requires that someone or some force has declared that you are sovereign and has given you the authority to exercise all of your powers over your subjects (citizens).

That could be done by God (as royalty claims to rule by divine right) or by being elected to that lofty position by your subjects.

Since none of us have been declared by God to be sovereign or elected to the position of sovereign by our fellow man, individually one cannot be sovereign, as many in the Patriot community profess. Not only would the declaration that you are sovereign be frivolous to the ears of the court, it would be a blasphemy to the Lord God of the Universe, as he is the only true Sovereign to whom we all owe our allegiance.

What you are is a unique species – a species described by God as a living soul.

"And the LORD God formed man of the dust of the ground, and breathed into his nostrils the breath of life; and man became a living soul."
– Genesis 2:8

That distinction is unique in the United States of America, because we all – collectively as living souls – were given the highest possible status: that of sovereign over the government we created. The authority for bestowing that authority was "We the People." When we act as a whole, then We the People are the Sovereign of the United States of America, exercising our power through our elected representatives. When we act as individuals, we are acting in the capacity of living souls, each responsible for ourselves. The court has described this concept as follows:

"A distinction was taken at the bar between a state and the people of the state. It is a distinction I am not capable of comprehending. By a state forming a republic (speaking of it as a moral person), I do not mean the legislature of the state, the executive of the state, or the judiciary, but all the citizens who compose the state, and are, if I may so express myself, integral parts of it; all together forming a body politic. The great distinction between monarchies and republics (at least our republic) in general is, that in the former the monarch is considered as the sovereign, and each individual of his nation as a subject to him, though in some countries with many important special limitations.

This, I say, is generally the case, for it has not been so universal. But in a republic, all the citizens as such, are equal, and no citizen can rightfully exercise any authority over another but in virtue of a power constitutionally given by the whole community, and such authority, when exercised, is in effect an act of the whole community, which forms such body politic. In such governments, therefore, the sovereignty resides in the great body of the people, but it resides in them not as so many distinct individuals, but in their political capacity only. Thus A, B, C, and D are citizens of Pennsylvania, and as such, together with all the citizens of Pennsylvania share in the sovereignty of the state. Suppose a state to consist exactly had a number of 100,000 citizens, and if it were practicable for them all to assemble at one time and in one place, and that 99,999 did actually assemble, the state would not be in fact assembled. Why? Because the state in fact is composed of all the citizens, not of a part only, however large the part may be, and one is wanting." – *Penhallow v. Doane*, 3 Dall. 93.

The protections we gave ourselves as living souls and a sovereign body politic were incorporated into the Constitution as the first ten Amendments, which are often referred to as the Bill of Rights. These rights were specifically enumerated because, from our colonial experience, these rights were the most often abused by the king and his agents and are deemed to be so fundamental, that without them, there would be no humanity.

The Constitution was written in order to protect the commerce of the independent sovereign states from foreign aggression and equal treatment among the contracting states. The individual living souls of the states that compacted together by the Constitution were protected in their fundamental rights from its creation, the federal government, in the exercise of the enumerated powers that we granted it and nothing more. The Constitution did not create a sovereign government over the member states to the compact or over the people of those states.

The Congress and the state legislatures are cognizant of the authority delegated them by "We the People" – the sovereign body politic – under the federal and state constitutions, and are specific when legislating law for the sovereign body politic and for subjects of the federal government. In order to gain control over us, "We the People," they use "word art," and by definitions such as "person," "including," "states," etc., they begin stripping away our basic fundamental rights by sophistry. For their success, they depend upon our apathy towards government and the general obscurity of knowledge regarding our status vs. the citizen subject of the District.

"Person: In general usage, a human being (i.e. natural person), though by statute term may include labor organizations, partnerships, associations, corporations, legal representatives, trustees, trustees in bankruptcy, or receivers." – *Black's Law Dictionary*, 6th Edition, page 1142

Notice that there are two types of person described:

1. A human being (natural person with natural rights)
2. May include… (artificial entities or legal fictions with legal rights)

The significance in our jurisprudence:

The word "person," in its primitive and natural sense, signifies the mask with which actors, who played dramatic pieces in Rome and Greece, covered their heads. These pieces were played in public places, and afterwards in such vast amphitheaters that it was impossible for a man to make himself heard by all the spectators. Recourse was had to art; the head of each actor was enveloped with a mask, the figure of which represented the part he was to play, and it was so contrived that the opening for the emission of his voice made the sounds clearer and more resounding, *vox personabat*, when the name "persona" was given to the instrument or mask which facilitated the resounding of his voice. The name "persona" was afterwards applied to the part itself, which the actor had undertaken to play, because the face of the mask was adapted to the age and character of him who was considered as speaking, and sometimes it was his own portrait. It is in this last sense of personage, or of the part which an individual plays, that the word persona is employed in jurisprudence, in opposition to the word man, homo. When we speak of a person, we only consider the state of the man, the part he plays in society, abstractly, without considering the individual". – 1 *Bouvier's Institutes*, note 1.

As you can see from the definition in *Bouvier's*, in our jurisprudence the part the "person" plays in society – the "mask" he wears – determines the natural or legal rights he may or may not have and the jurisdiction of the different courts over his persona.

Article 3, Section 2, of the Constitution for the United States defines the jurisdictions of the court. They are "Law," meaning the common law with all constitutional protections, "Equity," "Admiralty," and "Maritime," meaning contract law (private international law) with no constitutional protection. The common law has jurisdiction over the natural person (mask) by use of Article III courts; the remaining jurisdictions have jurisdiction over legal fictions

(MASK), i.e., NON-NATURAL PERSONS, under Article IV courts. A natural person can change his "acting role" in business and assume a different mask, if he for instance enters into a partnership, corporation or contract. He may still be a living soul, but his status (mask) under the Constitution has changed to that of a LEGAL FICTION or STRAWMAN (CORPORATE MASK), and the court's statutory jurisdiction over the STRAWMAN is now presumed.

PROGRESSION OF DECEPTION

During the early part of the 1800s up to the time of the War Between the States, the power brokers were busy putting together a plan that would increase the political jurisdiction of the United States. This plan was necessary in their opinion because the United States had a minimum number of subjects – the ones living in the District of Columbia and only the land ceded to it by the states. The District was only ten miles square, land ceded for the seat of government by Maryland and Virginia and some land outside the District by other States, as was necessary for forts, magazines, arsenals, and other needful buildings within the member states. So the acquisition of land was also on the agenda.

Between the 1860s and the early 1900s, banking and taxing mechanisms were changing through legislation sponsored by the European central banks. Clever politicians and agents of the central banks of Europe closely associated with the powers in England had enormous influence on the legislation being passed in the Congress. It was the responsibility of the people to understand their status with regard to the United States and the legislation being passed by the Congress and their state legislatures. The largest majority of the legislation did not apply to the states or to the people within the states, but Congress did not deem it their necessary duty to make the distinction as to which law applied to whom.

This distinction between the authority and jurisdiction of the United States and that of the states was critical and taught in the home, school and church. The true status was taught because there was no federal subsidy program for the schools with required subject matter or revisionist history that the government wanted taught and no incorporation of the church restricting what could be taught because of a tax exemption. The teaching of the Citizens' status was unobstructed and detailed. They understood the clear line established by the Constitution and the jurisdiction of the government that flowed from the enumerated powers granted to it by that compact.

The people were in control at that precise moment because they knew both their standing (mask) in relation to the United States and its legislative jurisdiction and that of their State. The Federal courts did not interpret legislation as broadly as they do now, because the people knew when the courts were overstepping their jurisdiction by entering into litigation that was reserved for the common law, as Admiralty is private International contract law under Article IV authority.

The 14th Amendment added some confusion about the basic understanding of status because it created a new class of citizen – United States citizens that had not existed previously. The newly freed black citizen knew nothing of the Constitution, let alone jurisdiction of the government over different classes of persons. Prior to its adoption, Citizens or persons of State status automatically were deemed Citizens of the American Empire, but first and foremost, State Citizenship was paramount and American Citizenship flowed from State Citizenship.

Before the 14th Amendment in 1868, there were no persons born or naturalized in the United States; naturalization was a state function. Each person had been born or naturalized in one of the several states. Following the Civil War, the new class of citizen was recognized, and this was the beginning of the departure from the Republic and the formation of a United States democracy, whose situs is the District of Columbia. The American people in the republic sited in the several republic states could choose the benefit of federal citizenship just as one of the new United States citizens if they chose to do so.

DUAL SYSTEM OF LAW CREATED BY THE 14TH AMENDMENT

This Chapter will cover the particulars of the "dual legal system" that has been established by the 14th amendment to the Constitution for the United States. Its subject matter will encompass a general overview of adverse conditions which affect the freedom and liberty of all Americans. Matters included herein will be in reference to the police power of the state in its relation and application to the Citizen (i.e., nationals) members of any given state; moreover, any such state's relations with other nationals of the American union.

NATIONALITY DE JURE

To grasp the true understanding of the United States of America's governmental system in the original premise, one must imagine that the government of the federation (the "United States") does not exist. In such case, each state in the Union would be a separate country; accordingly, under the rules of international law, a sovereign state is a nation, much as is the European continent at present.

STATE: A people permanently occupying a fixed territory bound together by common law habits and custom into one body politic exercising, through the medium of an organized government, independent sovereignty and control over all persons and things within its boundaries, capable of making war and peace and of entering into international relations with other communities of the globe. – *Black's Law Dictionary*, Sixth Edition

NATION: Nations or States are independent bodies politic; societies of men united together for the purpose of promoting their mutual safety and advantage by the joint efforts of their combined strength. – *Bouvier's Law Dictionary*, 1856 [i.e. state = nation]

The foregoing is the international definition of "state" and "nation." Now, adding the federal government back into the equation, the constitution for the united States of America is nothing more than an international agreement (or compact/charter) between the several republics of America and their respective nations.

Accordingly, in the forming of the American federation, each state of the Union gave up some of their inherent rights of statehood that they possessed under the general rules of international law. However, one such right they did not give up is the maintenance of their respective and individual nations. This is further found exemplified in the protection provisions that are set forth by the Ninth and Tenth Amendments in the Bill of Rights of the federal constitution.

To further expand on these premises, a citizen member of any particular nation carries the quality of that nationality.

NATIONALITY: The state of a person in relation to the nation in which he was born. A man retains his nationality of origin during his minority, but, as in the case of his domicile of origin, he may change his nationality upon attaining full age; he cannot, however, renounce his allegiance without permission of the government. – *Bouvier's Law Dictionary*, 1856

In reference to domicile, such is in direct relation to one's presence in a country. In reference to one's allegiance, such is to the nation or state of origin or his membership thereof. In further reference of nationality and allegiance that is inherent to our system of law, one has always been able to change his nationality within the Union; such terms below encompass this legal issue:

COUNTRY: By country is meant the state of which one is a member. Every man's country is in general the state in which he happens to have been born. – *Bouvier's Law Dictionary*, 1856

EXPATRIATION: The voluntary act of abandoning one's country and becoming the citizen (and national) or subject of another. – *Bouvier's Law Dictionary*, 1856

NATURALIZATION: The conferring of the nationality of a state upon a person after birth, by any means whatsoever. – *Ballentine's Law Dictionary*, 1969

Unknown to most Americans, such matter of natural right is available; however, for political reasons, it has been kept a secret, which will be briefly discussed in the next parts.

IN CONCLUSION:

In a clear sense, all such qualities make up the international and constitutional de jure premise of the Union – that is to say, each state is clearly a nation by right. Accordingly, the United States of America in a purely legal sense is based on the law of nations (natural law) – is not a state, nation or country; hence, one cannot have the nationality of such. To truly maintain nationality, land is required. The "United States" does (did) not possess land to support premise of nationality; hence, the "United States" is not a state or a nation, in regards to its composite stature as the government of the Union. The "United States" in simple sense is a "corporate body" that has been contracted by the several American nations to handle certain affairs.

FOURTEENTH AMENDMENT

It is common knowledge that after the American Civil War the Union went through some dramatic changes. Among these changes was a dominant makeover of the Union's constitutional system. Such changes included amendments to the federal Constitution, which are commonly known as the Reconstruction amendments – the 13th, 14th and 15th. As the people of America have been taught, they believe that these amendments were for the purpose of administering civil rights to the slaves. All such amendments have served such purpose; however, such measures have eroded the civil law of America – the common law.

Consequently, over the past one hundred thirty years, such civil law has been destroyed and has been tacitly transferred to the police power of the federal and state governments. This has been implicitly accomplished by section 1 of the Fourteenth Amendment, of and through which such legal operation is set forth:

"All persons born or naturalized in the United States, and subject to the jurisdiction thereof, are citizens of the United States and of the State wherein they reside."

In legal operation, it naturalizes everyone born in America to be federal citizens at birth. This clause is referred to as the "naturalization clause"; however, such citizenship is voluntary. It must be established that the Fourteenth Amendment citizenship develops a character that is somewhat repugnant to natural and international law.

In fact, said amendment induced a commercial-based constitutional system of law. That is to say, everything that is encompassed in the governmental de facto system is of a contractual nature, which imports the creation of legal fictions and creates several conflicts of law. Another repugnant factor that coexists with this de facto citizenship is the imposition of an unnatural allegiance to the "United States." Accordingly, Americans do not realize that they have given up their liberties by not expressly terminating the de facto citizenship at their age of majority; moreover, they further consent (in a tacitly made commercial style agreement) to the induced constitutional system and unnatural franchised citizenship by voting, pursuant to Section II of Amendment XIV.

Conformably, said section of the amendment further establishes the "new apportionment" of federal representation amongst the states of the Union and also sets up the new – or rather, alternate – state governments, which, as a matter of law, are de facto (insurgent). The law that is established under the Fourteenth Amendment is private international law; hence, the states and federal government represent only voting federal citizens, as set forth by the legal operation of Section II of the Amendment XIV.

Consequently, this is where the dual system of law is set forth: 1) the private law that is caused by the Fourteenth Amendment; and, 2) the public law that is inherent in the original form of the constitutional system, which includes the public law of each state (encompassed in their respective constitutions) and the public law that is set forth by the original form of the Constitution for the United States of America.

To further illustrate the establishment of the dual system of law, we must review what has truly transpired in relation to section 2 of the Fourteenth Amendment. Based on the rules that are set forth and established by the law of nations (and the alternate 13th Amendment), one cannot be subordinate to the dominion of another without his consent; hence, by using syntax (or rather, by applying sentence structure) to section 2 of the Fourteenth Amendment you will find the following relevant wording set forth in "word art": "...the right to vote...is denied...except for participation in rebellion, or other crime."

In essence, what this accomplishes is an unwitting contractual agreement by a native – now naturalized – "citizen of the United States" (federal citizen) to unwittingly give up his de jure law form and accept the de facto law form, which is in essence the police power of the federal and state legislatures (i.e. voluntary servitude), such as established by the diabolical Fourteenth Amendment system.

In reference to said system, in simple terms, the state legislatures are acting in a quasi-war mode due to the induced voting rebellion (i.e. police state). A U.S. citizen is in breach of allegiance to his native state by tacitly and unwittingly declaring that he accepts the alternate governmental system. Statutory law – state and federal – then controls him over his de jure law form, which is the common law.

All such citizens within the jurisdiction of the corporate United States are considered belligerents along with the nationals that run the de facto state governments. In the rudimentary form of the constitutional system of the Union, the legislatures could not create law that affected citizens at large (individual State Citizens); hence, some of the law established by the statutory scheme is pursuant to international rules of war.

As the law has been applied and is fundamentally being followed, the general constitutional provisions that have been craftily utilized to create this "silent hostility" can be found in the body of the original Constitution in Article IV, section 4 – "The United States shall ...protect each of (the several states) against Invasion; and on Application of the Legislature, or of the Executive, against domestic Violence."

In fact, this establishes a system of law that is based on maritime principles. Unknown to Americans, all courts of the United States – state and federal – are being operated under the principles of such law. Hence, note that all the courts in the United States of America display military flags (regular flags with gold fringe). Civil flags are hung vertically and never on a pole.

Accordingly, the states (governments) are acting in a quasi de jure capacity and asserting their sovereignty over their citizens de facto. Voting Americans – or, as they also have accepted this system, all United States citizens – have voluntarily been induced to unwittingly: 1) become enemies of the state; 2) become residents of their states (hence, not true nationals under the law of nations); 3) accept a feudal system of law (and land ownership); and thus, 4) give up their natural right to sovereignty that is protected by their state constitutions (and the law of nations).

Although the American governmental system is de facto, the de jure system of law, along with its several nationalities, is preserved. This is evident, as nothing in the original federal constitution has been repealed; thus, it is still in full force and effect. Under the rule of international law, the de facto governmental system cannot be forced on people of America that do not wish participate in it; thus, the de facto statutory construction can be applied only to consenting U.S. citizens (even if it is unwittingly so); hence, is not mandatory for – thus, cannot be forced on – those State Citizens who wish not to rebel against their de jure law to partake in the insurgent system.

FEDERALISM VERSUS NATIONALISM

In planned effect, these matters have created a legal or, rather, induced political phenomena – federalism. The antithesis of federalism is nationalism. To give a general background of the reasoning behind the two terms, the founding fathers, such as Thomas Jefferson, were concerned with the Federalists' ulterior motives. Jefferson sensed that the Federalists were primarily interested in turning America into one big commercial plantation under their rule. The Constitution reflects the general concerns of Jefferson: the document's predominate commerce clauses make obvious its commercial purpose.

Accordingly, if one would observe the political scheme that evolved in America, he would establish that in the early 1800s Jefferson ultimately overthrew the Federalist Party with his Democratic Republican Party. This took the Union out of the control of the elite (Federalist) and put it under the control of the American people. Soon after its establishment, the party split into two parties. The two parties are still in existence: today they are known as the Republicans and Democrats – the same snake with two heads.

These two parties, unbeknownst to most Americans, are acting secretly as the Federalists. Our real system of American law allowed too much freedom. On a mass basis, people could not be controlled to direct their labors toward the goals of the Elite. Instead, the current feudal system was induced unwittingly via the voluntary system put into place by the Fourteenth Amendment. To keep matters under the perpetual control of the Federalists (elitists), socialism was introduced. Karl Marx, drafter of the Communist Manifesto in 1848, said: "Socialism leads to Communism." To implement socialism on a Union-wide basis, the Fourteenth Amendment was enrolled via force of the Civil War. The general purposes of such obvious, yet covert, measures were to tame and train the masses to become a commercialistic economic slave force whereby the Elite would profit.

Communism is nothing more than another name for Federalism. It is basically a system that controls many nations centrally with the aim of commercialism. Accordingly, if one would investigate, all ten planks of the Communist Manifesto are applied in American law.

REMEDY OF NATURAL RIGHT AND PROTECTIONS

When societies, which are small local communities, are not allowed to govern themselves through their customs under the rule of natural law, they become prone to social breakdown. Many would agree that American society has seen a total breakdown. This is largely due to the combining of states (nations) to act as one under the dictatorial control of the federal government.

If America is to repair its apparent social degeneration, the police power of the states has to be negated and the civil common law has to be restored to the peoples (nations) of America. As the real intent of the Fourteenth Amendment took well over a century to accomplish, we can find that Congress passed law (found codified in Title 8 USC § 1401) that made America one nationality: "The following shall be nationals and citizens of the United States at birth – A person born in the United States, and subject to the jurisdiction thereof." Such is the language from the Fourteenth Amendment.

Fortunately, as this politically-imposed nationality is a fraud, a remedy is provided pursuant to international law. Under Title 8 of the United States Code, section 1481, the de facto federal nationality can be legally terminated. This returns one to his original status under the principles of the original constitutional system. Then, under de jure constitutional premise, interference by the "United States" is protected by the 9th and 10th Amendments in the

Bill of Rights of the federal constitution. Such is exemplified in the following legal definitions found in *Black's Law*, Sixth Edition.

Constitutional Liberty or Freedom: Such freedom as is enjoyed by the citizens of a country or state under the protection of its constitution, the aggregate of those personal, civil, and political rights of the individual, which are guaranteed by the Constitution and secured against invasion by the government or any of its agencies.

Constitutional Right: A right guaranteed to the citizens by the United States Constitution and state constitutions and so guaranteed as to prevent legislative interference therewith.

Once one corrects his status, he is no longer under the jurisdiction of the police power of the federal or state governments. One is then an alien as to the de facto political system, i.e. nation/body politic; moreover, one is also an alien in every state wherein he is not a national. This plays an important part in reference to the U.S. code in reference to protections and remedies. Accordingly, as one is no longer in breach of allegiance to his state government when his status is corrected, he is protected from its unlawful actions. Such unlawful actions are called actions done under color of law. The term "color of law" is another way of saying *private law*, or the law created under the police power of the state legislature (as it is not of the common law, i.e. custom and usage). Under the Fourteenth Amendment system, de jure nationals (a ward, in sense) are protected from such state actions by the federal government.

Title 18 USCA § 242.

Deprivation of rights under color of law. (Criminal) [In part]

"Who ever, under color of any law, statute, ordinance, regulation, or custom, willfully subjects any person in any State, Territory, or District to the deprivation of any rights, privileges, or immunities secured or protected by the Constitution or laws of the United States, or to different punishments, pains, or penalties, on account of such person being an alien, ... shall be fined under this title or imprisoned not more than one year, or both."

Note that a person has to be an alien to be protected from actions done under the color of law. This means that if a state employee or officer violates your natural rights that are secured by the federal and/or state constitutions, he can be put in jail; moreover, the state itself is not immune from such actions. They can be sued for their employees', officers', and their own actions. As the states are not paying their debts pursuant to money based on substance, as largely caused by the socialist system of government, the United States is bankrupt, and has been since 1933. All activity that they are involved in is fundamentally commercially based, such as their money system, traffic citations, taxes, etc. Accordingly, it has been held that the state governments are not immune from their commercial activities against lawful Americans. As the de facto law system fundamentally sets up a system that is based on commercial law, the states are liable for all damages that are done to a person that is not willfully participating in the de facto political system.

The state governments are basically quasi-political subdivisions of the federal government as they are composed of "rebelling" Americans (in treason). The state governments cannot violate the natural rights of a non-participatory American. If any such governments do violate anyone's rights thereof, they and their employees will be held liable for their actions. American's problems will not see any correction until either a peaceful or violent revolution is ceased and the original system put back in place. Until then, Americans must enforce their natural rights that are held under the law of nations and claim their true nationalities. It is the obligation of every American to enforce this right and make others aware of the hidden agenda that has been inflicted on us, which agenda is purely that of a commercial interest held by the World Elite.

In 1865, the 13th Amendment opened the floodgate for the people to volunteer into servitude in order to accept the benefits offered by the United States. The 13th Amendment prohibits involuntary servitude; it does not prohibit voluntary servitude. In 1870, the 15th Amendment gave that new class of citizen the right to vote in that democracy. Benefits came with this new citizenship, but with the benefits also came duties, liabilities and responsibilities that were totally regulated by the Congress for the District of Columbia and its subjects only.

In 1913, the United States began using international private law (Admiralty) because that facilitated an increase of "persons" and property for the United States, giving the District Courts booty and prize jurisdiction over enemy property within the confines of the American Republic; subject persons and property having the same status. Admiralty is a form of Military law, and jurisdiction is based upon contract. The adhesion contracts between the State Citizen and the federal government began to grow. This increase in subject citizen population became the cornerstone for the strategy of expansion, as now the federal government had many subjects because of the benefits derived from the contracts. Federal Admiralty jurisdiction was proper, because the former living soul (mask) was replaced with a legal fiction person (mask) voluntarily by contract.

Central banking for the United States was legislated into existence by the Federal Reserve Act and the 16th Amendment in 1913; it gave the central bankers all of the support they needed to finance their fiat money scheme. In 1917, the United States entered World War I and the Congress passed the Trading with the Enemy Act and the Emergency War Powers Act, opening the doors for the United States to suspend constitutional restrictions otherwise mandated by the Constitution. Even in times of peace, every contrived and created social, political, or financial emergency was sufficient authority for the officers of the United States to overstep its peace time power and implement volumes of "law" that would increase the wealth of the United States at the expense of the "persons" (mask) who were now duty bound to support it. All of the agencies that were created temporarily in time of war were not dismantled after the war, so the federal government got larger. The War Powers Act of 1917 was terminated after the war, but the agencies and departments created for that purpose still remain. There is always a declared emergency in the United States and its states since the resurrection of the War Powers Act of 1933, but when the statute is read carefully, it applies only to their 14th Amendment subject citizen. This is the main reason for obscuring the fact that there are two different classes of "person" within the American Empire, as well as two distinct United States. If you are not taught the facts in school, how else will you learn?

The statutory construction appears with crystal clarity when we consider the language used by the Supreme Court to describe the different definitions of the "United States."

"This term has several meanings. It may be merely [1] the name of a sovereign occupying the position analogous to that of other sovereigns in the family of nations, [2] it may designate territory over which sovereignty of the United States extends, or [3] it may be the collective name of the states which are united by and under the Constitution." *Hooven & Allison Co. v. Evatt.*

Thus, in *Hooven*, it is readily discernible that there are two literal UNITED STATES consisting of definitive landmasses or geographical areas. The third definition [3] in *Hooven* consists of the fifty States united under the Constitution. The second definition [2] designates the geographical area consisting of the District of Columbia and all territory over which the political sovereignty of the UNITED STATES extends. Congress expresses the sovereignty of this second UNITED STATES under authority of Article 1, §8, Clause 17 and 18, and Article 4, §3, Clause 2 of the Constitution with no constitutional restrictions placed on said plenary powers. Congress, in legislating for the District and its Territories, always defines the words "State" and "United States" in its public laws to only include such geographical areas.

Col. Edward Mandell House, who was the agent provocateur of Rothschild, the head of the European Central Banks, was assigned to oversee the President and the Congress in the implementation of the central bankers' plans. House is attributed with giving direction and strategy to be implemented by the president and the senators to enslave the American people with the passage of the Federal Reserve Act and Amendments 16 and 17.

Support for the legal presumption that the American people had volunteered to participate in the United States democracy was legislated with the 17th Amendment in 1913 in that participation in federal elections for U.S. Senator established the legal presumption necessary in determining that you were a federal citizen.

The scheme also provided for the control of the courts via the 1913 creation of the American Bar Association, whose parent organization was the European International Bar Association, which was the creation of Rothschild. This allowed the International Bankers to control the practice of law, in that the only ones permitted to practice before the courts were those who were educated under their brand of law, which was only Admiralty and Contract law. Common law of the people was to be replaced as it gave the natural man many jurisdictional protections from the bankers' legislation.

When the Congress made its first attempt to throw out the common law and replace it with Admiralty law, the Supreme Court rejected the proposed rules of court, explaining that the proposed rules would bring into existence a national police state. So, Roosevelt stacked the high Court and waited for a case upon which the demise of the common law could be accomplished. *Erie v. Tompkins* came along in 1938 and gave the court the opportunity that the Constitution did not. Thereafter, Common law at the federal level was to be no more.

The 1930s were an eat, drink and be merry time, with the majority of the population living the good life with no care in the world and no attention to what was happening in Congress. The stock market crashed, and those not on the inside were not warned to take their money out of the market and, as a result, lost everything. This set the stage for socialism and Roosevelt's New Deal. It was a new deal, all right – a one-sided deal, as you are about to learn.

Contract law is above the Constitution and under the jurisdiction of Equity/Admiralty courts, so the governments began to contract with everyone. The 1930s saw federal legislation providing for the registration of babies through applications for birth certificates. Government workers could get maternity leave with pay. The States pushed for registration of cars through applications for certificates of title and for registration of land through registration of deeds of trust. Constructive trusts were created secretly by adhesion contracts, giving benefits either present or future and as a result, each of the people blindly walked into the trap of United States democracy and its jurisdiction by the signing of contracts, thereby agreeing to be sureties for the debts of the United States and collateral for the Federal Reserve Bank, Inc.

The Great Depression supplied the diversion needed to keep the people's attention away from what the government was doing. The Social Security program was implemented, along with numerous other socialistic "New Deal" programs that invited the American people to volunteer to be the sureties behind the United States' new registered property and adhesion contracts through the legal presumption that they were 14th Amendment United States subjects. We are permitted to contract with anyone, even the government, so for the promise of benefits from the federal government, we traded away our unalienable rights and put on a mask of the subject person.

Massive registration of property through United States agencies, including the States of the Union as instrumentalities of the federal government in bankruptcy, assured the United States and its officers and instrumentalities (the states) that they would become wealthy beyond their wildest expectations, as predicted by Colonel House.

Edward Mandell House had this to say in a private meeting with Woodrow Wilson (President, 1913-1921) From the private papers of Woodrow Wilson:

"[Very] soon, every American will be required to register their biological property in a National system designed to keep track of the people and that will operate under the ancient system of pledging. By such methodology, we can compel people to submit to our agenda, which will affect our security as a charge back for our fiat paper currency. Every American will be forced to register or suffer not being able to work and earn a living. They will be our Chattel and we will hold the security interest over them forever, by operation of the law merchant under the scheme of secured transactions. Americans, by unknowingly or unwittingly delivering the bills of lading to us will be rendered bankrupt and insolvent, forever to remain economic slaves through taxation, secured by their pledges. They will be stripped of their rights and given a commercial value designed to make us a profit and they will be none the wiser, for not one man in a million could ever figure our plans and, if by accident one or two would figure it out, we have in our arsenal plausible deniability. After all, this is the only logical way to fund government, by floating liens and debt to the registrants in the form of benefits and privileges. This will inevitably reap to us huge profits beyond our wildest expectations and leave every American a contributor or to this fraud which we will call

"Social Insurance." Without realizing it, every American will insure us for any loss we may incur and in this manner; every American will unknowingly be our servant, however begrudgingly. The people will become helpless and without any hope for their redemption and, we will employ the high office of the President of our dummy corporation to foment this plot against America."

All of this was done without disclosure of the material facts that accompanied each application for contract registration. That fraud would have been sufficient reason to charge all the United States officers and elected officials with treason, unless a legal remedy could be legislated for the people to recoup their property and collect for the damages they suffered as a result of the fraud if ever discovered.

If a legal remedy was available, and the people chose not to or failed to secure their remedy, no charge of fraud could be brought, even to a common law court. The United States Congress needed only to provide the legal remedy. It was not required to explain it or even tell the people where the remedy could be found; if they did that then the entire conspiracy would be revealed and every cherry tree in Washington would be decorated with hanging bodies of Congressmen and bankers. The attorneys did not even have to be taught about the remedy in law school. Remaining quiet, Congress had plausible deniability if the people discovered the deception. The majority of the legislators did not have to have the intricate details of the law explained to them regarding the bills they were passing; the pressure was on by the leadership to pass this legislation, and that was all they needed to know. If the people failed to exercise due diligence, the United States became the holder in trust of all the land and labor of every subject in the American Empire. If, however, the people did discover their legal remedy, the United States would have to honor it and release the registered property back to the people, but only if the people were cognizant that they had a remedy, and only if they exercised it in the proper technical manner. It was a great plan, and it has worked for over 70 years.

Having established plausible deniability, even if the people became enlightened that they had a remedy and pursued it, the attorneys, judges, and legislators could claim that they did not understand the people's claims, especially if the technical requirements for achieving it were not followed pursuant to the statutory requirements. Requiring the public schools to teach civics, government, and history classes out of federally-approved politically correct textbooks written by the publishing houses owned by the owners of the Federal Reserve would assure that the people would not discover the remedy for a long time, if ever.

Passing state and federal statutes that subjugated the citizens to rules and regulations added another firewall of protection against the people ever discovering their remedy. The media, owned by the same people who own the Federal Reserve, was fashioned to report politically correct news day after day *ad nausea*, until few people believed there was any hope for relief from the system and totally forgot all of their previous history of liberty and freedom. If the people could be separated from their money and their time in pursuit of the remedy, it could be obscured long enough so that that the solutions could be lost in millions of law library books across the country and equitable estoppel by laches could be argued against the few who discovered it.

The majority of elder Americans know there is something terribly wrong with all the conflicts in the law and the "facts" they were taught in school; not so with the newer generation. How can the American people be free and subject to a government's fancy at the same time?

In 1933 the United States established its insurance policy with HJR 192 and recorded it in the Congressional Record. The Federal Register publication of that law was not required at that time. An Executive Order issued on April 5, 1933, paved the way for the withdrawal of all gold in the United States. Representative Louis T. McFadden brought formal criminal charges on May 23, 1933, against the Board of Governors of the Federal Reserve Bank system, the Comptroller of the Currency, and the Secretary of the United States Treasury (Congressional Record May 23, 1933, page 4055-4058). Those charges are still not acted upon and are still in committee. HJR 192 passed on June 3, 1933. Mr. McFadden claimed on June 10, 1933: "Mr. Chairman, we have in this country one of the most corrupt institutions the world has ever known. I refer to the Federal Reserve Board and the Federal Reserve Banks..."

HJR 192 is the insurance policy that protects the legislators from conviction for fraud and treason against the American people. It also protects the American people from damages caused by the actions of the United States.

HJR 192 provides that the one with the gold paid the bills. It removed the requirement that the United States subjects and employees had to pay their debts with gold. It actually prohibited the inclusion of any clause in all subsequent contracts that would require payment in gold. It also cancelled the clause in every contract written prior to June 5, 1933, that required an obligation to be paid in gold. It provided that the United States subjects and employees could use any type of coin and currency to discharge a public debt as long as it was in use in the normal course of business in the United States. For a time, United States Notes were the currency used to discharge debts because there was 40% gold and 60% Treasury guarantees behind the currency, but later the Federal Reserve and the United States provided a new medium of exchange through paper notes and debt instruments that could be passed on to a debtor's creditors to tender the debtor's debts. Tender and payment are not the same. Tender merely changes the legal character of the debt, where gold and silver would extinguish the debt.

In the 1950s, the Uniform Commercial Code was adopted in most of the States as a means of unifying the generally accepted procedures for handling the new legal system of dealing with commercial fictions as though they were real. Security instruments replaced substance as collateral for debts. Security instruments could be supported by presumptive adhesion contracts. Debt instruments with collateral and accommodating parties could be used instead of money. Money and the need for money was disappearing, and a uniform system of law had to be put in place to allow the courts to uphold the security instruments that depended on commercial fictions as a basis for compelling payment or performance. All this was accomplished by the mid-1960s.

The commercial code is merely a codification of accepted and required procedures which all people engaged in commercial activity must follow. The basic principles of commerce had been settled thousands of years ago, but were refined as commerce become more sophisticated over the years. In the 1900s, the age-old principles of commerce shifted from substance to form. Presumption became a major element of the law. Without giving a degree of force to legal presumption, the new direction in enforcing commercial claims could not be supported in Equity/Admiralty courts and had no chance in common law. If the claimants were required to produce their claims every time they tried to collect from the people, they would seldom be successful. The principles articulated in the commercial code combine the methods of dealing with substantive commercial activity with presumptive commercial activity. These principles work as well for us as they do for the entrenched powers. The rules are neutral and respect neither side of a dispute, as they are ancient in origin.

The entrenched powers that engineered the scheme for the people to register their property and person with the United States and its instrumentalities gained control of the peoples' property and right to property through registration and licensing. The United States became the trustee of the titles to everything. The definition of "property" is the interest one has in a thing. The thing is the principal. The property is the interest in the thing. Profits (interest) made from the property of another belong to the owner of the thing. The International Bankers made profits by pledging as surety the registered property of the people in commercial markets, but the profits do not belong to the Bankers. The profits belong to the owners of the thing. That is always the people. The corporation government shows only ownership of paper – titles to things. The substance cannot appear in the fiction. Sometimes the fiction is manufactured to appear as substance, but fiction can never become substance; it is an illusion. This is why the proper spelling of your name in upper and lower case is never used in court documents. The ALL CAPS spelling represents the legal fiction, which the government holds title to and jurisdiction over, as it is the creation of the government. The substance cannot appear in the fiction. What will happen when you appear and claim the name ascribed on the complaint? You and the fiction become one and the same; you have changed masks from a natural person to an artificial one.

The profits from all the registered property had to be put into trust for the benefit of the owners. If the profits were put into the general fund of the United States and not into separate trusts for the owners, the scheme would evidence fraud. The profits for each owner could not be co-mingled. If the owner failed to use his available remedy (fictional credits held in a constructive trust account, fund, or financial ledger) to benefit from the profits, it would not be the fault of the government or their banking co-conspirators. If the owner failed to learn the law that would open the door to his remedy, it would not be the fault of the swindlers. The owner is responsible for learning the law so he understands that the profits from his property are available for him to discharge debts or charges brought against his legal fiction person by the United States or other commercial entities.

If the United States has the "gold," the United States pays the bills (from the trust account, fund, or financial ledger). The definition of "fund" is money set aside to pay a debt. The fund is there to discharge the public debts attributed to the United States subjects, but ultimately back to the accommodating parties – the American people. The national debt is that which is due to the owners of the registered things – the American people – as well as to other creditors.

If the United States owes a debt to the owner of the thing, and the owner is presumed (by accommodation) to owe a public debt to the United States, the logical thing is to ask the United States to discharge that public debt from the trust fund. The way for the United States to get around having to pay the public debts for the people is to claim the owner cannot be an owner if he agreed to be the accommodating party for a debtor person. If the people are truly the principal, then they know how to handle their financial and political affairs (unless they have never been taught). If the owner admits by his actions of ignorance that he is an accommodating party, he has taken on the debtor's liabilities without getting consideration in exchange. Here lies the fiction again.

The owner of the thing does not have to knowingly agree to be the accommodating party for the debtor person; he just has to act like he agreed. The legal presumption that he is the accommodating party is strong enough for the courts to hold the owner of the thing liable for a tax on the thing he actually owns.

Debtors may have the use of certain things, but the things belong to the creditors. The creditor is the master. The debtor is the servant. The Uniform Commercial Code is very specific about the duties and responsibilities a debtor has. If the owner of the thing is presumed to be a debtor because of his previous admissions and adhesion contracts, he is going to have a difficult time convincing the United States that it has a duty to discharge public debts for him. In addition, the federal courts are staffed with loyal judges who will look for every mistake the people make when trying to use their remedy and use the mistake against them in dismissing any action they bring.

There is a very powerful tool the people can use to help them get to the real issues when they find themselves up against the power of presumption. The law provides for either party of an admiralty action to object to a line of questioning. When you object in that court setting, you must tell the judge why you object or he will overrule your objection. The reason is:

"This line of questioning assumes facts not in evidence."

You can request that evidence of the Plaintiff's claim be entered into evidence. If the judge overrules this fundamental principle of establishing subject matter jurisdiction and the right to make a charge, there is a major procedural error in the proceeding. Your objection has preserved the error for appeal. Granting in personam jurisdiction to get to the bottom of the issue is vastly better than arguing, "I'm not that person."

The owner of the thing, after learning the law and discovering who he is in relation to the United States, can file a UCC 1 Financing Statement and Security Agreement registering his interest in the artificial entity (PERSON) the United States created after Mom applied for a birth certificate. That was the act of registering her biological property, her baby (substance), with the State. The United States holds the paper title (form), not the substance (baby). Until your Financing Statement is filed, the United States is the holder of the title to the artificial entity. Its name is spelled in all capital letters – JOHN HENRY DOE. When John Henry Doe files the Financing Statement supported by a Security Agreement signed by the artificial entity (JOHN) and the owner (John), he becomes the holder in due course of the title to JOHN. The UCC and the State commercial law are very specific about the effect of a registered security interest. It has priority over most other interest claimed (only claimed) in the same thing. The evidence that is missing in the court is the registered claim over the person (JOHN).

The owner also must notify the Secretary of the Treasury that he is going to handle his own affairs in the future. He can file a "Bill of Exchange" with the Secretary through which he exchanges his person's accepted-for-value birth certificate and social security numbers for a charge-back of all the presumed charges brought against his person since the birth certificate was issued.

The owner can also reserve a non-cash Federal Reserve routing number and any number of non-cash instrument numbers by filing an amendment to his Financing Statement or just including his reservation on his original Financing Statement. Each bank account opened in the name of the owner's person has a routing number. If an account is open, it is available to process cash items. If you write a check to the plumber, it can be converted to cash at your bank. You cannot write a check on an account that has been closed. Those accounts and their routing numbers are reserved for non-cash items for the person (JOHN) that opened the account originally. Accounts that have been closed by the bank, instead of the person, should not be used for non-cash items. Once this is done, you are in a position to begin receiving reimbursements against the obligation the United States owes to you for money and time it has received that belong to you.

The owner of registered things who has learned the law and what his rights are and who has filed his Financing Statement, Security Agreement, and Bill of Exchange, and reserved his non-cash account routing numbers, can issue an instrument indicating his UCC registration number, his registered Federal Reserve routing number, the name of the public party making a charge against his person, and the amount of the debt to be discharged.

Think of the whole transaction in relation to a hot air balloon. The balloon represents your public person (JOHN), which is an empty entity that can function within the public maize of fiction, transmitting benefits from the public to you in the private IF it is filled with hot air. You cannot go into the public because you are not a fiction. JOHN has no lift until it is filled with hot air. That hot air comes from an IRS default notice, court judgment, credit card bill, utility bill, traffic ticket, or some other instrument that has a $ amount and JOHN's name on it as the presumed debtor. The bill is the hot air. It fills up the dead JOHN. You can now discharge JOHN and put JOHN's accrual account with the charging party back to a zero balance. You as the secured party over the assets put up as security by JOHN to you as collateral for the debt JOHN owes you, can discharge JOHN with a negotiable instrument for the same $ amount as the charging instrument. The charging party that receives your non-cash item can 1) process it through a United States department, 2) give it to a third party, 3) keep it to increase its liquidity.

When you, as the owner of a thing, registered it with the United States or one of its subdivisions, you let the United States hold the legal title to your thing based on misrepresentation and failure to disclose material facts to you at the time of registration. You probably retained possession of the thing. The United States invested the title and made a profit. If you did not specifically authorize the United States and its agents to invest the legal title, the profits made from that title belong to you, because as the owner, you remain the equitable titleholder. Legally all the profits from the investment of the titles to all your registered things must go into a fund for your benefit. If they did not put the profits in a trust fund of some sort, it would be fraud.

Just acquiring the titles through what is promoted as mandatory registration is fraud. If the scenario attributed to Mandell House is now in full application in the United States, which it is, the officers of the United States could be charged and convicted with treason IF they had not provided a remedy, which they did.

House Joint Resolution 192 on June 5, 1933, is their insurance policy to assure they are not convicted of treason. That does not mean they cannot be charged with treason, but the courts will dismiss based on failure to state a claim upon which relief can be granted. Because you have a remedy outside the court, you cannot sustain a charge of treason.

The problem in the past with trying to discharge public debts with instruments that could not be processed through your corner bank was that those discharge instruments did not route through the Federal Reserve, the bean counter for the federal debt. That debt is first and primarily owed to the people who are the equitable titleholders of all the substance in this country. If you try to discharge a public debt with your discharge instrument, and you do not route it through the Federal Reserve, it appears you are receiving a benefit from the United States without exchanging it for something of value. This is not technically correct because you have a right to be reimbursed, whether or not you apply it toward the debt the United States owes you. You are the substance; it is the fiction.

If you do route your discharge instrument through the Federal Reserve, where the national debt owed to you can be reduced by the amount of the instrument, you have made an exchange that fits nicely into their accrual bookkeeping system. Your PERSON's charge from the charging party within the United States commercial scheme is discharged, and the debt the United States owes to you is discharged by the same amount. That is a quid pro quo, and everyone is happy, EXCEPT those who are not interested in the money but just want to be in control from behind the scenes.

To accomplish this quid pro quo exchange:

1. Your claim to being one of the people must appear on a public register (the Secretary of State);
2. You must have an account with the banker for the United States (the Secretary of the Treasury);
3. You must have given notice of your reservation of routing numbers through the national debt accountant (the Federal Reserve);
4. You must refer to the insurance policy that covers your remedy (House Joint Resolution 192);
5. You must make your instrument negotiable so it can be used by the United States for a profit;
6. You must transmit your instrument back into the public through an agent (your registered debtor);
7. You must use only a non-cash item for this exchange;
8. You must do a banker's acceptance of a charging instrument to attach to your non-cash item; and
9. You must understand that you are not getting something for nothing.

Reserving your routing numbers to use on your discharge instruments is not as difficult as was thought during the previous decade. Every person has opened bank accounts in the past that have been closed for one reason or another. On the bottom of the checks for those closed bank accounts there is a routing number to the particular bank and a routing number to the particular account. Each check has a check number. When you put the check number together with the two routing numbers, you have a means of tracking each item that goes through the worldwide banking system. The routing numbers on the bottom of the checks from accounts your person has closed will never be reassigned. They are attached to your person's NAME forever and kept in the records of the Federal Reserve.

Bank accounts that are still open and active are used for cash items. Checks written on these open bank accounts can be taken to the particular bank and CASHED. This is the type of instrument used in commercial transactions everyday. There is a fund attached to the check from which the debt evidenced by the check can be paid.

Bank accounts that are no longer open and active cannot be used to process cash items. They can be used only to process non-cash items. They require special handling. Title 12 of USC and CFR explain how and when receiving banks are to process non-cash items. A closed bank account associated with your debtor's NAME has routing numbers that can route your discharge instrument through the Federal Reserve to reduce the national debt to you and increase the balance of the bank account of the party that is charging your debtor. It is a win-win situation.

The charging party is instructed to mail the discharge instrument to the Secretary of Transportation. Title 46 has sufficient evidence to support the proposition that the Secretary is the trustee over some or all vessels mortgaged by the United States. If your debtor PERSON is presumed to be a vessel, it is regulated by the Secretary of Transportation through the Maritime Ministries Administration; that is the proper party to assist in processing your non-cash item. The Secretary of Transportation can forward the item to the Secretary of the Treasury, who already has been notified to prepare for non-cash activity in your treasury direct account on the Bill of Exchange.

The Secretary of the Treasury is directly related to the Federal Reserve. Between the Treasury and the Federal Reserve, your non-cash item can be directed to the proper parties to settle the account and get everyone into that quid pro quo position we want.

The United States and its co-business partners are debtors to you. You are the creditor, not only over your debtor PERSON, but also over the United States, the legal titleholder over the registered things to which you are the equitable titleholder. You are the primary creditor, so if the United States has other creditors, like the international bankers, they cannot jump to the front of the line. Their claims are subordinated to your claims if your claims are registered and if you understand the law surrounding what you are doing.

Now that you have a better understanding of the "person" (mask) and "contract" and "jurisdiction" let's get back to the issue of sovereignty.

It is important to differentiate between sovereign power and unalienable rights. Sovereign power is subject to nothing, except what the sovereign expressly agrees to or consents may be done. Unalienable rights are simply those rights which cannot be taken away as they are deemed to be God-given and fundamental, without which no civilized society can exist, but they may be waived.

In this context it may be understood how the people may remain sovereign, even in the area where the federal government exercises its sovereign jurisdiction. By consent or by waiver, the people may be without those fundamental rights, as in those Federal jurisdictions; at least it appears that the federal government operates on that ideology. (*Hooven v. Evatt*, 324 US 652, 671-672)

Although there might be some waiver of rights, it is impossible to convert the natural born (sovereign) Citizen of this country into a subject (person) of his government. (*M'Ilvaine v. Coke's Lessee*, 8 US 209)

The framers acknowledged that the proposed Constitution for the united States of America was to be a document of "We the People," not of the States. It was to become a compact that provided for the people to be its beneficiaries in perpetuity. It was intended as a compact between the individual Citizen on the one hand and, on the other hand, the people as a whole, acting through their representatives. (*Glass v. The Sloop Betsey*, 4 US [4 Dall.] 8)

The Constitution was a compact drawn between the people and effective between the states. It created a union of States, not a union of people. The people are not members of the union; only the States are members. This is critical to your understanding of your proper relationship with the government. One is a Citizen of his state. National Citizenship is derived from state citizenship. Implicit to this process is the recognition that the true sovereignty was not with the States, but rather with the people as a whole. (*Gaines et al. v. Buford*, 31 KY 481, 500-501)

By virtue of this contract, three concepts of "United States" came into existence. First is the concept that the United States is a sovereign nation in the family of nations. This requires foreign governments to deal with the government of the United States of America rather than with each State or Citizen separately. Second is the idea that the United States is sovereign over its territory. This refers to the sovereignty of the government over that territory that is subject to its exclusive legislation, not to the territory of the fifty States. This is usually conceived to be the political jurisdiction of the United States. Third, the term is merely the collective name of the fifty States which are united under the Constitution. Federal sovereignty is not sovereignty over "We, the People."

Everything in our system operates on a contract principle. We give something to government and get something in return. If there is no benefit, there is not reciprocal obligation. It is a maxim of contract law that a contract is not enforceable, lacking equal consideration inuring to both parties of the agreement. No state and no citizen surrendered any sovereignty to any government. It was merely agreed that the national government, the state government and the people would be bound to obey proper laws made under the authority of that compact. They would suffer penalties if they did not. This is a common law viewpoint applicable among free men. It does not make the sovereign people subject to their government. The beneficiaries and their descendants remain bound because the compacts have created governmental entities pertaining to specific territories. If a person lives in the territory, either he obeys the common law of the territory thereof, or he is an outlaw.

Article 1 of the Constitution deals with the structure and powers of Congress. If Congress does not have a power to legislate in some area, then generally the other branches have no powers there either. If there is no law, there is nothing for the executive branch to enforce and nothing for the judiciary to interpret. The function of Congress is to make our laws, to the extent that the Constitution permits law making, and to make the laws for the municipal government of the District of Columbia, where there are no constitutional restrictions.

Article 1 also deprives the states of power to do those things for which the national government was formed. Our government is a limited government and this is made clear by the fact that it can act only within those powers that are specifically delegated. The enumerated rights are set forth in Article 1, Section 8, and Article IV, Section 3. By this enumeration Congress has power to make laws insofar as they are necessary and proper for the exercise of its enumerated power.

Particularly important is the power given to the government to have exclusive legislative jurisdiction over the seat of government and such other lands as are ceded to the government by the states for its military functions. This is a power limited in its territorial scope, but not otherwise. Because this special power has no constitutional limitation, unlike Congress' other enumerated powers, it is similar to the power of a sovereign. It is called the "political jurisdiction" of the United States. It operates in Washington, D.C., and in all areas ceded by the states to the federal government as enclaves. A similar power operates in the possessions and territories of the United States, but it has its source in a combination of the property power and the power to acquire territory. This is described as inherent powers. Sovereign power, like admiralty law, is deemed a necessity in those "uncivilized" territories. Such sovereign power of the federal government does not operate within the fifty states. As we will explore later, all federal courts are of Admiralty jurisdiction.

Constitutional guarantees do not generally apply in the sovereign federal areas, except insofar as Congress chooses to enforce them. Although a fundamental right should still exist since it is deemed unalienable, Congress can take the position that since "We the People" delegated sovereign power, all of the people must be subjects in those areas, because there cannot be two sovereigns ruling in the same place.

Having such power, it was not hard to predict that Congress would expand its power beyond proper Constitutional limitations. This expansion of power is manifestly evident in the application of the taxing power. That power is limited by the Constitution: direct taxes must be apportioned and indirect (excise) taxes must be uniform. These limitations, however, do not apply where the government has sovereign power. While enumerated powers are exercised all over the country, they are limited by the Constitution. The sovereign powers in territories and areas ceded by the states are not limited by the Constitution, and those citizens have little or no Constitutional protection.

Congressional power over federal funds has also been used to expand government authority. This is done by virtue of the practice of the federal government placing conditions on its grants of federal assistance. After all, the sovereign Citizen has the right to contract, even with the federal government. If you sell a right, it is gone, even though "unalienable." By this process the federal government has invaded every conceivable facet of the lives of citizens within the fifty states, regardless of the Constitution and its restrictions.

States, individuals and companies have all surrendered rights in exchange for Federal Reserve notes (fiat money) by entering into invisible contracts with the federal government. They do so by the use of such things as bank accounts, Social Security accounts, credit cards, etc. These invisible contracts have given the Federal Government jurisdiction over the majority of Americans, tried in Federal Equity/Admiralty Courts where the Constitution has no standing, as you have a contract with the government, and you never even knew it.

Powers not delegated to government by the Constitution belong to the people except to the extent that the people in their State constitutions have given them to States. The reality is that government has grabbed a lot more power than was given them under the Constitution and the Supreme Court has ratified the seizure. The Supreme Court in 1932 decided that any law enacted by Congress or the States was not open to challenge by anyone who had received any benefit under such law. Nor could the law be invalidated if there were some way to construe or apply such law in a manner not in conflict with constitutional limitations. (*Ashwander v. T.V.A.* (1932) 297 US 288)

However, whenever either a voluntary act or a questionable law appears to deprive the citizen of an unalienable natural right, if the Citizen is not aware that such is the effect of that act or law, the courts must prevent such deprivation. The Supreme Court has ruled that an unconscious and unintended waiver of any such right does not strip the Citizen of that right, but the district courts continually disregard that principle.

An example of the distinction is given by the Supreme Court in its requirement for unsworn declarations under penalty of perjury, located at 28 USC 1746. There is a different declaration for one who is within the United States used on all IRS 1040 Forms and one who is without the United States.

What is the only way one can be guilty of perjury? If one tells a lie under Oath or Oath of Office, period! There is no other way. How then can a Citizen who is filing his 1040 tax form be under penalty of perjury if he is not under Oath? The answer is he can't. The only ones who can file that form are government employees who are under Oath of Office.

CHAPTER THREE

COLLECTION AGENCY

AN OLD FASHIONED COLLECTION AGENCY

THE ABSENCE OF A STATUTE CREATING EITHER THE BUREAU OF INTERNAL REVENUE OR INTERNAL REVENUE SERVICE

The Constitution requires that law create offices or agencies. Pursuant to this mandate, on July 1, 1862, during the Civil War, Congress created several bureaus in branches of the federal government. But did it create during the same time the predecessor of the Internal Revenue Service, the Bureau of Internal Revenue?

In 1972, Internal Revenue Manual 1100 was published in both the Federal Register and Cumulative Bulletin (see 37 Fed. Reg. 20960, 1972-2 Cum. Bul. 836.) On the very first page of this Manual, published in the Bulletin, the following admission was made:

"(3) By common parlance [sic] and understanding of the time, an office of the importance of the Office of Commissioner of Internal Revenue was a bureau. The Secretary of the Treasury in his report at the close of the calendar year 1862 stated that, '*The Bureau of Internal Revenue has been organized under the Act of the last session...*'"

Also it can be seen that Congress had intended to establish a Bureau of Internal Revenue, or thought they had, from the act of March 3 1863, in which provision was made for the President to appoint with Senate confirmation a Deputy Commissioner of Internal Revenue "*...who shall be charged with such duties in the bureau of internal revenue as may be prescribed by the Secretary of the Treasury, or as may be required by law, and who shall act as Commissioner of internal revenue in the absence of that officer, and exercise the privilege of franking all letters and documents pertaining to the office of internal revenue.*"

In other words, "the office of internal revenue" was "the bureau of internal revenue," and the act of July 1, 1862, is the organic act of today's Internal Revenue Service.

This statement again appears in a similar publication appearing at 39 Fed. Reg. 11572, 1974-1 Cum. Bul. 440, as well as the current IRM 1100, essentially admitting that Congress never created either the Bureau of Internal Revenue or the Internal Revenue Service. That Congress *thought* it had created this agency is an admission that even the government itself cannot find anything that created either agency. The only office created by the act of July 1, 1862, was the Office of the Commissioner; that's an individual, not an agency consisting of over 100,000 employees. Neither the Bureau nor the Service was actually created by any of these acts. Congressman Pat Danner has acknowledged this deficiency: "You are quite correct when you state that an organization with the actual name 'Internal Revenue Service' was not established by law."

EXAMPLES OF THE CREATION OF PUBLIC OFFICES

Offices of the United States are extremely easy to create. To establish a public office, all Congress has done historically was to enact legislation that expressly declared that an office was being created. For example, on February 14, 1903, Congress created the Department of Commerce and Labor, 32 Stat. 825:

"That there shall be at the seat of government an executive department to be known as the Department of Commerce and Labor, and a Secretary of Commerce and Labor, who shall be the head thereof, who shall be appointed by the President, by and with the advice and consent of the Senate..."

Review of this particular statute demonstrates that this department was expressly created and that it plainly was one that constituted an office of the United States and its secretary was a cabinet officer.

But this is not the only example; there is a multitude of others. During the Civil War, Congress established a variety of bureaus. On July 5, 1862, Congress enacted a law which established several bureaus in the Navy Department, 12 Stat. 510:

"That there shall be established in the Navy Department the following bureaus, to wit:

"First. A Bureau of Yards and Docks.

"Second. A Bureau of Equipment and Recruiting.

"Third. A Bureau of Navigation.

"Fourth. A Bureau of Ordnance.

"Fifth. A Bureau of Construction and Repair.

"Sixth. A Bureau of Steam Engineering.

"Seventh. A Bureau of Provisions and Clothing.

"Eighth. A Bureau of Medicine and Surgery."

On June 20, 1864, Congress created a bureau to dispense military justice, 13 Stat. 144, 145:

"Sec. 5. And be it further enacted, that there shall be attached to, and made a part of, the War Department, during the continuance of the present rebellion, a bureau, to be known as the Bureau of Military Justice..."

Later on March 3, 1865, Congress established another similar bureau, 13 Stat. 507:

"That there is hereby established in the War Department, to continue during the present war of rebellion, and for one year thereafter, a bureau of refugees, freedmen, and abandoned lands... The said bureau shall be under the management and control of a commissioner to be appointed by the President, by and with the advice and consent of the Senate..."

Many public offices have been created as required by the Constitution. On May 29, 1884, Congress created the following bureau, 23 Stat. 31:

"That the Commissioner of Agriculture shall organize in his Department a Bureau of Animal Industry, and shall appoint a Chief thereof..."

See also 42 Stat. 139, 140: "Sec. 8. That there is hereby created and established in the Department of the Navy a Bureau of Aeronautics..."

On May 27, 1930, a bureau was established in the Justice Department, 46 Stat. 427: "There shall be in the Department of Justice a Bureau of Prohibition, at the head of which shall be a Director of Prohibition. The Director of Prohibition shall be appointed by the Attorney General, without regard to the civil service laws..."

These simple examples show that Congress is well aware of how to establish public offices pursuant to the Constitution. Congress surely knew how to and did create bureaus during the Civil War, but it has never seen any urgency in creating an "Internal Revenue Service."

OFFICERS OF THE UNITED STATES

The Constitution of the United States makes provision for the manner and method of appointing "Officers of the United States.

Art. II, §2, cl. 2 of the Constitution, the President "...shall nominate, and by and with the Advice and Consent of the Senate, shall appoint Ambassadors, other public Ministers and Consuls, Judges of the supreme Court, and all other Officers of the United States, whose Appointments are not herein otherwise provided for, and which shall be established by Law: but the Congress may by Law vest the Appointment of such inferior Officers, as they think proper, in the President alone, in the Courts of Law, or in the Heads of Departments."

Pursuant to the Constitution, an "Officer of the United States" is one who has been appointed with the Senate's consent to an office established by law. An inferior officer is appointed through the same method, except that consent of the Senate is not necessary.

How has the Supreme Court construed this provision of the Constitution? In *United States v. Mouat,* 124 U.S. 303, 8 S.Ct. 505 (1888), the Supreme Court was required to determine whether a Navy paymaster's clerk was an "officer" who could recover traveling expenses as allowed by law only for officers. Here, the Court was required to define the method for the appointment of officers of the United States, and it held:

"[U]nder the constitution of the United States, all its officers were appointed by the president, by and with the consent of the senate, or by a court of law, or the head of a department; and the heads of the departments were defined in that opinion to be what are now called the members of the cabinet. Unless a person in the service of the government, therefore, holds his place by virtue of an appointment by, the president, or of one of the courts of justice or heads of departments authorized by law to make such an appointment, he is not, strictly speaking, an officer of the United States."

Since in this case the president did not appoint Mouat, the Court found it essential to determine whether the head of a department had appointed him. There being no statute authorizing the Secretary of the Navy to approve Mouat's appointment the Court concluded that he was not even an inferior officer.

But there is no statute authorizing the secretary of the Navy to appoint a pay-master's clerk, nor is there any act requiring his approval of such an appointment, and the regulations of the navy do not seem to require any such appointment or approval for the holding of that position. The claimant, therefore, was not an officer, either appointed by the president or under the authority of any law vesting such appointment in the head of a department.

For this reason, it was held that Mouat was not entitled to travel expenses that were authorized to officers of the United States.

Another important case regarding the appointment of United States officers is *United States v. Smith,* 124 U.S. 525, 8 S.Ct. 595 (1888). Here, Smith was being prosecuted for embezzlement committed while he was employed as a clerk in the office of the collector of the customs. Since the statute under which Smith was being charged applied solely to officers of the United States, the Court was again required to define who was such an officer:

"An officer of the United States can only be appointed by the president, by and with the advice and consent of the senate, or by a court of law, or the head of a department. A person in the service of the government who does not derive his position from one of these sources is not an officer of the United States in the sense of the constitution."

In this case, Smith was found not to be an officer because neither the president nor the head of his department appointed him:

"There must be, therefore, a law authorizing the head of a department to appoint clerks of the collector before his approbation of their appointment can be required." No such law is in existence.

It is thus very clear that the constitution as well as a variety of decisions of the courts have provided the basic parameters to determine who is precisely an officer of the United States. See *United States v. Lee*, 106 U.S. 196, 220, 1 S.Ct. 240 (1882). ("All the officers of the government, from the highest to the lowest, are creatures of the law and are bound to obey it.") *Norton v. Shelby County*, 118 U.S. 425, 441, 6 S.Ct. 1121 (1886) ("There can be no officer, either de jure or de facto, if there be no office to fill"); and *N.L.R.B. v. Coca-Cola Bottling Co. of Louisville*, 350 U.S. 264, 269, 76 S.Ct. 383 (1956):

"Officers normally means those who hold defined offices. It does not mean the boys in the back room or other agencies of invisible government, whether in politics or in the trade-union movement."

This case is the reason why 26 U.S.C., §7803, exists. But, remember, *no statute exists regarding the appointment of others by the Commissioner.*

This is perhaps why you will not find any evidence that an IRS agent has taken an oath of office, required of all Officers of the United States Government. If one exhibits an oath, that individual is most likely serving in the capacity of a Federal Marshal.

If law did not create the IRS and the Officers of the IRS are not Officers of the United States Government, under what authority do they exist?

Congress did not create the Bureau of Internal Revenue and Internal Revenue Service. These are not organizations or agencies of the Department of the Treasury or of the federal government. They operate through pure trusts, administered by the Secretary of the Treasury (Trustee). The Settlor of the trusts or the Beneficiary or Beneficiaries are unknown. According to the law governing trusts, that information does not have to be revealed.

TITLE 31 USC

The organization of the Department of the Treasury can be found in Title 31 USC, §3. You will not find the Bureau of Internal Revenue, the Internal Revenue Service, the Secret Service, or the Bureau of Alcohol Tobacco and

Firearms listed. I learned that the Bureau of Internal Revenue, a.k.a., Internal Revenue, internal revenue, Internal Revenue Service, the Bureau of Internal Revenue Service, internal revenue service, Official Internal Revenue Service, the Federal Alcohol Administration, Director Alcohol Tobacco and Firearms Division, and the Bureau of Alcohol, Tobacco and Firearms are one and the same organization. Their organizational offices and field offices have not been recorded in the Federal Register. They are all invisible as a matter of law.

Constructive Fraud

My investigation discovered that, except for the very few who are engaged in specific or licensed activities, the Citizens of the fifty States of the united States of America have never been required to file or to pay "income taxes." The Federal government is engaged in constructive fraud on a massive scale. Americans who have been frightened into filing and paying "income taxes" have been robbed. Millions of lives have been ruined. Thousands of innocent people have been imprisoned on the pretense they violated a law that does not exist. Marriages have been destroyed; property has been levied upon to pay taxes that were never owed. Many have been driven to suicide or insanity. The home of the free and land of the brave is not a description that I would give to the modern day United States.

Lincoln's War Powers Tax

During the Civil war, Abraham Lincoln imposed what would later be termed a "War Powers Act" and a war tax upon the citizens of the Federal Government. The War tax lawfully applied only to those citizens who were considered to be in rebellion against the Union or who resided within the federal District of Columbia or the federally owned territories, dockyards, naval bases, and forts. Many Citizens of the several States volunteered to pay believing they were required to do so or simply because they wanted to help in the war effort. After the war the tax was repealed. This left the impression with the general population of the country that the President and Congress had the constitutional authority to levy an unapportioned direct tax upon the Citizens of the several States. In fact, no such tax had ever been imposed. The Tax was not fraud on the part of Mr. Lincoln or the Congress, as nothing was done to deceive the people. Those who volunteered, in fact, deceived themselves just as we do today.

Philippine Trust #1

By conquest of Spain, the United States acquired the territory of the Philippine Islands, Guam, and Puerto Rico as war reparations. The Philippine Commission passed the Philippine Customs Administrative Act during the period from September 1, 1900, to August 31, 1902. The Act was for the regulation of trade with foreign countries and designed to generate revenue in the form of duties, excises and imposts. The Act created the federal government's first trust fund titled Trust fund #1, Philippine special fund or customs duties, (31 USC § 1321).

The Act was administered under the general supervision and control of the Secretary of Finance and Justice.

Philippine Trust #2

Bureau of Internal Revenue

The Philippine Commission passed another act known as the Internal Revenue Law of 1904. This Act created the Bureau of Internal Revenue and the federal government's second trust fund called Trust fund #2, the Philippine special fund (internal revenue) and the IRS were born. [31 USC §1321]. Article I, Section 2.

"There shall be established a Bureau of Internal Revenue, the chief officer of which Bureau shall be known as the Collector of Internal Revenue. He shall be appointed by the Civil Governor, with the advice and consent of the Philippine Commission, and shall receive a salary at the rate of eight thousand pesos per annum. The Bureau of Internal Revenue shall belong to the Department of Finance and Justice."

Section 3 states, "The Collector of Internal Revenue, under the direction of the Secretary of Finance and Justice, shall have general superintendence of the assessment and collection of all taxes and excises imposed by this Act or by any Act amendatory thereof, and shall perform such other duties as may be required by law."

Customs & Bureau of Internal Revenue Merged

The Customs Administrative Act was to fall within the jurisdiction of the Bureau of Internal Revenue, which was to be responsible for "...all taxes and excises imposed by this Act." The Act clearly included import and export excise taxes. This effectively merged Customs and Internal Revenue in the Philippines.

Prohibition

When Prohibition was ratified in 1919 with the18th Amendment, the government created federal bureaucracies to enforce the new law. As social protest and resistance mounted against Prohibition, new federal laws and the number of bureaucrats hired to enforce them increased. This seems to be the only way this de facto government can operate – more laws and more cops. After much public dissent, imprisoned citizens and loss of life, Congress repealed Prohibition with the ratification of the 21st Amendment to the Constitution in 1933.

For the purpose of our analysis on the demise of the Republic and the birth of a Democracy, the year 1933 will be as good as any. This country had elected a dedicated socialist, who by his actions would effectively destroy the Republic.

As one of his first acts as President, Franklin Delano Roosevelt declared a "Banking Emergency" to bail out the Federal Reserve Bank, which had embezzled this country's gold supply. The Congress gave the President dictatorial powers under the "War Powers Act of 1917" (amended 1933), written, by the way, by the Board of Governors of the Federal Reserve Bank of New York.

Congress used the economic emergency as the excuse to give blanket approval to any and all presidential executive orders, making Roosevelt a constitutional dictator. Roosevelt, a devout socialist, with a little help from his socialist friends, was prolific in his production of new legislation and executive orders, as has every president since. It is he who placed the federal and state governments and all of the people into perpetual bankruptcy, pledging their labor and property as collateral to the creditors, the International Banking families.

Who owns the Federal Reserve central banks? The ownership of the twelve central banks, a very well kept secret, has been revealed. They are all members of the Council on Foreign Relations, Trilateral Commission, or their European counterparts, the Bilderbergers:

Rothschild Bank of London
Warburg Bank of Hamburg
Rothschild Bank of Berlin
Lehman Brothers of New York
Lazard Brothers of Paris
Kuhn Loeb Bank of New York
Israel Moses Self of Italy
Goldman Sachs of New York
Warburg Bank of Amsterdam
Chase Manhattan of New York

These bankers are connected to the London banking houses, which ultimately control the Federal Reserve central bank. When England lost the Revolutionary War with America, they planned to control us by controlling our banking system, the printing of our money, and our debt. The individuals listed below owned banks which, in turn, owned shares in the FED. They have incestuously passed this legacy on to their progeny, so the names remain the same with little deviation. The banks and individuals listed have significant control over the New York FED, which controls the other 11 FED Districts.

First National Bank of New York: James Stillman
National City Bank, New York: Mary W. Harnman
National Bank of Commerce, New York: A.D. Jiullard
Hanover National Bank, New York: Jacob Schiff
Chase National Bank, New York: Thomas F. Ryan, Paul Warburg, William Rockefeller, Levi P. Morton, M.T.Pyne, George F. Baker, Percy Pyne, Mrs. G.F. St. George, J.W. Sterling, Katherine St.George, H.P. Davidson, J.P. Morgan (Equitable Life/Mutual Life), Edith Brevour Baker

It was estimated that, in 1933, these individuals represented one fifth of the entire world's wealth. You can imagine what that number is today, after nearly seventy years of draining the wealth from this nation and our future generations.

The families that control the FED are the creators of and members of the Council on Foreign Relations. They have recruited some peons from amongst us to "take the heat" and have rewarded them lavishly for that treason.

In 1935 the Public Administration Clearinghouse wrote, and Roosevelt introduced, the "Federal Alcohol Act." Congress passed it into law. The Act established the Federal Alcohol Administration. That same year, in a monumental ruling, the Supreme Court struck down the act among many others on a long list of draconian "New Deal" laws. The Federal Alcohol Administration did not go away; it became involved in other affairs, placed in a sort of standby status, which we will examine later on in the book.

Internal Revenue (Puerto Rico)

At some unknown date prior to 1940, another Bureau of Internal Revenue was established in Puerto Rico. The 62nd trust fund was created and named Trust Fund #62 Puerto Rico special fund (Internal Revenue). Note that the Puerto Rico special fund has Internal Revenue, capital "I" and capital "R," whereas the Philippine special fund (internal revenue) is in lower case letters.

Between 1904 and 1938 the China Trade Act was passed to deal with opium, cocaine and citric wines shipped from China. It appears to have been administered in the Philippines by the Bureau of Internal Revenue.

China Trade Act

In studying a copy of The Code of Federal Regulations of the United States of America that was in force on June 1, 1938, Title 26 – Internal Revenue, Chapter I – (Parts 1-137), I found reference to the China Trade Act on page 65. This is when the IRS first began to use their special brand of speak, with such terms as "income," "credits," "withholding," "Assessment and Collection of Deficiencies," "extension of time for payment," and "failure to file a return."

The entire substance of Title 26 deals with foreign individuals, foreign corporations, foreign insurance corporations, foreign ships, income from sources within possessions of United States, citizens of the United States, and domestic corporations deriving income from sources within a possession of the United States, and China Trade Act Corporations. Nowhere does an income tax on any natural person of any of the Republic States appear.

Narcotics, Alcohol, Tobacco, Firearms

All of the taxes covered by these laws concerned only the imposts, excise taxes and duties to be collected by the Bureau of Internal Revenue for such items as narcotics, alcohol, tobacco, and firearms. The Internal Revenue Service likes to make much ado about the fact that Al Capone was jailed for tax evasion, but that is not what he was jailed for. The IRS will not tell you that the tax Capone evaded was not "income tax" as we know it but the tax due on the income generated from the alcohol that he had imported from Canada. If he had paid that tax, he would not have been convicted.

The Internal Revenue Act of 1939 was clearly concerned with all taxes, imposts, excises and duties collected on trade between the Possessions and Territories of the United States. In addition to foreign individuals, foreign corporations or foreign governments, the income tax laws have always applied only to the Philippines, Puerto Rico, District of Columbia, Virgin Islands, Guam, Northern Mariana Islands, American Samoa, territories and insular possessions; never to the Republic States of the American Union.

FAA becomes BIR

Under Reorganization Plan Number 3 of 1940, which appears at 5 United States Code Service Section 903, the Federal Alcohol Administration and offices of members and Administrator thereof were abolished and their functions directed to be administered under direction and supervision of Secretary of Treasury through Bureau of Internal Revenue. I found this history in all of the older editions of 27 USCS, Section 201. It has been removed from current editions. Only two Bureaus of Internal Revenue have ever existed: one in the Philippines and another in Puerto Rico. The evolution that has transpired tells us that the Federal Alcohol Administration was absorbed by the Puerto Rico Trust # 62 (Internal Revenue).

Victory Tax Act

In 1939, Congress passed the Public Salary Tax Act (PSTA), apparently to tax only the salaries of federal employees. Soon afterward (in the early days of World War II) a "one time only" Victory Tax was levied on all citizens.

Somehow, it never went away, however; only the name changed. At the time, almost no one connected the income tax with the PSTA.

World War II created for the International Bankers a golden opportunity. Americans were willing to sacrifice almost anything for the United States fighting forces if they thought that sacrifice would win the war. In that atmosphere Congress passed the Victory Tax Act. It mandated an income tax for the years 1943 and 1944 to be filed and paid in the years 1944 and 1945. The Victory Tax Act automatically expired at the end of 1944; it was renewed for an additional two years and then again for five additional years. The federal government, with the clever use of language, created the myth that the tax was applicable to all Americans and hid the fact that it was a tax only on Government employees.

Nowhere does the Internal Revenue Code define the "individual" who is liable to pay the tax. This may explain why Congress has never converted Title 26 of the U.S. Code into positive law. It contains no liability statute; that is, it does not state who is liable to pay. Imagine the IRS taking someone to court on tax charges who then argues that he is exempt because he works for a private company, while the income tax depends on the Public Salary Tax Act. Now imagine what would happen if the judge decided against him, saying, "Everyone is subject to the PSTA." He would have to admit publicly that the government – rather, its creditors – owns every business in the United States and that everyone is working for them! Either way he ruled, the Government would lose!

Because of their desire to win the war and their ignorance of the law, Americans filed and paid the tax. The government promoted the fraud and threatened those who objected with jail or confiscation of their property. Americans forgot or never knew the law had expired. When the date of expiration had come and gone, they continued to keep "records," continued to file and continued to pay the tax. The federal government continued to print returns and collect the tax, never mind the fact that no Citizen of any of the several States of the Union was ever liable to pay the tax in the first place.

Federal Power Limited

The fiction that "because it was an excise tax, it was legal" is not true. The power of the federal government is limited to its own property as stated in Article 1, Section 8, paragraph 17, and to "regulate Commerce with foreign

Nations, and among the several States, and with the Indian tribes;" as stated in Article 1, Section 8, paragraph 3.

18 USC, Section 921, Definitions, states: "The term 'interstate or foreign commerce' includes commerce between any place in a State and any place outside of that State or within any possession of the United States (not including the Canal Zone) or the District of Columbia, but such term does not include commerce between places within the same State but through any place outside of that State. The term 'State' includes the District of Columbia, the Commonwealth of Puerto Rico, and the possessions of the United States (not including the Canal Zone)."

Only employees of the federal government, residents of the District of Columbia, residents of naval bases, residents of forts, U.S. Citizens of the Virgin Islands, Puerto Rico, territories, and insular possessions were lawfully required to file and pay the Victory Tax.

Bureau of Internal Revenue becomes IRS

The year 1953 saw the United States relinquish control over the Philippines. Several nagging questions remain:

1. Why do the Philippine Pure Trusts #1 (customs duties) and #2 (internal revenue) continue to be administered by the Secretary of Treasury today?
2. Who are the Settlors of the Trusts?
3. What is done with the funds in the Trusts?
4. What businesses, if any, do these Trusts operate?
5. Who are the Beneficiaries?

On July 9, 1953, the Secretary of the Treasury, G. M. Humphrey, by "virtue of the authority vested in me," changed the name of the Bureau of the Internal Revenue (BIR) to Internal Revenue Service when he signed what is now Treasury Order 150-06. This was an obvious attempt to legitimize the Bureau of Internal Revenue without the approval of Congress or the President. Without any legal authority, Humphrey turned a pure trust into an agency of the Department of the Treasury. His actions were illegal but went unchallenged. Did he change the name of the BIR in Puerto Rico or the BIR in the Philippines?

Along came Guam

In 1954 the United States and Guam became partners under the Mutual Security Act. The Act and other documents make reference to the definition of Guam and the United States as being mutually interchangeable. In the same year the Internal Revenue Code of 1954 was passed. The Code provides for the United States and Guam to coordinate the "Individual Income Tax." Pertinent information on the tax issue may be found in 26 CFR 301.7654-1: Coordination of U.S. and Guam Individual income taxes, 26 CFR 7654-1(e): Military personnel in Guam, 48 USC § 1421(i): "Income-tax laws" defined.

The Constitution forbids un-apportioned direct taxes upon the Citizens of the several States of the fifty States of the Union; therefore, the federal government must coerce (defraud) people into volunteering to pay taxes as "U.S. citizens" of either Guam, the Virgin Islands, or Puerto Rico. It sounds insane, and it is, but it is absolutely true. Each time we sign a 1040 Form, with its approved Office of Management and Budget (OMB) number, we are saying under penalty of perjury that we are residents of the Virgin Islands. Check out the number on the form and ask the Director of the OMB if that number is not a designation for the Virgin Islands. One other point of interest on the 1040: how can you sign a form under penalty of perjury? The only way possible for you to have committed perjury is if you were under an Oath or an Oath of Office. If you are not a government employee, you are not under Oath of Office.

The Metamorphosis continues

On June 6, 1972, Acting Secretary of the Treasury Charles E. Walker signed Treasury Order Number 120-01, which established the Bureau of Alcohol, Tobacco and Firearms. He did this with the stroke of his pen, citing "by virtue of the authority vested in me as Secretary of the Treasury, including the authority in Reorganization Plan No.26 of 1950." He ordered the "transfer, as specified herein, the functions, powers and duties of the Internal Revenue Service arising under laws relating to alcohol, tobacco, firearms, and explosives (including the Alcohol, Tobacco and Firearms Division of the Internal Revenue Service) to the Bureau of Alcohol, Tobacco and Firearms (hereinafter referred to as the Bureau) which is hereby established. The Bureau shall be headed by the Director, Alcohol, Tobacco and Firearms (hereinafter referred to as the Director). The Director shall perform his duties under the general direction of the Secretary of the Treasury (hereinafter referred to as the Secretary) and under the supervision of the Assistant Secretary (Enforcement, Tariff and Trade Affairs, and Operations) (hereinafter referred to as the Assistant Secretary)."

Transformation complete

Treasury Order 120-01 assigned to the new BATF Chapters 51, 52, and 53 of the Internal Revenue Code of 1954 and sections 7652 and 7653 of such code, chapters 61 through 80 inclusive of the Internal Revenue Code of 1954. The Federal Alcohol Administration Act (27 USC Chapter 8), which in 1935 the Supreme Court had declared unconstitutional within the several States of the Union. 18 USC Chapter 44, Title VII Omnibus Crime Control and Safe Streets Act of 1968 (18 USC Appendix, sections 1201-1203, 18 USC 1262-1265 1952 and 3615).

Mr. Walker then made a statement within TO 120-01 that is very revealing:

"The terms 'Director, Alcohol, Tobacco and Firearms Division' and 'Commissioner of Internal Revenue' wherever used in regulations, rules, and instructions, and forms, issued or adopted for the administration and enforcement of the laws specified in paragraph 2 hereof, which are in effect or in use on the effective date of this Order shall be held to mean 'the Director.'"

Walker seemed to branch the Internal Revenue Service (IRS), creating the Bureau of Alcohol, Tobacco, and Firearms (BATF), and then with that statement joined them back together into one. In the Federal Register, Volume 41, Number 180, of Wednesday, September 15, 1976, we find, "The term 'Director Alcohol, Tobacco and Firearms Division' has been replaced by the term 'Internal Revenue Service.'"

Incredible!

It appears that without any authority from Congress or the President, an Agency of over 100,000 employees is created by replacing "The term 'Director Alcohol, Tobacco and Firearms Division.'"

I found this pattern of deception and invisibility everywhere I looked during my investigation. For further evidence of the fact that the IRS and the BATF are one and the same organization, reference 27 USCA Section 201.

THE ART OF PUTTING LIGHTNING IN A BOTTLE

This is how the lightning master performed his light show. Secretary Humphrey, with no constitutional authority, created an agency of the Department of the Treasury called "Internal Revenue Service" out of thin air from an offshore pure trust called "Bureau of Internal Revenue." The "Settlor" and "Beneficiaries" of the trust are still unknown. The "Trustee" is the Secretary of the Treasury. Acting Secretary Walker further laundered the trust by creating, from the alleged "Internal Revenue Service," the "Bureau of Alcohol, Tobacco, and Firearms."

Unlike Humphrey, however, Walker assuaged himself of any guilt when he nullified the order by proclaiming: "The terms 'Director, Alcohol, Tobacco and Firearms Division' and 'Commissioner of Internal Revenue' wherever used in regulations, rules, and instructions, and forms, issued or adopted for the administration and enforcement of the laws specified in paragraph 2 hereof, which are in effect or in use on the effective date of this Order, shall be held to mean 'the Director.'"

Walker created the Bureau of Alcohol, Tobacco, and Firearms from the Alcohol, Tobacco and Firearms Division of Humphrey's Internal Revenue Service. He then said that what was transferred is the same entity as the Commissioner of Internal Revenue. He knew he could not legally create something from nothing without the authority of Congress and/or the President – only God can do that – so he made it look like he did something that he had, in fact, not done. To compound the fraud, he had the Federal Register publish the unbelievable assertion that a person had been replaced with a thing: "the term 'Director Alcohol, Tobacco, and Firearms Division' has been replaced with the term 'Internal Revenue Service.'" Incredible!

The Federal Alcohol Administration, which administered the Federal Alcohol Act, and offices of members and Administrator thereof, were abolished and their functions were directed to be administered under direction and supervision of Secretary of Treasury through Bureau of Internal Revenue, now Internal Revenue Service. The Federal Alcohol Act was ruled unconstitutional within the fifty States and was immediately transferred to the BIR, which is an offshore trust.

This became the IRS, which gave birth to the BATF and somehow the term "Director, Alcohol, Tobacco, and Firearms Division," which is a person within the BATF, spawned the Internal Revenue Service via another flick of the pen on September 15, 1976. I asked the BATF, by use of a freedom of information request, to identify the person who now administers the Federal Alcohol Act. If I was wrong, a reply should have been sent stating that no record exists as to any name of any person who administers the Act. The request was submitted to the BATF. The reply came on July 14, 1994, from the Secret Service, an unexpected source, which disclosed a connection I had not suspected.

The reply stated that John Magaw of the Bureau of Alcohol, Tobacco, and Firearms, of the Department of the Treasury, administers the Federal Alcohol Act. You may remember from the Waco hearings that John Magaw is the Director of the Bureau Alcohol, Tobacco, and Firearms – the man in charge of the heroic deed accomplished by the BATF with the execution of 86 human beings in Waco, Texas. That source and admission confirmed all of my research.

Smoke and Broken Mirrors

Despite all the smoke and mirrors, there is no such organization of the Department of the Treasury known as "Internal Revenue Service" or the "Bureau of Alcohol, Tobacco, and Firearms." Title 31 USC is "Money and Finance" and therein are published the laws pertaining to the Department of the Treasury (DOT). 31 USC, Chapter 3 is a statutory list of the organizations of the DOT. Internal Revenue Service and/or Bureau of Alcohol, Tobacco, and Firearms are not listed within 31 USC as agencies or organizations of the Department of the Treasury. They are referenced, however, as "to be audited" by the Controller General in 31 USC § 713.

Puerto Rico Home of BATF

Puerto Rico is a small but beautiful Island in the Caribbean which became U.S. Territory as war reparations from Spain. Ever since that day it has been a place where Congress could play games with the Constitution without much interference from the Supreme Court and a place where most of the Congress and other federal agencies still play games with the American people.

I have already demonstrated that both of these organizations are, in reality, the same organization. Where we find the Yin, we will surely find the Yang. In 27 CFR 26.11 (formerly 27 CFR, Chapter 1, Section 250.11), Definitions, we find: "United States Bureau of Alcohol, Tobacco and Firearms office. The Bureau of Alcohol, Tobacco and Firearms office in Puerto Rico" and "Secretary – The Secretary of the Treasury of Puerto Rico." and "Revenue Agent – Any duly authorized Commonwealth Internal Revenue Agent of the Department of the Treasury of Puerto Rico." Remember that "Internal Revenue" is the name of the Puerto Rico Trust #62. It is perfectly logical and reasonable that a Revenue Agent works as an employee for the Department of the Treasury of the Commonwealth of Puerto Rico, but in Cincinnati or Saint Augustine?

Under Which Shell hides the IRS?

Where is the alleged "Internal Revenue Service"? The Internal Revenue Code of 1939, a.k.a. Internal Revenue Code of 1954, etc., etc., etc. 27 CFR refers to Title 26 as relevant to Title 27, as per 27 CFR, Chapter 1, Section 250.30, which states that 26 USC 5001(a)(1) is governing a 27 USC law. In fact, 26 USC Chapters 51, 52, and 53 are the alcohol, tobacco and firearms taxes, administered by the Internal Revenue Service; alias, Bureau of Internal Revenue; alias, Virgin Islands Bureau of Internal Revenue; alias, Director, Alcohol, Tobacco and Firearms Division; alias, Internal Revenue Service.

Must be Noticed

According to 26 CFR Section 1.6001-l(d), Records... No one is required to keep records or file returns unless specifically notified by the district director by notice served upon him to make such returns, render such statements, or keep such specific records as will enable the district director to determine whether or not such person is liable for tax under subtitle A of the Code. 26 CFR states that this rule includes state individual income taxes.

Don't get fooled here, because in IRS-speak, "state" means "the District of Columbia, U.S. Virgin Islands, Guam, Northern Mariana Islands, Puerto Rico, territories, and insular possessions." ONLY!

No Implementation of Law

Title 44 USC states that every regulation or rule must be published in the Federal Register. It also states that the Secretary of the Treasury must approve every regulation or rule. If there is no regulation there can be no implementation of the law. There is no regulation governing "willful failure to file a return." There is no computer code for "failure to file." The only thing I could find was a requirement stating "where to file an income tax return". It can be found in 26 CFR, Section 1 6091-3, which states that, "Income tax returns required to be filed with Director of International Operations."

Who is the Director of International Operations?

Delegation of Authority

No one in government is allowed to do anything unless they have been given specific written authority by law, or unless someone who has been given authority in the law gives that person a delegation of authority order spelling out exactly what they can and cannot do under that specific order.

I researched the Department of the Treasury's Handbook of Delegation Orders and found that no one in the IRS or BATF has any authority to do most of the things they have been doing for years. The IRS cites Treasury Order 150-10, dated April 22, 1982, as the delegation of authority to the Commissioner of the Internal Revenue Service for the collection of taxes. Close examination of the documents created serious doubts with this researcher as to the legality of the Order 150-10.

Delegation of Authority Order 150-37, dated April 22, 1982, superseded the previous Treasury Order 150-37, dated March 17, 1955. Treasury Secretary Ronald T. Regan duly signed treasury Order 150-37, dated April 22, 1982. The Official Seal of the Department of the Treasury was affixed to the letterhead. The stationary date at the lower left hand corner of the document was (2-81).

The Internal Revenue Service relied upon the Delegation of Authority Order 150-10 as its current authority. Upon close inspection of this Order, the Official Seal of the Secretary of the Treasury has been modified and was not the actual seal of the Secretary as was depicted on Order 150-37. Furthermore the date of this order was April 22, 1982, which is the same date that the former Delegation of Authority Order 150-37 was signed. The Secretary did not sign this Delegation of Authority Order, and the stationary date at the lower left-hand corner of the document, is (11-85). The tree from which the order's paper was manufactured was growing for over three years, all the while purportedly giving authority.

I have serious concerns that indicate fraud with these documents:

1. That the Official Seal on 150-10 was not the same Seal as the one depicted on 150-37, even though they were allegedly administered the same day.
2. That the Secretary had not signed this important order (150-10) upon which the IRS currently relies as their official Delegation of Authority, whereas the Secretary felt it important to sign (150-37) which was to be superseded the same day by Order (150-10).
3. That the stationary date on Order 150-37 was fourteen months prior to the date of signature which seems appropriate from harvest to manufacture; however, the stationary date on 150-10 was forty-three months after the Order was allegedly issued as the Delegation of Authority. I believe that, on its face, this constitutes fraud with malicious intent to defraud the American people.

No Authority to Audit

Delegation Order Number 115 (Rev. 5), of May 12, 1986, is the only delegation of authority to conduct audit. It states that the IRS and BATF can audit only *themselves* and only for amounts of $750 or less. The Comptroller General, according to Title 31 USC, must audit any amount above that amount. No other authority to audit exists. No IRS or BATF agent or representative can furnish me with any law, rule, or regulation which gives the IRS the authority to audit anyone other than himself. Order Number 191 states that they can levy on Property but only if that Property is in the hands of third parties.

Authority to Investigate

The manual states on page 1100-40.2 of April 21, 1989, Criminal Investigation Division, that "the Criminal Investigation Division enforces the criminal statutes applicable to income, estate, gift, employment, and excise tax laws involving United States citizens residing in foreign countries and nonresident aliens subject to Federal income tax filing requirements by developing information concerning alleged criminal violations thereof, evaluating allegations and indications of such violations to determine investigations to be undertaken, investigating suspected criminal violations of such laws, recommending prosecution when warranted, and measuring effectiveness of the investigation processes."

Why then have all prosecutions for individuals related to income tax law violations been prosecuted when they are not among the class of individuals identified in the above manual?

Authority to Collect

On page 1100-40.1 it states in 1132.7 of April 21, 1989, Director, Office of Taxpayer Service and Compliance: "Responsible for operation of a comprehensive enforcement and assistance program for all taxpayers under the immediate jurisdiction of the Assistant Commissioner (International) ...Directs the full range of collection activity on delinquent accounts and delinquent returns for taxpayers overseas, in Puerto Rico, and in United States possessions and territories."

Fifty States not included

1132.72 of April 21, 1989, Collection Division says: "Executes the full range of collection activities on delinquent accounts, which includes securing delinquent returns involving taxpayers outside the United States and those in United States territories, possessions and in Puerto Rico."

U.S. Attorney's Manual

The United States Attorney's Manual, Title 6 Tax Division, Chapter 4, page 16, October 1, 1988, 64.270, Criminal Division Responsibility, states: "The Criminal Division has limited responsibility for the prosecution of offenses investigated by the IRS. Those offenses are: excise violations involving liquor tax, narcotics, stamp tax, firearms, wagering, and coin operated gambling and amusement machines; malfeasance offenses committed by IRS personnel; forcible rescue of seized property; corrupt or forcible interference with an officer or employee acting under the Internal revenue laws; and unauthorized mutilation, removal or misuse of stamps." See 28 CFR § 0.70.

So why is the Attorney General prosecuting all of these innocent Americans?

"Act of Congress"

I found this revelation in 28 USC Rule 54c, Application of Terms:

"As used in these rules the following terms have the designated meanings. 'Act of Congress' includes any act of Congress locally applicable to and in force in the District of Columbia, in Puerto Rico, in a territory or in an insular possession."

Title 28 USC is the "Rules of Courts" and was written and approved by the Justices of the Supreme Court. The Supreme Court in writing 28 USC has already ruled upon this issue. It is the law.

It would appear, then, that any Act of Congress is applicable only to the District of Columbia and its instrumentalities unless specifically designated for the general population of the Union.

CHAPTER FOUR

THE FEDERAL RESERVE, INCORPORATED

THE FEDERAL RESERVE BANK

MONUMENTAL FRAUD IN AMERICA'S HISTORY

"Man can live and satisfy his wants only by ceaseless labor; by the ceaseless application of his faculties to natural resources. This process is the origin of property. But it is also true that a man may live and satisfy his wants by seizing and consuming the products of the labor of others. This process is the origin of plunder. Since man is naturally inclined to avoid pain and since labor is pain in itself, it follows that men will resort to plunder whenever plunder is easier than work.

"When plunder becomes a way of life for a group of men living in society, they create for themselves, in the course of time, a legal system that authorizes it and a moral code that glorifies it."

– *The Law*, by Frederick Bastiat, Economist and Statesman (June, 1850)

Banks are established for one reason and one reason only: to plunder the wealth of diligent, honest, hardworking people. Impenetrable secrecy shrouds the issue of money, banking, finance and economics. Each year thousands of students spend enormous sums of money and time attending Ivy League schools in a futile attempt to exalt and legitimize a system that, at its very core, is based upon the blackest of evil, theft and usury. Our Founding Fathers had no difficulty whatsoever understanding the agenda of the bankers, and they constructed our Constitution to protect us from that force of darkness.

They hated the Bank of England in particular and felt that even if we were successful in winning our independence from King George, we could still never truly be a nation of freemen unless we started with an honest money system. Only a $50,000 education could convince a man that a thief is honest, that wrong is right and day is night. Most of these Ivy League club members become lawyers. These lawyers and judges then populate the justice system of this country protecting the international bankers. On one side of this justice highway stand these warped intellects; we, the American people, stand on the other. The only things in the middle of the road are dead skunks and ignorant people.

For some strange reason, the men who have created this elaborate scheme, whose sole purpose is the plunder of our national wealth, are the same morons who claim to be brilliant, educated, and informed. Even they cannot seem to agree on much of anything when it comes to banking or money.

"An International Monetary Fund seminar of eminent economists couldn't agree on what money is and how banks create it." – Wall Street Journal (September 24, 1971)

After reading this book, you will understand more about money and banking than the average banker knows. You will be equipped with information that you need to know and of which were deprived by your government-funded public education. You can stop living as though someone else held your destiny in his hands.

"Those who create and issue credit and money, direct the policies of government, and hold in the hollow of their hands the destiny of the people." – The Right-Honorable Reginald McKenna, Midland Bank of England, Secretary of the Exchequer

"Whoever controls the money in any country is master of all its legislation and commerce." – President James Garfield

EXPOSING THE FRAUD

"Centralization of credit in the hands of the State, by means of a national bank with State capital and an exclusive monopoly." – 5th Plank of the Communist Manifesto, by Karl Marx (1848)

What is the "Federal Reserve Banking System"? The "Fed," as it is commonly referred to, is privately owned. It is part of an international banking cartel, owned by an exclusive cadre of the most wealthy and powerful individuals on the face of the earth. The Fed is not in any demonstrable way part of our federal government, any more than is Federal Express. Federal Express will, however, give you service for purchase. The Federal Reserve Banks' intended purpose is to fleece the American people by stealing our wealth under the pretext of a "government-regulated central banking system" that calls itself "Federal."

75 Congressional Record 12595-12603: "The Federal Reserve Banks are privately owned, locally controlled corporations." *Lewis vs. U.S.*, 680 F2d 1239, 1241 (1982)

"From a legal standpoint these banks are private corporations, organized under a special act of Congress, namely, the Federal Reserve Act. They are not in the strict sense of the word, 'Government banks.'" – William P.G. Harding, Governor of the Federal Reserve Board (1921)

The U.S. Constitution, Art. 1 § 8 states: "The Congress shall have Power... To coin Money, regulate the Value thereof...

This power is granted by the People and vested only in the United States Congress. Yet Congress re-delegated this power, contrary to the Supreme Law of the Land, the Constitution for the United States.

The Federal Reserve Act is in direct violation of the Constitution, because no provision was ever made by the People for Congress to do so.

"Congress cannot delegate or sign over its authority to any individual, corporation or foreign nation." – 16th Corpus Juris Secundum, § 141

"The powers of the legislature are defined, and limited; and that those limits may not be mistaken, or forgotten, the constitution is written. To what purpose are powers limited, and to what purpose is that limitation committed to writing, if these limits may, at any time, be passed by those intended to be restrained? The distinction, between a government with limited and unlimited powers, is abolished, if those limits do not confine the persons on whom they are imposed, and if acts prohibited and acts allowed, are of equal obligation. It is a proposition too plain to be contested, that the constitution controls any legislative act repugnant to it; or, that the legislature may alter the constitution by an ordinary act." – U.S. Supreme Court in *Marbury v. Madison, 5 U.S. 368*

"The general rule is that an unconstitutional statute, whether federal or state, though having the form and name of law, is in reality no law, but is wholly void, and ineffective for any purpose, since unconstitutionality dates from the time of its enactment, and not merely from the date of the decision so branding it. No one is bound to obey an unconstitutional law and no courts are bound to enforce it." – 16th American Jurisprudence, § 256, 2nd Ed.

The Federal Reserve Act, as passed by Congress, December 23, 1913, has since become the biggest fraud in the history of this country. Its passage occurred because of self-serving politicians that were more interested in lining their pockets than upholding their oath of office.

This is how it started.

TREASON'S RESORT

This day of infamy ended like most in the small town of Hoboken, New Jersey. The sky was overcast this 22nd day of November, 1910; there was a damp chill in the air. A train moving southwest left its vapor trails in the evening sky and moved off into the sunset on a journey that would within the near future change the world forever.

On the train, as it sped secretly into the blackness of night and into a malevolent future, were several of the most influential, powerful, financial and political men in the world. Many hours went by in silence; all men present knew they were to play a part in the development of a master plan that would alter forever their destiny, the destiny of the United States and of the entire world.

For some of these men, traveling in the sealed railcar with the windows blacked out, doubt crept into their minds as they pondered what would happen to them if identified. They would certainly be branded by some a traitor to the country, for clearly this act they were undertaking was treason. The others among them had no latent sentiment of patriotism. Their only allegiance was to their families (Rothschild, Rockefeller, Morgan) and money – money beyond imagination that was soon to be theirs. The train moved steadily south, consuming mile after mile of rail, bringing the collection of traitors, bankers and politicians closer to their destiny at Jekyll Island, Georgia.

Conditions precedent to the Jekyll Island meeting unfolded several years earlier with the 1907-08 financial panics, which had been secretly orchestrated by J.P. Morgan. Morgan de-stabilized the currency by starting a rumor about a competitor to eliminate competition and consolidate his power. This experience unnerved the entire country. President Theodore Roosevelt signed into law a bill which created the National Monetary Commission. This Commission was charged with the formulation of plans for stabilization of the U.S. currency. Senator Nelson Aldrich (grandfather to Nelson Rockefeller) was appointed its chairman.

Senator Aldrich, along with the entire Commission, departed for Europe seeking solutions to the problems of U.S. banking and currency stabilization. Their trip lasted nearly two years. The committee visited with heads (Rothschild) of all the European central banks. Upon their return no results of the trip were published; no legislation was offered to Congress. All that was known was that the bill for the trip was $300,000.

There were, however, some interesting immigrants landing on our shores along with the returning banking committee. One of them, Paul Warburg, a German and member of the Rothschild banking family (German division), immediately gained employment at the banking house of Kuhn, Loeb and Company as an advisor at a salary of $500,000. Warburg and Aldrich developed a plan, which Aldrich submitted to Congress, entitled the "Aldrich Plan," which was soundly rejected by the Western and Southern Congressmen.

As the train approached the Brunswick, Georgia, station, several dark limos were present, awaiting the arrival.

A small group of newspaper reporters were waiting to interview some VIPs. None were sure who they were or what they could possibly want in this small Georgia town. As the train came to a noisy, steamy stop, the reporters gathered around the sealed car with the drawn windows.

Down through the clouds of steam stepped Senator Aldrich to lead the resistance and offer answers to the annoying questions he knew were sure to follow. The reporters gathered around and to his side listening to the senator's story on the glory of duck hunting at Jekyll Island. Meanwhile, the other members of the coach disembarked and silently entered the waiting cars, unseen and unidentified.

The "duck hunters" included: Benjamin Strong, known as J.P. Morgan's lieutenant; America's recent German immigrant, Paul Warburg; Charles D. Norton, president of the Morgan-dominated First National Bank of New York; Shelton, Aldrich's private secretary; A. Piatt Andrew, Assistant Secretary of the Treasury; Frank Vanderlip, president of the National City Bank of New York and Rockefeller's agent; and Henry P. Davison, senior partner of J.P. Morgan Company.

Jekyll Island was a pleasant getaway from the turmoil of a busy banker's day. You can imagine how exhausting the denial of loans, foreclosures on homes, and collection of bad debts can be. Several years prior to the meeting, the island had been purchased by J.P. Morgan and a few of his wealthy New York banking and industrialist friends for the purpose of a vacation spot, spicy parties, winter golf and an occasional duck hunting expedition. The launch trip to the island was uneventful and relaxing after the rail car journey from New York. This was the perfect spot for such a high level meeting, which would direct the course of future human events. The owners of the Jekyll Island Hunting Club, in and of themselves, represented one-fifth of the total wealth of the world and some of them were soon to get richer.

Of course there was no intention for this group of high rollers to duck hunt. Their agenda was strictly focused on the development of a central bank and its funding. Out of this gathering were to spring plans for implementing the 16th and 17th amendments to the United States Constitution and a central bank (Federal Reserve Bank).

Senator Aldrich was expected to develop a monetary reform plan to submit to Congress. The "plan" that was to be developed here by these assembled must, by any means, keep the author's identities secret from Congress and the American people. Southern Senators would rebel if it were known that the very people they feared (Wall Street bankers) were developing the plan, the same plan that Congress had just rejected.

The heart of the reform plan was the creation and funding of a central bank. Approximately one year prior to the meeting, joint resolutions had been sent to the states for ratification to become part of the Constitutional body of law. The 16th amendment was the tool necessary to fund the Federal Reserve banking system. This amendment would mean the success or failure of their monetary plans. No matter what, this amendment must become law.

President Woodrow Wilson, along with his watchdog, Colonel House (who was an agent of Rothschild), had to enlist the aid of Secretary of State Philander Knox. Together, these three would proclaim that the 16th amendment had been ratified, even though they knew it had little or no chance of ratification. This had to be done! After the proclamation, the amendment file would be hidden away and no one would ever know that a little detail like non-ratification ever happened.

"No one will ever go out to the states and check," and no one did until two men named Bill Benson, of South Holland, Illinois, and M.J. "Red" Beckman of Butte, Montana, came along (*The Law That Never Was*).

Thomas Jefferson had struggled against Alexander Hamilton's scheme for the First Bank of the United States, which was backed by James Rothschild. He stated, "A central bank is a greater threat to our freedom than a standing army"

Later, President Andrew Jackson was successful in removing the Second Bank of the United States; again Rothschild was attempting to gain a foothold on this continent. President Jackson stated, "You are a nest of vipers and thieves, and by the grace of the all mighty God, I will root you out." And so he did. We were saved once again by a wise and assertive leader.

I am afraid the crop of presidents, beginning with Wilson to the present day, were not cut from the same cloth as our former presidents and are directly under the influence and control of the same evil financiers of the original central banks of our past.

With a negative history of central bank activity in America, Paul Warburg had warned the group not to call it a central bank. He convinced the group of conspirators to use the name "Federal Reserve Bank." The word "Federal" had the inference of government, and the word "Reserve" gave a warm, fuzzy feeling of confidence that there was something set aside that would stabilize the currency in hard times.

Nothing in the words "Federal Reserve Bank" has, in fact, any of the substance that the words suggest. The "Federal Reserve Bank" is not Federal and has no true governmental authority. The word "Reserve" is misleading in that there are no reserves of any kind.

The controllers of our currency and our lives are those same secret society members who control Europe, Japan, and now, Russia. Their plans of world domination are nearly perfected. The only concerns they have are that the American people who are armed to the teeth, having tasted freedom, would fight to the death to preserve it. This is why they desperately seek the outright banning of guns in America. (State Dept. Document 7277)

In referencing the Jekyll Island meeting, Bertie Charles Forbes, the founder of *Forbes* magazine, six years after the event, wrote:

"Picture a party of the nation's greatest bankers stealing out of New York on a private railroad car under cover of darkness, stealthily hiding hundreds of miles South, embarking on a mysterious launch, sneaking onto an island deserted by all but a few servants, living there a full week under such secrecy that the names of not one of them was once mentioned lest the servants learn the identity and disclose to the world this strangest, most secret expedition in the history of American finance. I am not romancing; I am giving to the world, for the first time, the real story of how the famous Aldrich currency report, the foundation of our new currency system, was written....

"The utmost secrecy was enjoined upon all. The public must not glean a hint of what was to be done. Senator Aldrich notified each one to go quietly into a private car of which the railroad had received orders to draw up on an unfrequented platform.

"Off the party set. New York's ubiquitous reporters had been foiled...

"Nelson (Aldrich) had confided to Henry, Frank, Paul and Piatt that he was to keep them locked up at Jekyll Island, out of the rest of the world, until they had evolved and compiled a scientific currency system for the United States, the real birth of the present Federal Reserve System, the plan done on Jekyll Island in the conference with Paul, Frank, and Henry.... Warburg is the link that binds the Aldrich system and the present system together. He, more than any one man, has made the system possible as a working reality."

The Federal Reserve System was, from the day of its inception, unconstitutional. The administrators of the system were to be appointed directly by the President, giving the Congress no say in its construction. Had this been known, the western and southern states would have had an all-out rebellion.

The last things in the world they trusted were the Wall Street bankers who had created the 1907-08 panic. Now, to have these men at the control of America's currency would never have been permitted. This was the major concern of Aldrich and the reason for the high secrecy concerning the meeting.

Under the proposed system, there would be four (later twelve) regional Federal Reserve banks throughout the country, the New York bank being in control of all the regions. This gave the public the impression of regional reserves and independence, along with a feeling of security, albeit false.

And so on December 22, 1913, when Congress was more interested in adjourning for the Christmas holiday than on the currency issue, they approved the Federal Reserve Act. The international agents had control of the United States of America. At that time, the nation had zero national debt. As of this writing, the national debt is over nine trillion dollars. If all off-budget items were truthfully presented, the debt would be double that figure or greater.

The money barons have drained America of its national wealth and stolen the American dream from all future generations. Every man, woman, and child in this country, upon birth, has a personal debt to these international agents of over $30,000. The interest alone is over one billion dollars each day and rising. The principal will never be repaid, and their miracle of compound interest will ensure the control of these "New World Order" masters over the American people forever.

"The current Fed structure is difficult to justify in a democracy. It's an oddly undemocratic institution. Its organization is so dated that there is only one Reserve Bank west of the Rocky Mountains, and two in Missouri. Having a central bank with a monopoly over the issuance of the currency in a democratic society is a very difficult balancing act." – *Wall Street Journal*, Feb.8, 1993

That is the story of creation of the Federal Reserve Bank. Now we will explore the creation of their private "money."

CHAPTER FIVE

MONEY

And [said unto them], What will ye give me, and I will deliver him unto you? And they covenanted with him for thirty pieces of silver. (Matthew 26:15)

WHAT IS MONEY vs. FEDERAL RESERVE NOTES

"A Federal Reserve Note (is) merely an IOU." Here's how it works. When the politicians want more money, they dispatch a request to the Federal Reserve for whatever sum they desire. The Bureau of Printing and Engraving then prints up bonds indenturing taxpayers to redeem their debts. The bonds are then 'sold" to the Federal Reserve. But note this unusual twist. The bonds are paid for with a check backed by nothing! It is just as if you were to look into your account and see a balance of $505 and then, hearing that government bonds were for sale, write a check for $1billion. Of course, if you or I did that, we would go to jail. The Federal Reserve bankers do exactly that, with no fear of losing their freedom. In effect, they print the money that enables their check to clear." – James Dale Davidson, Director, National Taxpayers Union

"The creation of a loan is little different when you go to your neighborhood bank. Again, the 'money' that is loaned is created out of thin air, with nothing more than a book entry! Let us see how a bank creates a mortgage lien on a house: A man who owns a building lot and has $20,000 needs an additional $75,000 to build a house. If the banker finds the collateral sufficient, he may credit the man's checking account with $80,000 – minus several 'points' for expenses – against which checks can be written to pay for construction. When the house is completed, it will have a thirty-year lien at 12 or 15 percent. After working 30 years to liquidate the debt, the owner will have paid perhaps $300,000 for something that did not cost the banker a dime in the first place. This is the magic of fractional reserve banking." – *The Battle for the Constitution*, Dr. Martin A. Larson

Some 97% of the money supply is made up predominantly of book entries, about 3% actual coin and paper currency. The system needs a continuous and increasing cycle of borrowing, debt, and refinancing, or the entire system will collapse:

"If all the bank loans were paid off tomorrow morning, no one would have a bank deposit and there would not be a dollar or coin or currency in circulation. This is a staggering thought. We are completely dependent on the commercial banks. Someone has to borrow every dollar we have in circulation. If the banks create ample synthetic money, we are prosperous; if not, we starve. We are absolutely without a permanent money system. When one gets a complete grasp of the picture, the tragic absurdity of our hopeless position is almost incredible, but there it is. It is the most important subject intelligent persons can investigate and reflect upon. It is so important that our present civilization may collapse unless it becomes widely understood and the defects remedied very soon." – Robert Hemphill, former Credit Manager, Fed Bank of Atlanta (in testimony before the Senate)

IMPOSSIBLE TO PAY THE NATIONAL DEBT

"The one aim of these financiers is world control by the creation of inextinguishable debts." – Henry Ford

The money to pay the interest on a debt must come from the same source as the debt principal. The only problem is that the money to pay the usury has never been created! Loan repayments to banks reduce the money supply. The Federal Reserve removes the money from circulation when a debt is repaid. To keep the money supply from shrinking, more borrowing is necessary. It is mathematically impossible to pay off the debt principal plus the interest. In your attempt to avoid the day of reckoning, you are forced to take on increasing amounts of debt to pay not only the principal of the debt, but the onerous interest. Your debt escalates until you are forced into bankruptcy. This phenomenon is not unique to government borrowing; it also applies as well to individuals and businesses. We need to recognize the perils of a private sector debt that is now at least five times greater than that of the Federal government's debt!

A Myth We Live By – The reason we have a $6 trillion national debt and $17 trillion private debt is because people, government, and business have spent beyond their means, right?

Wrong!

The fact is, our monetary system guarantees that debt must increase regardless of what people, business or government do or do not do, whether or not they balance their budgets. Suppose I lend you ten ball bearings, the very last ten in existence, with the condition that you return ten to me plus one more ball bearing as interest. If you knew there were only ten in existence, you would not accept this offer. But suppose you are naive about the creation and circulation of ball bearings and you accept the terms; when repayment time comes, you possess only ten, having been unable to get the nonexistent eleventh ball bearing. You lose your house, which was pledged as collateral.

A silly story, you say; no one would do that. Don't be so sure; our monetary system works the same way! Another example: Suppose you deposit $1,000 into a bank at 10% compound annual interest, which means that each year you will make interest on the interest. In 145 years you will have over $1 billion – an exponential growth of 1,000,000 times. The moral: A small amount, held as a perpetual debt, quickly compounds to astronomical amounts.

Our money supply was loaned into existence, and you don't pay back a money supply. Compound interest payments will cause this debt to rise to astronomical amounts (it already has). Furthermore, just like my ball bearing example, there is always more debt than there is money to pay it back, so it can never be paid back. The best we can do is refinance it.

Explained another way:

How the Federal Reserve creates money out of thin air.

Centuries ago in the city of Babylon, a goldsmith named Jebidiah had the only safe in the entire city and was proud to show it off to all of his friends. The friends were so impressed with Jebidiah's safe, they asked him if he would take their gold for safekeeping, as crime was on the rise and they feared its loss by burglars.

Jebidiah was glad to share his resource with his friends, and issued them receipts in the form of shares.

One pound of gold on deposit would equal one hundred shares in the form of receipts. As more customers took advantage of the safe, the receipts were passed out among the townspeople for payment of services, and the need to withdraw the gold was nearly eliminated. Jebidiah noticed that there was never more than 10% of the gold ever withdrawn; 90% remained safe in the vault. So, in discussion with his wife, Jebidiah began issuing to many people receipts for gold, ten times the quantity of actual gold in the vault, while charging interest for the receipts. Needless to say, Jebidiah prospered. This was one of the first experiments with fractional reserve banking.

Unfortunately for Jebidiah the king signed, with his neighbor to the south, a trade treaty which removed all trade tariffs. The result was that all of the businesses in Babylon moved south to the neighboring country. There the labor rate was one tenth that of Babylon, and with no trade barriers the businessmen could send their products back across the border and make huge profits from the reduced labor costs and no tariffs. (Sounds a great deal like the NAFTA and GATT agreements, doesn't it?) The businessmen, however, needed capital to establish their new businesses in the new business community to the south.

They went to Jebidiah and presented him with their receipts to reclaim their gold. The other customers, to whom he had sold receipts, also wanted gold for them so that they also might invest and take advantage of this new treaty. The result was, of course, a disaster for Jebidiah. There was not sufficient gold on deposit to cover the demand. He was dragged from his shop and crucified on the spot.

That is how things were done in the criminal justice system of the time.

One night at the dinner table, Jebidiah's two sons discussed the recent events and decided that their father's idea was still a viable option if it were modified. The next day they opened their vault for business once again with a few changes. First, the brothers demanded up to 200% security for all of the receipts they issued to the customers who did not deposit actual gold with them. The borrower pledged twice the value of what he received and also paid an interest on the principle value borrowed. Another requirement was that the receipts would not be redeemable except by giving a 90-day notice of withdrawal. In addition, the brothers inserted on the loan contract a clause which gave them a right to declare the loan immediately due and payable, regardless of the due date on the note, and repayable only in gold.

Business, because of the treaty, was good for all and business prospered until the king had a dispute with the neighboring sovereign and canceled the treaty. The brothers began calling in the loans, foreclosed on all security, liquidated the securities at a discount for a profit of 60% and were still able to deliver to the depositors all of their gold within 90 days, per the deposit agreement. They grew rich beyond belief and began to branch out to other towns and countries. They were the worlds' first fractional reserve bankers, and the business plan hasn't changed substantially for centuries.

This is how the Federal Reserve Bank and all of your local friendly bankers operate today. Now you know how the system of fractional banking works and how destructive it has been to any nation that has been foolish enough to permit it.

Fractional reserve banking has been scientifically reconstructed for the present needs of today. The receipts are now legally determined by our government to be a replacement for the gold. If you look closely at your "money," you will notice that it is a "Federal Reserve Note." A note is a debt instrument. In the past, the receipt was an acknowledgment of the banker's debt to you, and the gold you had on deposit was payable on demand. Your money (note) has no such payable on demand notice on it, and all you will receive from the bank on payment demand is a blank stare. What we have now is a debt instrument being used to pay off other debt instruments.

When you make a loan, the money that you borrow is on ledger as a credit to your account by a journal entry on the creditor's record. If you wrote a check on the account and deposited that check in another bank, Bank Two considers this new money, and it can lend against that deposit at a ten to one ratio. If Bank Two lends this new money to another individual who then writes a check on Bank One, Bank One lends against this deposit at the same ten to one ratio and the multiples of ten to one go on and on and on to infinity.

The courts or Congress have never repealed that provision in the Uniform Commercial Code, but go stone cold deaf and blind to the use of Federal Reserve Notes to pay off debt. When you mortgage your home for a loan by executing a mortgage deed, whether you receive a credit on your account or are given the cash (Federal Reserve Notes), you have given the bank something of value – your promise of labor – in return for nothing of value.

All across the country, property owners are having their mortgages canceled because they can prove that no equal consideration was given for their support of the mortgage. The banks are scared to death you will find out about this fraud. When a government owns the press and can print an unlimited number of worthless notes and can borrow with no limit on the notes it legalizes, there is no need to tax the citizens. The only reason for the government to go through the ritual of taxing you is to control you. The sole purpose of the tax they exact from you is to get all of that worthless paper out of circulation; otherwise inflation would consume the economy within a matter of months. The Federal Reserve can create inflation or deflation at its whim. It creates prosperity, inflation or depression anytime it wishes. IT CONTROLS ALL OF US.

The people in control of the presses (FED) can pay old debts with the inflated currency. They just keep the presses rolling. Just to survive, the rest of us are then required to spend all that we have before its devaluation makes it worthless. Mexico, Argentina and Brazil are prime examples of what awaits this country. In a central banking system, the only ones who profit are the owners of the central bank. If our government officials had one honest bone in their body, which is doubtful, they would buy back the Federal Reserve franchise and do what they are Constitutionally-required to do: print money by and for the Treasury, interest free.

Legal taxes on things properly taxable would be ample revenue to secure that money. It is not a widely published fact, but America has been in bankruptcy since 1933. (12 USC 9 (a); Executive Orders 6073, 6102, 6111, 6260).

Our Secretary of the Treasury is both the receiver in that bankruptcy and the Governor of the International Monetary Fund. This organization, made up of international bankers, pays the Secretary's salary, not us. Doesn't that make him an agent of a foreign power? You bet it does, and I can assure you that the Honorable Secretary has the best interests of the bankers in mind and not that of We the People. If he is an agent of the International Monetary Fund, then are not his sub-agents the IRS also foreign agents? You bet they are. By law, a foreign agent who does not file as such is committing a felony. (Section 64 of Title 22 of the United States Code) You now know how the FED creates money with the stroke of a pen. Now I will explain mankind's eternal curse – usury, commonly known as interest.

Many civilizations have lived productive lives on this earth having no knowledge of interest or the repayment of money loaned. Men such as Jebidiah's sons developed the concept of usury in order for them to get rich on their brethren's labor. Usury is illegal in the Moslem world and punishable by death if detected.

Outlawed in Europe and other continents for over three centuries, the penalty for anyone charging interest was severe: sometimes the death penalty was administered to those lazy and greedy loan sharks who wished to inflict usury on their neighbors.

How I long for the good old days once again!

William Patterson, an English banker, coined the term "interest" in the year 1694. The Crown, in need of additional revenue sources, gave license to Patterson to form his private bank. The Crown would authorize the money and the credit provisions of usury for the innocent English citizen.

This is a fair representation of what happened next. The first month that Patterson opened his bank, he made loans to ten farmers who needed the money to buy seed stock, livestock and supplies. The farmers borrowed one hundred pounds for one year at an interest rate of six percent. That was simple interest, as the concept of compound interest had not as yet been visualized. After one year the farmer was required to repay the hundred pounds plus the interest of six pounds. The only problem was that Patterson had created only a thousand pounds, and some of the farmers, although able to repay the original hundred pounds, were unable to come up with the additional six pounds. They tried to borrow it from some of the other farmers, but they too were having difficulty trying to find the interest.

One of the farmers had died and Patterson had taken the farm as the security for the loan. The deceased farmer's family had used some of the money to live on and was holding on to the rest of it because now they had no provider. So, in the village, there were some of the farmers who were able to sell products or services to the deceased farmer's family for some of Patterson's money and to repay the loan principle and interest. There were six farmers who could not come up with the interest. Patterson foreclosed on their farms and, under the protection of the Crown (for the King's unlimited credit), became the first central bank. Patterson realized that if he did not create any more money than he loaned out for the debt interest of the borrower, a large percentage of his customers would not be able to repay the loan and he could take their property at great profit to himself.

If you were to take this example and apply it to our present time, multiplied by the trillions, you can quickly see why the national debt will never be repaid.

The money for the repayment has never been created, and if they were to print money for it, that created money would have no money created to pay it off. This monstrous system is perpetual in its destruction. It has destroyed entire nations. The time has come for We the People to understand the system and demand a stop to this dishonest finance forever.

I prepare many bankruptcies each year. The large majority of these are the result of credit card purchases and abuse. The interest on the debt compounds itself, and the lender loves it when you pay only the minimum payment each month. Once caught in the interest trap of credit cards, the only way out for many is to file bankruptcy, but Congress has passed new legislation that will not allow for an individual to remove his credit card debt through bankruptcy. Credit cards should be made illegal, and our nation must return to the honest and Constitutional no-interest Treasury note, or we will not survive into the new millennium as a free people.

At exactly 6:00 p.m. on December 23rd, 1913, three United States Senators who had been recruited by Colonel House to commit treason voted into law the Federal Reserve Act of 1913 by voice vote only. America had been betrayed. Our Founding Fathers must have rolled over in their graves with anger. America was on a fast track to financial destruction. At the time of the FED's creation there was no National debt, and now we are approaching debt in the unbelievable amount of ten trillion dollars.

I was discussing a newspaper article with a friend who was concerned with what the paper described as the reason the Federal Reserve was going to replace the existing money with new issue notes. The reason given in the article was that Iran was in the counterfeit money business and the new currency would put an end to their plans. My friend believed that the paper was correct in the given explanation that if this were not done, the phony money would wreck our economy.

The newspaper and my friend would have been correct if the Federal Reserve notes were indeed backed by gold held by the Treasury. But the FED has no such gold reserve requirement and the Iranians don't charge us any interest for the money they print.

The Federal Reserve charges us 100% of the face value of the currency printed, which costs them 9/10 of a cent regardless of the face value amount, and Federal Reserve Notes give no consideration in return. Heaping on us another indignity, we are charged an additional surcharge of 10% for every dollar of our money they print. Every one of their dollars drags us further into debt. This being the case of two opposing criminal factions, one of which does not charge you for its product and the other one which does; who is the worse enemy of this country, the Iranians or the Federal Reserve Bank? I personally appreciate all the extra DEBT FREE money in circulation at no cost to We the People.

Iran, keep it coming! Run three shifts; I'll spend as much of it as you will give me. That's a promise!

In 1933, as expressed in Roosevelt's Executive Orders 6073, 6102, and 6260, the United States first declared bankruptcy. The bankrupt U.S. went into receivership in 1933. America was turned over via receivership and reorganization in favor of its creditors. These creditors, the International Bankers, from the beginning stated their intent, which was to plunder, bankrupt, conquer and enslave America and return it to its colonial status.

Congressman Lewis T. McFadden, Chairman of the House Banking Commission, speaking to Congress at the very time the conspiracy was taking place said, "We have in this country one of the most corrupt institutions the world has ever known. I refer to the Federal Reserve Board and the Federal Reserve Banks, hereinafter called the FED. They are not government institutions. They are private monopolies which prey upon the People of the United States for the benefit of themselves and their foreign and domestic swindlers, rich and predatory money lenders."

McFadden died mysteriously in 1936 after three attempts on his life.

At the time of the passage of the Federal Reserve Act of 1913, Congressman Charles Lindberg, Sr., said, "This Act establishes the most gigantic trust on earth. When the President signs this Act the invisible government by the Money Power, proven to exist by the Money Trust Investigation, will be legalized. The new law will create inflation whenever the trusts want inflation. From now on, depressions will be scientifically created."

And then we have an admission from Franklin Delano Roosevelt, in a letter to Colonel Edward Mandell House, the chief architect of the Federal Reserve Act and the fraudulent 16th Amendment, revealed in *The Intimate Papers of Colonel House*: "The real truth of the matter is, as you and I know, that a financial element in the large centers has owned the government of the

U.S. since the days of Andrew Jackson. History depicts Andrew Jackson as the last truly honorable and incorruptible American Presidents."

At least I must give FDR some credit in admitting that profound statement. The shame of it is that it is still true.

If we don't force Congress to rectify the matter soon, the whole house of cards is going to fall down around our heads in a few short years. The inevitable result is depression or hyperinflation, the worst possible economic crisis. Those who refuse to learn the lessons of history are bound to repeat the mistakes. History is replete with examples of nations whose governments permitted private centralized banks to control and debauch their currency. The ultimate mathematical equation is complete and total bankruptcy for all but the elite few. Widespread poverty, lawlessness, anarchy – much the same environment as paved the way for the second World War – is being visited upon us again and by the same people. *When*, not if, our own economy collapses, the people will accept anyone, even a despot like Hitler, who claims he can save you from financial ruin.

The International Bankers have historically been responsible for crisis after crisis and have invariably had their man waiting in the wings with the "solution" for the "problem" they created.

"In the case of the federal government, we can print money to pay for our folly for a time. But we will just continue to debase our currency, and then we'll have financial collapse. That is the road we are on today. That is the direction in which the 'humanitarians' are leading us. But there is nothing 'humanitarian' about the collapse of a great industrial civilization. There is nothing 'humanitarian' about the dictatorship that must inevitably take over as terrified people cry out for leadership. There is nothing 'humanitarian' about the loss of freedom. That is why we must be concerned about the cancerous growth of government and its steady devouring of our citizens' productive energies... I speak of this so insistently because I hear no one discussing this danger. Congress does not discuss it. The press does not discuss it. Look around us, the press isn't even here! The people do not discuss it – they are unaware of it. No counter-force in America is being mobilized to fight this danger. The battle is being lost, and not a shot is being fired." – Congressman William E. Simon, in a speech to the House of Representatives (April 10, 1976)

"I believe that if the people of his nation fully understood what Congress has done to them over the past 49 years, they would move on Washington, they would not wait for an election... It adds up to a preconceived plan to destroy the economic and social independence of the United States." – Senator George W. Malone, speaking before Congress about the Federal Reserve Bank (1962)

"The best way to destroy the capitalist system is to debauch the currency." – Vladimir Ilyich Ulyanov, commonly referred to as "Lenin."

Why should we Americans be paying a consortium of private international banking families and their stockholders for use of what we have been led to believe is our own medium of exchange?

Why is it that we find ourselves indebted to these already incomprehensibly wealthy people?

Isn't the U.S. Treasury responsible for the nation's money supply?

Doesn't the U.S. Bureau of Engraving print the "money"?

Why then do we borrow it from a <u>private</u> banking system?

Do we somehow need the bankers' permission to create and use our own money supply?

"The privilege of creating and issuing money is not only the supreme prerogative of Government, but is the Government's greatest creative opportunity. By the adoption of these principles, the tax payers will be saved immense sums of interest." – President Abraham Lincoln

United States Congressional Record March 17, 1993 Vol. #33, page H-1303, Congressman James Traficant, Jr. (Ohio) addressing the House:

"Mr. Speaker, we are here now in chapter 11. Members of Congress are official trustees presiding over the greatest reorganization of any Bankrupt entity in world history, the U.S. Government. We are setting forth, hopefully, a blueprint for our future.

"There are some who say it is a coroner's report that will lead to our demise. It is an established fact that the United States Federal Government has been dissolved by the Emergency Banking Act, March 9, 1933, 48 Stat. 1, Public Law 89-719; declared by President Roosevelt, being bankrupt and insolvent. H.J.R. 192, 73rd Congress in session June 5, 1933 – Joint Resolution To Suspend The Gold Standard and Abrogate the Gold Clause dissolved the Sovereign Authority of the United States and the official capacities of all United States Governmental Offices, Officers, and Departments and is further evidence that the United States Federal Government exists today in name only.

"The receivers of the United States Bankruptcy are the International Bankers, via the United Nations, the World Bank and the International Monetary Fund.

"All United States Offices, Officials, and Departments are now operating within a de facto status in name only under Emergency War Powers. With the Constitutional Republican form of Government now dissolved, the receivers of the Bankruptcy have adopted a new form of government for the United States. This new form of government is known as a Democracy, being an established Socialist/Communist order under a new governor for America. This act was instituted and established by transferring and/or placing the Office of the Secretary of Treasury to that of the Governor of the International Monetary Fund. Public Law 94-564, page 8, Section H.R. 13955 read in part:

"The U.S. Secretary of Treasury receives no compensation for representing the United States."

In the United States Congressional Record, May 4, 1992, page H 2891, Chairman of the House of Representatives Committee on Banking, Finance and Urban Affairs, Henry Gonzalez (Texas) speaking on "NATIONAL AND INTERNATIONAL THIEVERY IN HIGH PLACES," said:

"We are bankrupted. We are insolvent on every level of our national life, whether it is corporate, whether it is just plain you and I out there with the life of debt that we have all piled up, private debt, credit cards and what not, or whether it is the government. We are insolvent. How long will it take before that nasty Megatruth is conveyed?"

United States Congressional Record January 19, 1976, page 240, Marjorie S. Holt (Maryland):

"Mr. Speaker, many of us recently received a letter from the World Affairs Council of Philadelphia, inviting members of Congress to participate in a ceremonial signing of 'A Declaration of Interdependence' on January 30 in Congress Hall, adjacent to Independence Hall in Philadelphia. A number of Members of Congress have been invited to sign this document, lending their prestige to its theme, but I want the record to show my strong opposition to this declaration.

"It calls for the surrender of our national sovereignty to international organizations. It declares that international authorities should regulate our economy. It proposes that we enter a 'New World Order' that would redistribute the wealth created by the American people. Mr. Speaker, this is an obscenity that defiles our Declaration of Independence, signed 200 years ago in Philadelphia. We fought a great Revolution for independence and individual liberty, but now it is proposed that we participate in a world socialist order. Are we a proud and free people, or are we a carcass to be picked by the jackals of the world, which want to destroy us? When one cuts through the high-flown rhetoric of this 'Declaration of Interdependence,' one finds key phrases that tell the story.

"For example, it states that 'The economy of all nations is a seamless web, and that no one nation can any longer effectively maintain its processes of production and monetary systems without recognizing the necessity for collaborative regulation by international authorities.' How do you like the idea of 'international authorities' controlling our production and our monetary system, Mr. Speaker?

"How could any American dedicated to our national independence and freedom tolerate such an idea? America should never subject her fate to decisions by such an assembly, unless we long for national suicide. Instead, let us have independence and freedom.... If we surrender our independence to a 'New World Order' ...we will be betraying our historic ideals of freedom and self-government. Freedom and self-government are not outdated. The fathers of our Republic fought a revolution for those ideals, which are as valid today as they ever were.

"Let us not betray freedom by embracing slave masters; let us not betray self-government with world government; let us celebrate Jefferson and Madison, not Marx and Lenin."

A dollar is a measure of weight defined by the Coinage Act of 1792 and 1900, which is still in force today. A "dollar" specifies a certain quantity – 24.8 grains of gold, or 371.25 grains of silver. In *Black's Law Dictionary*, Sixth Edition, Dollar: "The money unit employed in the United States of the value of one hundred cents, or of any combination of coins totaling 100 cents." Cent: "A coin of the United States, the least in value of those now minted. It is the hundredth part of a dollar."

Gold and silver were such powerful money during the founding of the United States of America that the founding fathers declared that only gold or silver coins can be "money" in America. Since gold and silver coinage was heavy and inconvenient for a lot of transactions, they were stored in banks and a claim check was issued as a money substitute. People traded their coupons as money or "currency." Currency is not money, but a money substitute. Redeemable currency must promise to pay a dollar equivalent in gold or silver money. Federal Reserve Notes (FRNs) make no such promises and are not "money." A Federal Reserve Note is a debt obligation of the federal United States government, not "money." The federal United States government and the U.S. Congress were not and have never been authorized by the Constitution for the united States of America to issue currency of any kind, but only lawful money – gold and silver coin.

It is essential that we comprehend the distinction between real money and paper money substitute. One cannot get rich by accumulating money substitutes; one can only get deeper into debt. We the People no longer have any "money." Most Americans have not been paid any "money" for a very long time, perhaps not in their entire life. Now do you comprehend why you feel broke? Now do you understand why you are "bankrupt" along with the rest of the country?

Federal Reserve Notes (FRNs) are unsigned checks written on a closed account. FRNs are an inflatable paper system designed to create debt through inflation (devaluation of currency). Whenever there is an increase of the supply of a money substitute in the economy without a corresponding increase in the gold and silver backing, inflation occurs.

Inflation is an invisible form of taxation that irresponsible governments inflict on their citizens. The Federal Reserve Bank, who controls the supply and movement of FRNs, has everybody fooled. They have access to an unlimited supply of FRNs, paying only for the printing costs of what they need. FRNs are nothing more than promissory notes for U.S. Treasury securities (T-Bills) – a promise to pay the debt to the Federal Reserve Bank.

There is a fundamental difference between "paying" and "discharging" a debt. To pay a debt, you must pay with value or substance (i.e., gold, silver, barter or a commodity). With FRNs, you can only discharge a debt. You cannot pay a debt with a debt currency system. You cannot service a debt with a currency that has no backing in value or substance. No contract in Common law is valid unless it involves an exchange of "good and valuable consideration." Unpayable debt transfers power and control to the sovereign power structure that has no interest in money, law, equity or justice because they have so much wealth already.

Their lust is for power and control. Since the inception of central banking, they have controlled the fates of nations. The Federal Reserve System is based on Canon law and the principles of sovereignty protected in the Constitution and the Bill of Rights. In fact, the international bankers used "Canon Law Trust" as their model, adding stock and naming it a "Joint Stock Trust." The U.S. Congress had passed a law in 1873 making it illegal for any legal "person" to duplicate a "Joint Stock Trust." The Federal Reserve Act was legislated post-facto (to 1870), although post-facto laws are strictly forbidden by the Constitution (1:9:3). The Federal Reserve System is a sovereign power structure separate and distinct from the federal United States government. The Federal Reserve is a maritime lender and/or maritime insurance underwriter to the federal United States operating exclusively under Admiralty/Maritime law.

The lender or underwriter bears the risks, and the Maritime law compelling specific performance in paying the interest, or premiums are the same. Assets of the debtor can also be hypothecated ("to pledge something as a security without taking possession of it") as security by the lender or underwriter. The Federal Reserve Act stipulated that the interest on the debt was to be paid in gold. There was no stipulation in the Federal Reserve Act for ever paying the principle.

Prior to 1913, most Americans owned clear, allodial title to property, free and clear of any liens or mortgages, until the Federal Reserve Act of 1913 "hypothecated" all property within the federal United States to the Board of Governors of the Federal Reserve, in which the Trustees (stockholders) held legal title. The U.S. citizen (tenant, franchisee) was registered as a "beneficiary" of the trust via his birth certificate. In1933, the federal United States hypothecated all of the present and future properties, assets and labor of their "subjects," the 14th Amendment U.S. citizen, to the Federal Reserve System. In return, the Federal Reserve System agreed to extend to the federal United States Corporation all of the credit "money substitute" it needed.

Like any other debtor, the federal United States government had to assign collateral and security to their creditors as a condition of the loan. Since the federal United States didn't have any assets, they assigned the private property of their "economic slaves," the U.S. citizens, as collateral against the unpayable federal debt. They also pledged the unincorporated federal territories, national park forests, birth certificates, and nonprofit organizations, as collateral against the federal debt. All has already been transferred as payment to the international bankers.

Unwittingly, America has returned to its pre-American Revolution feudal roots whereby a sovereign holds all land and the common people have no rights to hold allodial title to property. Once again, We the People are the tenants and sharecroppers renting our own property from a sovereign in the guise of the Federal Reserve Bank. We the People have exchanged one master for another.

This has been going on for over eighty years without the "informed knowledge" of the American people, without a voice protesting loud enough. Now it is easy to grasp why America is fundamentally bankrupt. Why don't more people own their properties outright? Why are 90% of Americans mortgaged to the hilt and have little or no assets after all debts and liabilities have been paid? Why does it feel like you are working harder and harder and getting less and less?

We are reaping what has been sown, and the results of our harvest are a painful bankruptcy and a foreclosure on American property, precious liberties, and way of life. Few of our elected representatives in Washington, D.C., have dared to tell the truth. The federal United States is bankrupt. Our children will inherit this unpayable debt and the tyranny to enforce paying it.

CHAPTER SIX

ABOVE THE LAW

Horror hath taken hold upon me because of the wicked that forsake thy law. (Psalm 119:53)

FEDERAL RESERVE NOT ACCOUNTABLE TO CONGRESS

The Federal Reserve's income each year is well over a trillion dollars. Congress holds them exempt from paying taxes on their illegally obtained income. They pay only real estate taxes. In order to perpetuate this ongoing fraud on the American public, it is imperative that the Fed's financial activities never be subject to public scrutiny, and so, in its eighty-six year history, the Fed has never been audited by Congress or by any other government agency and never will be.

"Neither Presidents, Congressmen, nor Secretaries of the Treasury direct the Federal Reserve. In the matters of money, the Federal Reserve directs them." – *None Dare Call It Conspiracy*, by Gary Allen

"In the United States we have, in effect, two governments... We have the duly constituted Government... Then we have an independent, uncontrolled and uncoordinated government in the Federal Reserve System, operating the money powers which are reserved to Congress by the Constitution." – Congressman Wright Patman, Chairman, House Banking and Currency Committee

"By law, the seven members of the Federal Reserve Board are appointed by the President for a term of fourteen years each. In spite of the incredible length of these appointments, nevertheless, they are supposed to create the illusion that the people, acting through their elected leaders, have some voice in the nation's monetary policies. In practice, however, every President since the beginning of the Federal Reserve System has appointed only those men who were congenial to the financial interests of the international banking dynasties. There have been no exceptions." – *The Capitalist Conspiracy*, by G. Edward Griffin

"In its 60-year history, the Federal Reserve System has never been subjected to a complete, independent audit, and it is the only important agency that refuses to consent to an audit by the Congress' agency, the General Accounting Office... GAO audits of the Federal Reserve will, moreover, fill the glaring gap that now exists in our information about the Fed's activities and programs. As things now stand, the only information that we get on programs of the Fed is what the Fed itself wants us to have." – Congressman Wright Patman, Congressional Record (May 5, 1975)

THE FED WILL TELL YOU ALL ABOUT THEIR MONEY

I found that of the most informative information available on the topic of money, debt, inflation, borrowing, interest, and banking are given freely by the Federal Reserve District Banks.

THE STORY OF THEIR MONEY

What we carry in our wallets, Federal Reserve Notes, would be disqualified as money, even if they were notes. A note is an IOU, a promise to pay – an evidence of debt. Even the Fed itself does not refer to FRNs as money. Their own publications, however, often refer to FRN's as "forms" of money. Other possible forms of money might include credit cards, bank drafts, checks, electronic funds transfer, pretty colored rocks, etc. None of these, however, can in any way be construed as "money," and it is arguable whether they are even a legitimate promise to pay money.

Legal Tender

Look at a Federal Reserve Note, and you will find the statement: THIS NOTE IS LEGAL TENDER FOR ALL DEBTS PUBLIC AND PRIVATE.

The Fed has been careful so as not to perpetrate an outright fraud (Congress did that for them), at least in so far as what they state on their "notes." They have never asserted that their currency is "lawful money," for that would be a direct violation of the Constitution and the Coinage Act. Instead, they have called it "legal tender." One is a noun (money = substance); the other a verb (tender = action).

Legal. The form of law; posited by the courts as the inference or imputation of the law, as a matter of construction, rather than established by actual proof.

Tender. An offer of money. The act by which one produces and offers to a person holding a claim or demand against him the amount of money which he considers and admits to be due, in satisfaction of such claim or demand, without any stipulation or condition. As used in determining whether one party may place the other in breach of contract for failure to perform.

The actual proffer of money as distinguished from mere proposal or proposition to proffer it. Hence, mere written proposal to pay money, without offer of cash is not tender. (*Black's Law Dictionary*, 6 Ed.)

The Law Ignored

Was the Constitution amended?

Have the laws been changed?

What happened to all the money?

Government would argue that no person has the right to financial transactions that are private in nature – only criminals; like drug dealers, care about privacy. The argument goes "if you don't have anything to hide, why would you care about privacy?" However, *YOUR* right to privacy supersedes government's right to know!

Privacy is a Constitutionally-protected right, not so that real criminals will go unpunished, but because governments have historically demonstrated a propensity for using information gained against its citizens as a means of control and intimidation. The real objective of implementing an electronic cash devoid of real money is not at all about the elimination of real and legitimate crime in society. It is about seizing control of every imaginable area of our lives!

Smart cards and neural implants (microchip implants) are a technologic and practical reality today. All that is really necessary to break down the widespread reluctance to implementing them is an economic collapse. It's the old game of government creating the problem, like Waco, Texas, and then providing the solution. Did you realize that we are already living in a cash-void society? Cash is money, isn't it? How could we possibly have a free market, cashless society, without any real money?

"The legal tender acts do not attempt to make paper a standard of value. We do not rest their validity upon the assertion that their emission is coinage, or any regulation of the value of money; nor do we assert that Congress may make anything which has no value money." – *Bates v. United States*, 108 F2d 407 408 (1939)

"Are silver dollars really made of silver? Not anymore. Silver is too expensive, so today's silver dollars are really made of silver-looking metal outside that is 75 % Copper and 25% nickel. The inside is 100% copper." – First Bank exhibit, Denver Children's Museum, Denver

Payment vs. Discharge of Debt

Did you realize that when you "tender" a debt with a Federal Reserve Note, or a bank draft, check, credit card, or other forms of money as opposed to actual money, you are not in any way making payment? You simply made a promise to pay. The Constitution and the law establish that the only lawful money is gold and silver coin. You cannot lawfully make payment with anything but gold and silver coin, unless the parties agree in advance to some other form of equitable value barter exchange. An FRN has no intrinsic value and is not evidence of wealth; it is evidence of debt, and unfortunately for the one who accepts them, they are not even legitimate notes. FRNs fail the test of legitimacy for notes, because there isn't a promise to pay anything, and they're not redeemable for anything:

Note, n. An instrument containing an express and absolute promise of signer (i.e. maker) to pay to a specified person or order, or bearer, a definite sum of money at a specified time. A note not meeting these requirements may be assignable but not negotiable. – *Black's Law Dictionary*, 6 Ed

"A note is a specific and unconditional promise to pay." – UCC-304-I

"Intrinsically, a dollar bill is just a piece of paper." – *Modern Money Mechanics*, Federal Reserve Bank of Chicago

FRNs Do Not "Make Payment."

What exactly happens then when you make a transaction using an FRN and acquire property or services?

You have not in fact made payment, but the debt incurred for the "goods" is thereby discharged. The distinction is significant:

"There is a distinction between a debt discharged and one paid. When discharged, the debt still exists, though divested of its character as a legal obligation during the operation of the discharge. Something of the original vitality of the debt continues to exist, which may be transferred even though the transferee takes it subject to the disability incident to the discharge. The fact that it carries something which may be a consideration for a new promise to pay, so as to make an other wise worthless promise a legal obligation, makes it the subject of transfer by assignment" – *Stanek v. White*, 215 N.W 784

"About all a Federal Reserve note can legally do is wipe out one debt and replace it with itself, another debt; a note that promises nothing. If anything has been paid, the payment occurs only in the minds of the parties in the idea sphere, not the real world." – *The Miracle on Main Street*, by F. Tupper Saussy

A bona fide note can be used in a financial transaction to discharge the debt, only because it is an unconditional promise to pay by the issuer to the bearer. Is a Federal Reserve Note a contract note, an unconditional promise to pay? At one time the Federal Reserve issued bona fide contractual notes and certificates, redeemable in gold and silver coin. Most people never saw or comprehended the contract. It went largely unread because the Federal Reserve very cunningly hid the contract on the face of the note by breaking it up into five separate lines of text with a significantly different typeface for each line, and placing the President's picture right in the middle of it. They even used the old attorney's ruse of obscuring the most important text in fine print! Over time, the terms and conditions of the contract were diluted, until eventually they literally became an I.O.U. *Nothing.*

Lincoln and Kennedy Assassinated

By 1964, there were no more Federal Reserve Notes being issued that were redeemable for money. In fact fifty million of the very first non-redeemable notes were shipped on November 26, 1963, the very day JFK was being buried! Could there be a connection? President Kennedy had issued Executive Order 11110, on June 4, 1963, ordering the Treasury to print United States Notes. The most memorable of these notes was the $2 issue.

These notes couldn't be redeemed for anything any more so than could Federal Reserve Notes, but at least they had not indebted the People, because they were issued without debt owing to the Federal Reserve Bank.

Abraham Lincoln also made a similar daring move, ordering the Treasury to issue paper notes (know as "Lincoln Greenbacks") rather than borrow bank notes from the Bank of England. Both Presidents were promptly assassinated. One of the very first Executive Orders issued by Lyndon B. Johnson as newly-appointed dictator was for the mints to stop producing silver coins and to start issuing clad coins made out of copper, nickel and zinc, and other cheap metals. In this order, Johnson recalled all of the non-interest bearing scrip. Johnson was demonstrably responsible for the debauching of the U.S. currency.

"The high office of President has been used to foment a plot to destroy the Americans' freedom, and before I leave office I must inform the citizens of this plight." – John F. Kennedy at Columbia University, 10 days before his assassination

It is my firm belief that President Kennedy was removed by the same organization that removed Lincoln, by the same method, for the same reason. If he had not issued EO 11110 and made that statement, he most likely would have lived.

INSTITUTIONS OF BLUE SMOKE AND MIRRORS

For the past thirty years I have known that the owners of the Federal Reserve Bank control the entire world economy, not just the United States. Until only recently, however, did I understand the extent of the fraud and the far-reaching implications it presents throughout the entire world banking system. I began my research in preparation for writing *High Priests of Treason: The Federal Reserve* by talking to judges, bankers and attorneys about the money and banking system.

I was appalled to discover that most of those learned people did not know the truth about our money or banking system. Further, I found that schools of all levels do not teach that banks create money out of thin air. I researched throughout history, accounting, and law books on the high school and college level. The truth is not to be found there. No one I talked to knew that banks create money out of thin air, or they weren't talking if they did.

I did find the truth verified in an unlikely source and in a form that cannot be contradicted – The Federal Reserve Bank of Chicago's own publication, *Modern Money Mechanics*, and a companion comic book for young children titled *The Story of Money*. These books have been used as exhibits in lawsuits against banks and are no longer available.

THE TRUTH OF HOW MONEY IS CREATED FROM THE MOUTH OF THE FEDERAL RESERVE

"Money is an ordinary, routine part of our lives. Its existence and acceptance are taken for granted by each of us every day. A user of money may on occasion sense that money must come into being either automatically as a result of economic activity and labor or as an outgrowth of government.

But just how this happens all too often remains a mystery, and our schools do not attempt to lift the veil of darkness.

"The actual process of money creation takes place primarily in the bank ... In the absence of legal reserve requirements, a bank can build up deposits by increasing loans and investments so long as they keep enough currency on hand to redeem whatever amounts the holders of deposits want to convert into currency. This unique attribute of the banking business was discovered many centuries ago. (emphasis added)

"It started with goldsmiths. As early bankers, they initially provided safe keeping services, making a profit from vault storage fees for gold and coins deposited with them. People would redeem their 'deposit receipts' whenever they needed gold or coins to purchase something, and physically take the gold or coins to the seller who, in turn, would deposit them for safekeeping. Often, with the same banker. Everyone soon found that it was a lot easier simply to use the deposit receipts directly as a means of payment. These receipts, which became known as notes, were acceptable as money since whoever held them could go to the banker and exchange them for metallic money.

"Then, bankers discovered that they could make loans merely by giving their promises to pay, or bank notes, to borrowers. In this way, banks began to create money. More notes could be issued than the gold and coin on hand because only a portion of the notes outstanding would be presented for payment at any one time. Enough metallic money had to be kept on hand, of course, to redeem whatever volume of notes was presented for payment.

"Transaction deposits are the modern counterpart of bank notes. It was a small step from printing notes to making book entries, crediting deposits of borrowers, which the borrowers in turn could spend, by writing a check, thereby printing their own money."

- *Modern Money Mechanics – A Workbook on Bank Reserves and Deposits Expansion*, Pages 2 and 3, Feb. 1994, Federal Reserve Bank of Chicago.

Reading *Modern Money Mechanics* will absolutely astound you and finally fill in some of your brain cavity that which was purposefully left empty by our federally-funded public educational system. Whoever authorized this booklet to be written, published, and placed into distribution is owed a great debt of gratitude. This booklet, read, understood, and acted upon by you, will return the system back to Constitutionally-sound money if you do your part to free We the People from our present economic slavery.

CHAPTER SEVEN

THE SWINDLE

HOW THE BANKERS SWINDLE YOU ON A HOME MORTAGE

Now apply what we have just learned about money and banking to buying a home. Let us presume that after years of saving and months of looking you finally find and select a home in which you want to raise your family. Interest rates vary from bank to bank, so you must shop around until you find the best deal. We are all nervous when we sit before the loan officer at the bank. But you have always paid your debts and for years have had excellent credit, so there should be no problem getting the loan. The loan officer calls you a week later with the news that you are a new homeowner (you and the bank).

In a few weeks, you go to the scheduled closing and are greeted with a mountain of papers in triplicate. After forty-five minutes, you have finished the paper work and the home is yours *and the bank's*. Now the hard part begins – paying for it!

Your loan was for $85,000 at 8.5% interest, agreeing to pay it back at $653 per month for the next 30 years. In the next 30 years (assuming that you earn $10 per hour), 23,500 hours of your labor will go toward paying for that house. This works out to about 11 3/4 years at 40 hours per week.

This is the system of usury in all of its evil glory and this is how it works.

What you did not know and would never have believed is that the bank just defrauded you. This is how they did it. As a typical bank customer, you presumed that the money you borrowed from the bank came from its depositors or investors. *That is what the bank wants you to believe.* But that is not the truth.

Before you took out the loan from the bank, *that money did not exist.* The bank took your loan application and renamed it a "promissory note." The bank then took your "promissory note" and attached it to the title of the property. *Using the home as collateral, the bank wrote a check.*

The moment the bank wrote the check, it created the money out of thin air. If you doubt that the bank is writing checks to create money using your promissory note as an asset read the following again. In the Federal Reserve Bank's own words:

"Bankers discovered that they could make loans merely by giving their promises to pay, or bank notes, to borrowers. In this way, banks began to create money."

Returning to our example, the bank made a check payable to the seller. The seller accepted the check and deposited it back into the system. No armored cars ever delivered money to anyone.

You believe the bank approved your loan because you are a splendid example of credit risk and would make good on your promise to pay. Actually, the bank doesn't give a flip whether you pay or not; it doesn't really matter to the bank whether you keep your promise or not. After all, if you don't, they just foreclose and take your home.

What took the bank moments to create will take you 23,500 hours of labor to pay back.

Your intellect should be telling you about now that there is something terribly wrong in River City.

Now let's create a legitimate scenario for a moment and, using the same numbers, make the transaction honest.

You want to buy the same home on a land contract, directly from the seller. You would pay the seller directly.

Would the exchange of the home for money be honest? Yes.

Would it be legal? Yes, of course it would be. Why? Because the home is a direct product of someone's labor. The money you exchanged for the home has value because you exchanged your labor for it. Unlike the first example with the bank, it was not something which you created out of thin air. When you exchange your labor for money, the money has value and substance, because you exchanged your labor for it. *It is labor which gives value to the money.* In this example, value for value is exchanged.

Financing a home through a bank could be an honest transaction. Years ago it was. But the bank must lend you money that was either invested by its owners or placed on deposit by its customers. We all presume when we borrow from a bank that this is where the money comes from. It doesn't, but this is exactly what the bankers want you to believe.

THE BUYER-THE CONTRACT – THE FRAUD

Every contract must have six elements in order to be legally binding. If any one of the elements is missing, then there is no legally binding contract:

1. Offer by person qualified to make the contract.
2. Acceptance by a party qualified to make and accept the contract.
3. Agreements, full disclosure, and complete understanding by both parties.

Did you know that when you took out a bank loan or used a credit card, the bank was creating the money out of thin air? If you didn't, then there was no "full disclosure and complete understanding." Therefore, there is no legally binding contract.

4. *Consideration given.*

When you borrow from a bank that created money out of thin air, there can be no consideration. *No equal consideration, NO CONTRACT.*

5. Every contract must have the element of time to make it lawful.
6. All parties must be of lawful age, usually 21 years old.

YOUR REMEDY

You have been lied to, cheated and stolen from each and every time you borrowed money from a bank. If you want to help restore this country to a constitutional money system, then here is something practical that you might consider. You can sue every bank and credit card company that has ever stolen from you and force them to cancel your loans with respect to the credit cards and return all of the money you have given them. Some have taken the banks to court and had their mortgages canceled and kept possession of the home. This type of suit will stop a foreclosure if the judge knows anything about law.

Here on the following pages are a few suggested letters samples that you might use to get the process started in removing the debt on your credit cards. A bank, by the way, is always in back of a credit card issue.

1st letter

Bank
Manager, Customer Service
Credit Card Division
P.O. Box .
City and State

Certified Mail #

Month, 200_

Dear Sir or Madam:

It has come to my attention after reading a publication titled *Modern Money Mechanics* published by the Federal Reserve Bank of Chicago that (Name) Bank and other banks within the Federal Reserve System may be perpetrating a fraud on the American public. I have some questions which need to be answered before I continue to make payments on or use my (Type) Bank credit card. My account number is (Number). The following are my questions:

1. Was an individual depositor's money deposit used in order to pay the vendors when I made charges to my account?
2. Was the money that was loaned created by my signing of the voucher when I made the purchase?
3. Is it (Name) Bank policy to create checkbook money in amounts equal to the charges made by Bank customers?
4. Does (Name) Bank have on file a contract signed by me with a bona fide signature?
5. Will (Name) Bank provide a copy of the journal entry that is made when I charge to my account?

Please answer these questions within ten (10) days so that I am not late in making my payment. If I do not hear from you, I will assume that what I have learned is the truth and will, therefore, rescind my contract with (Name) Bank, as I do not wish to be a party to fraudulent practices.

Thanking you in advance for your cooperation, I look forward to your immediate response to this most disturbing revelation. My hope is that you can dispel my fears and refute this troubling circumstance in which we find ourselves.

Sincerely,

Your Name
c/o Your Street
Your City, Your State, Your Postal Zone

2nd letter

Date

Certified Mail No.

Credit Card Company Address
City, State, Zip

Dear Manager,

I wrote you a letter on (date), a copy of which is attached, asking that you supply me with information regarding how (credit card company) operates and how charges made by me are handled within your system. As of this date my questions remain unanswered. Since that writing I have done an exhaustive amount of research regarding the subject matter of that letter. (Credit card company) has refused to answer my questions. I have taken this to mean that your bank is doing as other banks are, loaning or creating credit on its books, then using my debt as an asset of the bank.

I am withholding any future payment based on your refusal to answer the questions contained in that letter of (date). If you can evidence to me that your bank actually gave me or the vendors involved something other than an electronic entry using my charge as a deposit on your books in order to create an electronic deposit to the vendors' accounts (checkbook money), then I will be willing to pay the balance(s) due.

In addition to my original requests, I would also like you to provide me with the following information:

A copy of your bank charter.

The names of the Board of Directors.

As I indicated in my first writing I am in possession of a booklet published by the Federal Reserve Bank of Chicago called *Modern Money Mechanics*. The booklet describes who creates money.

Please respond within ten (10) days with the information I have requested. Unless I hear from you refuting my stated facts, I will consider my account with you closed and this matter settled. Please be sure to have the person replying sign any further correspondence under penalty of perjury, and send it only to the address exactly as it appears below by certified mail. Thanking you in advance for your cooperation.

Sincerely,

Your Name
c/o Your Street
Your City, Your State, Your Postal Zone

Attach to 2nd Letter

STATE OF
COUNTY OF

Affidavit of Revocation of Signature for Cause

Comes now Affiant having full, first-hand knowledge of the facts herein and, by making this affidavit of his own first-hand knowledge, affirms that the facts stated herein are true and correct to the best of his knowledge and belief.

On or about (date you signed your credit card application), Affiant signed documents without knowledge that a fraud was being perpetrated upon Affiant:

That Affiant was coerced into signing documents without any knowledge that a fraud was being perpetrated upon Affiant;

That Affiant's revocation of signature constitutes a recession of signature. Thus, the contract no longer exists.

Affiant hereby revokes and makes void all signatures for cause pursuant to UCC 3-501.

Now Affiant is formally and timely removing the aforementioned signature(s) for all time and removing any nexus that (credit card company) may presume to have over Affiant by virtue of said signature(s).

Further Affiant sayeth not.

____

(your name

__________________________ __________________________

(name of witness) (name of witness)

STATE OF
COUNTY OF

On this ____ day of ______________,200_, before me personally appeared Affiant , ________________________, who under oath attests to the truth of the aforementioned Affidavit and identified by a valid Drivers license, is hereby acknowledged by me.

____

NOTARY PUBLIC

3rd letter

Date
Certified Mail No.
Credit Card Company
Address
City, State, Zip

Dear Sir or Madam:

I am returning your correspondence, which is enclosed. This matter has been settled. Please reference the attached copies of my correspondence of (dates). To date I have not received a satisfactory response to questions asked of you within these letters. A complete response from you is necessary in order to comprehend a full understanding of my contractual relationship with your bank. In the absence of a satisfactory reply, I have, therefore, concluded that (credit card company) is operating fraudulently and has not loaned me anything but a liability.

Until you prove to me that your bank has advanced to me a bank asset, I am under no obligation to repay the bank whatsoever. (Credit card company) has not fulfilled its contract with me.

I know that your bank's records still show that it owes me an asset because what (credit card company) loaned me was created by my note to them. If (credit card company) wants payment in like funds, I will be pleased to send you a promissory note, which is all that (credit card company) ever gave me.

I will consider this matter to be closed on your part also, unless (credit card company) truthfully answers my questions. Any further contact from you will be considered harassment and will be dealt with accordingly. If you find it necessary to contact me, please do by certified mail so only at the address below, exactly as it appears, and have the person supplying the answers sign under penalty of perjury. All other correspondence will be refused, and telephone calls will not be accepted.

Sincerely,

Your Name
c/o Your Street
Your City, Your State, Your Postal Zone

4th Letter

Date
Certified Mail No.

Attn: Legal Department Credit Card Company
Address City, State, Zip
Manager Legal Department:

REFUSED FOR CAUSE WITHOUT DISHONOR UCC 3.501

Enclosed please note my returned credit card issued by your bank (card number). I demand proof of its cancellation. In addition I demand that all related computer-generated bookkeeping entries concerning my account be destroyed. Failure on your part to comply with my demands will result in court action to compel performance of said demands. Further, be advised that any action by you or your agents in any attempt to collect on this account will result in immediate court action.

My actions are taken in a timely manner with this refusal for cause, pursuant to UCC 3-501.

Refusal for Cause Without Dishonor, UCC 3-501(b)(3) states: "Without dishonoring the instrument, the party to whom presentment is made may (i) return the instrument for lack of a necessary endorsement, or (ii) refuse payment or acceptance for failure of the presentment to comply with the terms of the instrument, an agreement of the parties, or other applicable law or rule.

The reasons for my refusal for cause are as follow:

Constructive Fraud

When applying for my credit card, I was under the mistaken belief that (credit card company) would be loaning me depositor's money, which it received from its depositors or investors. I have found by researching relevant case law on the matter and reading *Modern Money Mechanics*, published by the Federal Reserve Bank of Chicago, that (credit card company) created the money I borrowed by using my promise to pay. It generated computer entries to my account, listing the loan as a credit, in effect, creating money out of thin air.

In none of my transactions with (credit card company) did any officer or employee notify me that your bank created money by a journal entry (out of thin air). After discovering this, I am prepared to proceed against (credit card company) for bank fraud. The bank's transactions relating to me lacked two necessary elements of a valid contract.

Perhaps you should be aware of the following:

United States Code, Title 32, Section 24, Paragraph 7 confers upon a bank the power to lend its money, not its credit. In *First National Bank of Tallapoosa v Monroe*, 135 Ga.614; 69 S.E. 1123 (1911), the court stated:

"(T)he provisions referred to do not give power to a national bank to guarantee the payment of the obligations of others solely for their benefit, nor is such power incidental of the business of banking. A bank can lend its money but not its credit."

Again in: *Howard & Foster Co. v Citizens National Bank of Union*, 133 S.C. 202; 130 SE 758, (1927) "It has been settled beyond controversy that a national bank, under federal law, being limited in its power and capacity, cannot lend its credit by guaranteeing the debt of another. All such contracts being entered into by its officers are ultra vires and not binding upon the corporation. See also *Merchants Bank of Valdosta v Baird*, 160 F 642; 17 Lns 526 (1876).

(Credit card company) did not notify me that it created money by journal entry (out of thin air), defined as "bank credit." To do so would have disclosed that there was no consideration from (credit card company) to me.

"A lawful consideration must exist and be tendered, to support the note." See *Anheuser Busch Brewing Co. v Emma Mason*, 44 Minn. 318, 46 NW 558 (1890).

If there is no full disclosure and no consideration, there is no contract.

Peonage

(Credit card company's) manner of transacting business has made me a debt slave, in violation of the Thirteenth Amendment to the Constitution of the United States, which expressly forbids involuntary servitude. The United States Supreme Court addressed involuntary servitude, also called peonage, in *Clyatt v. U.S.*, 197 U.S. 207, 215-216; 25 S.Ct. 429; 43 L. Ed. 726 (1905), when it said:

"Peonage is sometimes classified as voluntary or involuntary, but this implies simply a difference in the mode of origin, but none of the character of the servitude. The one exists where the debtor voluntarily contracts to enter the service of his creditor. The other is forced upon the debtor by some provision of law."

In addition, (credit card company)'s method of creating money out of thin air and charging interest upon the transaction is a violation of the Biblical law of "just weights and measures." (Credit card company) created in moments money which takes me years of labor to pay off. (Credit card company) made me a debt slave by controlling my labor when it loaned me "bank credit" and not money.

BE NOTICED that I no longer consent to accepting (credit card company)'s demands upon me for my money. Your manner in the conduct of your banking business is in direct violation of the laws of contracts, the Constitution of the United States of America, God's law and my civil rights.

Revocation of Signature

By my refusal of (credit card company)'s statement in a timely manner pursuant to UCC 3-501, I hereby revoke, rescind, and repudiate my signature on the original application presented to (credit card company). The original application was fraudulent on its face, as full disclosure was not provided. The application did not inform me that (credit card company) was loaning me "bank credit" created out of thin air.

Had (credit card company) so disclosed this fact to me, that I was in fact borrowing "bank credit," I would have known that the element of consideration was missing from the contract and would have not entered into that agreement. It is a well-established principle of law that fraud has no statute of limitations and that its presence vitiates any and every contract or agreement. I make demand upon your bank to cancel our agreement and to return to me every dollar of my labor plus all interest I have ever paid to you for the duration of the agreement. I will contact the vendors directly and pay them for the products or services I purchased from them.

CONSPIRACY

You and your fellow bankers have been allowed to defraud the American public for many years. This can be explained only by the knowledge that the Federal Reserve Banks are a privately owned, operating for profit, corporation. Because of your inter-relationship and practices, all banks in this country are to be considered in law as one and the same, in that each bank in the Federal Reserve System is obligated to accept the checks of other member banks as if they issued it. I find it unconscionable that (credit card company) has been able to transfer my labor to its balance sheet by mere bookkeeping entries into its computer. This egregious violation of law and my civil rights shocks the conscience of all law-abiding citizens.

NOTICE

UCC 3-503 allows you thirty (30) days from receipt of this Refusal for Cause Without Dishonor notice to state under oath your rebuttal to my following causes:

That (credit card company) did not create money by loaning its credit and charging interest upon that loan, in violation of the law of contracts.

If you do not respond within thirty (30) days from the date of your receipt of this NOTICE, a default will be created by your material misrepresentation which vitiates any transaction occurring from the beginning of our doing business together until thirty (30) days from the date first above written. UCC 1-103.

If, within thirty (30) days, you do not either answer the above under oath or provide me proof of the cancellation of this computer-generated debt, the return or destruction of my application, and the return of all Federal Reserve Notes that I have paid to you since the beginning of our business relationship, I will seek damages against your bank for fraud. The Uniform Commercial Code allows me to seek the return of all Federal Reserve Notes paid to (credit card company) plus triple damages.

GOVERN YOURSELF ACCORDINGLY.

I will guarantee you only this: this set of letters will get their attention at the very highest level. You will get one heck of an education reading their replies. What will you do with all of the extra money, after you pay off the vendors?

CHAPTER EIGHT

A HOUSE FOR FREE

The same fraud used for Mortgages

The subject of money is a complex one and a subject that directly effects all of our lives, from the cradle to the grave. Home ownership is one of the American dreams that we have all sought but few will ever truly achieve. The following action at law concerned the Federal Reserve Notes and that relationship as equal consideration for the purposes of a binding contract as related to a home mortgage. This knowledgeable litigant won his home from the bank. Enjoy the story.

The following is the Memorandum of Law submitted by Judge Mahoney in that case. It should have the effect of a cold water shower to your intellect and a sobering realization of the gigantic fraud that has been fostered on the American people for the past eighty-six years. This case cannot be used as precedent, as the Supreme Court of Minnesota has reversed it, not because the judge was wrong (they did not comment on his analysis of the law), but because, they said, his court did not have jurisdiction. They were, in my opinion, attempting to save this evil banking system from collapse.

Judges are not permitted to make a judgment if that judgment would create chaos in society. The Supreme Court of Minnesota, in reversing this decision, was merely maintaining the status quo – We the people as slaves and the bankers as the masters. Anything else would be chaos as far as the government and bankers are concerned.

STATE OF MINNESOTA
IN JUSTICE COURT
COUNTY OF SCOTT
TOWNSHIP OF CREDIT RIVER

MARTIN V. MAHONEY, JUSTICE

FIRST BANK OF MONTGOMERY,
Plaintiff, CASE NO: 19144

vs. JUDGMENT AND DECREE

Jerome Daly,
Defendant.
______________________/

The above entitled action came on before the Court and a Jury of 12 on December 7, 1968, at 10:00 a.m. Plaintiff appeared by its President Lawrence V. Morgan and was represented by its Counsel Theodore R. Mellby. Defendant appeared on his own behalf.

A jury of Talesmen were called, impaneled and sworn to try the issues in this Case. Lawrence V. Morgan was the only witness called for Plaintiff and Defendant testified as the only witness in his own behalf.

Plaintiff brought this as a Common Law action for the recovery of the possession of lot 19, Fairview Beach, Scott County, Minn. Plaintiff claimed titled to the Real Property in question by foreclosure of a Note and Mortgage Deed dated May 8, 1964, which Plaintiff claimed was in default at the time foreclosure proceedings were started.

Defendant appeared and answered that the Plaintiff created the money and credit upon its own books by bookkeeping entry as the legal failure of consideration for the Mortgage Deed and alleged that the Sheriff's sale passed no title to Plaintiff.

The issues tried to the jury were whether there was a lawful consideration and whether Defendant had waived his rights to complain about the consideration having paid on the note for almost 3 years.

Mr. Morgan admitted that all of the money or credit which was used as a consideration was created upon their books, that this was standard banking practice exercised by their bank in combination with the Federal Reserve Bank of Minneapolis, another private bank, further that he knew of no United States Statute of Law that gave the Plaintiff the authority to do this. Plaintiff further claimed that Defendant by using the ledger book created credit and by paying on the Note and Mortgage waived any right to complain about the consideration and that Defendant was estopped from doing so.

At 12:15 on December 7, 1968, the Jury returned a unanimous verdict for the Defendant.

Now therefore, by virtue of the authority vested in me pursuant to the Declaration of Independence, the Northwest Ordinance of 1787, the Constitution of the United States and the Constitution and laws of the State Minnesota not inconsistent therewith;

IT IS HEREBY ORDERED, ADJUDGED AND DECREED:

1. That Plaintiff is not entitled to recover the possession of lot 19, Fairview Beach, Scott County, Minnesota, according to the Plat thereof on file in the Register of Deeds office.
2. That because of failure of a lawful consideration the Note and Mortgage dated May 8, 1964, are null and void.
3. That the Sheriff's sale of the above-described premises held on June 26, 1967, is null and void, of no effect.
4. That Plaintiff has no right, title or interest in said premises or lien thereon, as is above described.
5. That any provision in the Minnesota Constitution and any Minnesota Statute limiting the Jurisdiction of this Court is repugnant to the Constitution of the United States and to the Bill of Rights of the Minnesota Constitution and is null and void and that this Court has Jurisdiction to render complete Justice in this Cause.
6. That Defendant is awarded costs in the sum of $75.00 and execution is hereby issued therefore.
7. A 10 day stay is granted.
8. The following memorandum and any supplemental memorandum made and filed by this Court in support of this judgment is hereby made a part hereof by reference.

Dated December 9, 1968

BY THE COURT

MARTIN V. MAHONEY
JUSTICE OF THE PEACE
CREDIT RIVER TOWNSHIP
SCOTT COUNTY, MINNESOTA
Scott County, Minnesota

MEMORANDUM

The issues in this case were simple. There was no material dispute on the facts for the Jury to resolve.

Plaintiff admitted that it, in combination with the Federal Reserve Bank of Minneapolis, which are for all practical purposes, because of their interlocking activity and practices, and both being Banking Institutions incorporated under the Laws of the United States, are in the Law to be treated as one and the same Bank, did create the entire $14,000.00 in money or credit upon its own books by bookkeeping entry. That this was the Consideration used to support the Note dated May 8, 1964 and the Mortgage of the same date. The money and credit first came into existence when they credited it. Mr. Morgan admitted that no United States Law of Statute existed which gave him the right to do this. A lawful consideration must exist and be tendered to support the note. See *Anheuser Busch Brewing Co. v. Emma Mason*, 44 Minn. 318. 46 N.W. 558. The Jury found there was no lawful consideration and I agree. Only God can create something of value out of nothing.

Even if defendant could be charged with waiver or estoppel, as a matter of Law this is no defense to the plaintiff. The Law leaves wrongdoers where it finds them. See sections 50, 51, and 52 of Am Jur 2d "Actions" on page 584 – "no action will lie to recover on a claim based upon, or in any manner depending upon, a fraudulent, illegal, or immoral transaction or contract to which plaintiff was a party.

Plaintiff's act of creating credit is not authorized by the Constitution and Laws of the United States, is unconstitutional and void, and is not lawful consideration in the eyes of the Law to support any thing or upon which any lawful rights can be built.

Nothing in the Constitution of the United States limits the jurisdiction of this Court, which is one of original Jurisdiction with right of trial by Jury guaranteed. This is a Common Law Action. Minnesota cannot limit or impair the power of this Court to render Complete Justice between the parties. Any provisions in the Constitution and laws of Minnesota which attempt to do so are repugnant to the Constitution for the United States and void. No question as to the Jurisdiction of this Court was raised by either party at the trial. Both parties were given complete liberty to submit any and all facts and law to the Jury; at least in so far as they saw fit.

No complaint was made by Plaintiff that Plaintiff did not receive a fair trial. From the admissions made by Mr. Morgan the path of duty was made direct and clear for the Jury. Their Verdict could not reasonably have been otherwise. Justice was rendered completely and without denial, promptly and without delay, freely and without purchase, conformable to the laws in this Court on December 7, 1968.

BY THE COURT

December 9, 1968

MARTIN V. MAHONEY
JUSTICE OF THE PEACE
CREDIT RIVER TOWNSHIP
SCOTT COUNTY, MINNESOTA

Note: It has never been doubted that a Note given on a Consideration which is prohibited by law is void. It has been determined, independent of Acts of Congress, that sailing under the license of an enemy is illegal. The emission of Bills of Credit upon the books of these private Corporations, for the purposes of private gain is not warranted by the Constitution of the United States and is unlawful. See Craig v. Mo. 4 Peters Reports 912, This Court can tread only that path which is marked out by duty. M.V.M.

Judge Martin Mahoney's decision was as follows:

"For the Justice fees, the First National Bank deposited with the Clerk of the District Court the two Federal Reserve Notes. The Clerk tendered the Notes to me. My sworn duty compelled me to refuse the tender. This is contrary to the Constitution of the United States. The States have no power to make bank notes a legal tender. See American Jurist on Money, sec. 13. Only gold and silver coin is a lawful tender."

"Bank Notes are a good tender as money unless specifically objected to. Their consent and usage is based upon the convertibility of such notes to coin at the pleasure of the holder upon presentation to the bank for redemption. When the inability of a bank to redeem its notes is openly avowed they instantly lose their character as money and their circulation as currency ceases. (See 36 Am. Jur. on Money, Section 9).

"There is no lawful consideration for these Federal Reserve Notes to circulate as money. The banks actually obtained these notes for cost of printing. There is no lawful consideration for said Notes.

"A lawful consideration must exist for a Note. As a matter of fact, the "Notes" are not Notes at all, as they contain no promise to pay. (See 17 American Jurist section 85, 215)

"The activity of the Federal Reserve Banks of Minnesota, San Francisco and the First National Bank of Montgomery is contrary to public policy and contrary to the Constitution of the United States and constitutes an unlawful creation of money, credit and the obtaining of money and credit for no valuable consideration. Activity of said banks in creating money and credit is not warranted by the Constitution of the United States.

"The Federal Reserve Banks and National Banks exercise an exclusive monopoly and privilege of creating credit and issuing their Notes at the expense of the public, which does not receive a fair equivalent. This scheme is obliquely designed for the benefit of an idle monopoly to rob, blackmail, and oppress the producers of wealth.

"The Federal Reserve Act and the National Bank Act is in their operation and effect contrary to the whole letter and spirit of the Constitution of the United States, for they confer an unlawful and unnecessary power on private parties; they hold all of our fellow citizens in dependence; they are subversive to the rights and liberation of the people.

"These Acts have defiled the lawfully constituted Government of the United States. The Federal Reserve Act and the National Banking Act are not necessary and proper for carrying into execution the legislative powers granted to Congress or any other powers vested in the Government of the United States, but, on the contrary, are subversive to the rights of the People in their rights to life, liberty, and property. (See Section 462 of Title 31 U. S. Code).

"The meaning of the Constitutional provision, 'NO STATE SHALL make any Thing but Gold and Silver Coin a tender in payment of debts' is direct, clear, unambiguous and without any qualification. This Court is without authority to interpolate any exception. My duty is simply to execute it, as written, and to pronounce the legal result. From an examination of the case of *Edwards v. Kearsey*, 96 U.S. 595, the Federal Reserve Notes (fiat money), which are attempted to be made a legal tender, are exactly what the authors of the Constitution of the United States intend to prohibit. No State can make these Notes a legal tender. Congress is incompetent to authorize a State to make the Notes a legal tender. For the effect of binding Constitution provisions see *Cooke v. Iverson*. This fraudulent Federal Reserve System and National Banking System has impaired the obligation of Contract, promoted disrespect for the Constitution and Law and has shaken society to its foundations. (See 96 U.S. Code 595 and 108 M 388 and 63 M 147)

"Title 31, U.S. Code, Section 432, is in direct conflict with the Constitution insofar, at least, that it attempts to make Federal Reserve Notes a Legal Tender. The Constitution is the Supreme Law of the Land. Section 462 of Title 31 is not a law which is made in pursuance of the Constitution. It is unconstitutional and void, and I so hold. Therefore, the two Federal Reserve Notes are null and void for any lawful purpose in so far as this case is concerned and are not a valid deposit of $2.00 with the Clerk of the District Court for the purpose of effecting an Appeal from this Court to the District Court.

"However, there is a second ground of invalidity of these Federal Reserve Notes previously discussed and that is that the Notes are invalid because on no theory are they based upon a valid, adequate or lawful consideration.

"At the hearing scheduled for January 22, 1969, at 7:00 p.m., Mr. Morgan, nor anyone else from or represent the Bank, attended to aid the Court in making a correct determination.

"Mr. Morgan appeared at the trial on December 7, 1969, he appeared as a witness to be candid, open, direct, experienced and truthful. He testified to 20 years of experience with the Bank of America in Los Angeles, the Marquette National Bank of Minnesota and the First National Bank of Minnesota. He seemed to be familiar with the operation of the Federal Reserve System. He freely admitted that his Bank created all of the money and credit upon its books with which it acquired the Note and Mortgage of May 8, 1964. The credit first came into existence when the Bank created it upon its books. Further, he freely admitted that no United States Law gave the Bank the authority to do this. There was obviously no lawful consideration for the Note. The Bank parted with absolutely nothing except a little ink. In this case the evidence was on January 22, 1969, that the Federal Reserve Banks obtain the Notes for the cost of the printing only. This seems to be conferred by Title 12 USC, Section 420. The cost is about 9/10t^{hs} of a cent per Note, regardless of the amount of the Note. The Federal Reserve Banks create all of the money and credit upon their books by bookkeeping entries by which they acquire United States and State Securities. The collateral required to obtain the Note is, by section 412 USC, Title 12, a deposit of a like amount of Bonds – Bonds which the Banks acquire by creating money and credit by bookkeeping entry.

"No rights can be acquired by fraud. The Federal Reserve Notes are acquired through the use of unconstitutional statutes and fraud.

"The Common Law requires a lawful consideration for any Contract or Note. These Notes are void for failure at a lawful consideration at Common Law, entirely apart from any Constitutional Considerations. Upon this ground, the Notes are ineffectual for any purpose. This seems to be the principal objection to paper fiat money and the cause of its depreciation and failure down through the ages. If allowed to continue, Federal Reserve Notes will meet the same fate. From the evidence introduced on January 22, 1969, this Court finds that as of March 18, 1968, all Gold and Silver backing is removed from Federal Reserve Notes.

"The law leaves wrongdoers where it finds them. See Amer. Jur. 2nd on Actions, Sections 50, 51 and 52.

"Slavery and all its incidents, including Peonage, thralldom and debt created by fraud is universally prohibited in the United States. This case represents but another refined form of Slavery by the Bankers. Their position is not supported by the Constitution of the United States. The People have spoken their will in terms which cannot be misunderstood. It is indispensable to the preservation of the Union and independence and liberties of the people that this Court adhere only to the mandates of the Constitution and administer it as it is written. I therefore hold these Notes in question void and not effectual for any purpose."

January 30, 1969

BY THE COURT
/s/ Martin V. Mahoney
MARTIN V. MAHONEY
JUSTICE OF THE PEACE
CREDIT RIVER TOWNSHIP
SCOTT COUNTY, MINNESOTA

If we as a nation only had a few of these remarkable men in the judiciary we cannot even imagine the prosperity we would enjoy. Judge Mahoney died of mysterious causes several months after this decision.

The American People held as collateral

Why does there exist within the borders of the United States of America a system that appears to be predicated upon the enslavement of its citizens for the benefit of the favored few international bankers?

Perhaps we should revisit the time period of 1933 for the answer.

Perpetual Bankruptcy for America

Soon after the federal government's departure from common law in 1938, the United States entered the Second World War. The League of Nations was re-instituted under the pretence of the "United Nations" (22 U.S.C.A. 287 et. seq.). The Bank for International Settlements was re-instituted under pretense of the Bretton Woods Agreement (60 Stat. 1401, 22 U.S·C·A. 286 et seq.) as the "International Monetary Fund" (The Fund) and the "International Bank For Reconstruction And Development" (The Bank).

The United States as a corporate body politic (artificial entity) emerged from World War II in worse economic condition than when it entered.

In 1950, again the US declared bankruptcy and "reorganization." The reorganization is located in Title 5 of United States Code Annotated. The "explanation" at the beginning of 5 U.S.C.A. is immensely informative. The "Secretary of Treasury" was appointed as the "Receiver" in Bankruptcy. (Reorganization Plan No. 26. 5 U.S.C.A. §903, Public Law 94-564, Legislative History, page 5967.)

The United States subsequently and periodically filed further reorganizations. Conditions and situations worsened and Congress, having done what they were commanded not to do (Madison's Notes, Constitutional Convention, August 16, 1787; *Federalist Papers* No.44), in 1965 passed the "Coinage Act," completely debasing the Constitutional Coin (gold and silver, i.e. "dollar"). (18 U.S.C.A, §§331 and 332, U.S. vs. Marigold, 50 U.S. 560, 13 L.Ed. 257.)

At the signing of the Coinage Act on July 23, 1965, President Lyndon B. Johnson stated in his press release:

"When I have signed this bill before me, we will have made the first fundamental change in our coinage in 173 years. The Coinage Act of 1965 supersedes the Act of 1792. And that Act had the title: 'An Act Establishing a Mint and Regulating the Coinage of the United States...'

"Now I will sign this bill to make the first change in our coinage system since the 18th Century. To those members of Congress who are here on this historic occasion, I want to assure you that in making this change from the 18th Century we have no idea of returning to it."

It is important to take full cognizance of the fact that no Constitutional Amendment was ever obtained to fundamentally change, amend, abridge, or abolish the constitutional mandates, provisions, or prohibitions contained in the organic Constitution for the United States regarding our money. But due to internal and external pressures and divisions surrounding the Vietnam conflict, etc., the usurpation and breach of their constitutional mandate, Congress' actions went basically unchallenged and unnoticed by the general public at large. They, the de jure people of the United States of America, that day, became "a wealthy man's cannon fodder or cheap source of slave labor." (*Silent Weapons for Quiet Wars*, TM-SW7905.1, pages 6-13, 56).

Congress is clearly mandated the power and authority to regulate and maintain true and inherent "value" of the Coin within the scope and authority of Article I, Section 8, Clauses 5 and 6, and Article I, Section 10,

Clause 1, of the ordained Constitution (1787). Further, Congress had a corresponding obligation to maintain gold and silver Coin and Foreign Coin at the necessary and proper "equal weights and measures" clause. (Public Law 97-289, 96 Stat. 1211.)

Those exercising the public offices of the Union States all knew such de facto transitions were unlawful and unauthorized. Regardless, they sanctioned, implemented, and enforced the complete destruction of the American people's wealth. Inevitably resulting in destructive "governmental, social, industrial economic change" in the de jure States of the United States of America. (Public Law 94-564, Legislative History, pages 5936, 5945; 31 U.S.C.A §314, 31 U.S.C.A·§321, and 31 U.S.C.A. §5112). Under the delusion that they may, lawmakers now as then, both directly and indirectly, continue to do with impunity what they are absolutely prohibited from doing. (*Federalist Papers* No. 44, *Craig vs. Missouri*, 4 Peters 903.)

The International Bankers and Corporations take control of America

In 1966, Congress being then as severely compromised by campaign contributions from banks and corporations as they are now, passed the "Federal Tax Lien Act" by which the entire taxing and monetary system, the "essential engine" (*Federalist Papers* No. 31), was placed under the Uniform Commercial Code. (Public Law 89-719, Legislative History, page 3722) The Uniform Commercial Code was promulgated by the National Conference of Commissioners on Uniform State Laws, in collusion with the American Law Institute, for the benefit of banking and business interests. (*Handbook Of The National Conference of Commissioners on Uniform State Laws*, 1966, pages 152 and 153).

The United States became engaged in numerous conflicts, including Korea and the Vietnam, that were under the direction and control of the United Nations (22 U.S.C.A. §287 [d]), and Congress agreed to foot the bill. (22 U.S.C.A. §287 [i]). Not being able to honor their obligations, Congress re-hypothecated debt credit, openly and publicly dishonored and disavowed their "notes" and "obligations" at (12 U.S.C.A. §411), i.e., "Federal Reserve Notes" through Public Law 90-269, Section 2, 82 Stat. 50 (1968), to wit:

"Sec. 2. The first sentence of section 15 of the Federal Reserve Act (12 U.S.C. 391) is amended by striking 'and the funds provided in this Act for the redemption of Federal Reserve notes.'"

Our Republic began to crumble. On March 28, 1970, President Richard M. Nixon issued Proclamation No. 3972, declaring an "emergency" because the postal employees struck against the de facto government for higher pay, due to inflation of the paper "bills of credit." (Senate Report No. 93-549, page 596). President Nixon then placed the U.S. Postal Department under control of the "Department of Defense" (*Department of the Army Field Manual*, FM 41-10 [1969 ed].).

The Federal Reserve System's reserve policy had been faltering for more than a decade, but the benchmark date of the collapse is put at August 15, 1971. On that day, President Nixon reversed U.S. international monetary policy by officially declaring the non-convertibility of the U.S. dollar (F.R.N.) into gold (Public Law 94-564, Legislative History, page 5937, and Senate Report No. 93-549, Foreword, Page III, Proclamation No. 4074, Page 597, 31 U.S.C.A. §314 and 31 U.S.C.A. §5112). There was simply no longer any gold left in Fort Knox with which to pay the country's international debt to its foreign creditors. You know why? That chapter is coming up.

On September 21, 1973, Congress passed Public Law 93-110, amending the Bretton Woods Par Value Modification Act, 82 Stat. 116, 31 U.S.C.A. §449, and reiterated the "emergency" at *12 U.S.C.A. §95(a)* and amended section 8 of the Bretton Woods Agreement Act of 1945 (22 U.S.C.A. §286 (f), which included "reports on foreign currency transactions." (Also see: Executive Order No. 10033.) This Act further declared in section 2(b) that:

"No provision of any law in effect on the date of enactment of this Act, and no rule, regulation, or order under authority of any such law, may be construed to prohibit any person from purchasing, holding, selling, or otherwise dealing with gold."

The United Nations: Good or Evil

On January 19, 1976, Congresswoman Marjorie S. Holt noted for the record a second "Declaration of Interdependence," which clearly identified the UN as a "Communist" organization, the UN seeking both production and monetary control over the Union and the People, using the international organization (UN), by promoting the "One World Order." (Congressional Record, January 19, 1976, Extension of Remarks. Also see 8 U.S.C.A. §1101(40), 50 U.S.C.A. §§781 and 783.)

First the Federal Judges roll over for their 20 pieces of silver

Social and economic conditions steadily worsened as noted in the Complaint/Petition filed in the U.S. Court of Claims, Docket No. 41-76, on February 11, 1976, by 44 federal judges. *Atkins, et al. vs. U.S.* Atkins complained that:

"As a result of inflation, the compensation of federal judges has been substantially diminished each year since 1969, causing direct and continuing monetary harm to plaintiffs... The real value of the dollar decreased by approximately 34.5 percent from March 15, 1969, to October 1, 1975. As a result, plaintiffs have suffered an unconstitutional deprivation of earnings..." and in the prayer for relief claimed "damages for the constitutional violations enumerated above, measured as the diminution of his earnings for the entire period since March 9, 1969."

It is quite apparent that the persons holding and enjoying offices of public trust, honor and/or profit knew of the emergency and emergent problem. They sought protection for themselves to the damage and injury of "We the People" and our children who were classified as "a club that has many other members who have no remedy." Knowing that "heinous" acts had been committed, the judges stated that they (judges/lawyers) would not apply the law, nor would any substantive remedy be applied "until all of us (judges) are dead."

Such persons fraudulently swore an oath to uphold, defend, and preserve the sovereignty of the Nation and the Republic States of the Union and the Constitution. They breached their duty to protect the Citizens and their posterity from fraud, imposition, avarice, and stealthy encroachment. *Atkins et al. vs. U.S.* 556 F.2d 1028, pages 1072, 1074; *The Tempting of America*, supra, pages 155-159; 5 U.S.C.A. §§5305 and 5335, Senate Report No. 93-549, pages 69-71.) This is verified in Public Law No. 94-564, Legislative History, Page 5944, and states:

"Moving to a floating exchange rate for international commerce means private enterprise and not central governments bear the risk of currency fluctuations."

Numerous serious debates were held in Congress, including but not limited to Tuesday, July 27, 1976, (Congressional Record – House, July 27, 1976), concerning the international financial institutions and operations. Representative Ron Paul, Chairman of the House Banking Committee, made numerous references to the true practices of the "international" financial institutions, including but not limited to the conversion of $27,000,000 (27 million) in gold (today that's $9.5 billion in FRNs factoring the price of gold at $352 per ounce), contributed by the United States as part of its "quota obligations" which the International Monetary Fund (Governor-Secretary of Treasury) sold (Public Law 94-564, Legislative History, pages 5945 and 5946) under questionable terms and concessions. (Also see: *The Ron Paul Money Book*, (1991), by Ron Paul, Plantation Publishing, 837 W. Plantation, Clute, Texas 77531.)

Invisible Contracts you have with the Secretary of the Treasury for the use of the Federal Reserves private money

On October 28, 1977 the passage of Public Law 95-147, 91 Stat. 1227 declared most banking institutions, including State banks, to be under direction and control of the corporate "Governor" of the International Monetary Fund. (Public Law 94-564, Legislative History, page 5942, *United States Government Manual*, 1990/91, pages 480-481.) The Act further declared:

"(2) Section 10(a) of the Gold Reserve Act of 1934 (31 U.S.C. §822 a [b]) is amended by striking out the phrase 'stabilizing the exchange value of the dollar'..."

"(c) The joint resolution entitled 'Joint resolution to assure uniform values to the coins and currencies of the United States', approved June 5, 1933, (31 U.S.C. §463) shall not apply to obligations issued on or after the date of enactment of this section."

The international organizations, corporations, and associations could not pay and refused to pay their debts. They determined that they could pass the loss of their non-redeemable, non-current notes, bonds, and evidences of debt off onto others and thereby crown their fraud with success. (Letter from Department of Treasury, Russell L. Hunk, Assistant General Counsel (International Affairs), October 26, 1989, as recorded in the office of Clerk and Recorder, Baca County, Colorado, at Book 540 page 364). The de facto United States as Corporators, (22 U.S.C.A. §286 [e], et seq.) and "state" had declared "insolvency" (26 USC § 1651[g][1], Westfall vs. Bralev, 10 Ohio 188, 75 Am. Dec. 509, Adams vs. Richardson, 337 SW 2d 911; Ward vs. Smith, 7 Wall 447).

In 1980 Congress passed among other things Public Law 96-221, providing for the furtherance and expansion of the profligate re-hypothecated debt pyramid scheme and reduced the reserve requirements on "transaction accounts" to a minimum of three percent (3%) to a maximum of (14%) percent. Institutions Deregulation And Monetary Control Act of 1980, Section 103[b][E][2].

And you thought it was money

"In the United States neither paper currency nor deposits have value as commodities. Intrinsically, a dollar bill is just a piece of paper. Deposits are merely book entries. Coins do have some intrinsic value as metal, but generally far less than their face amount...

"In the absence of legal reserve requirements, banks can build up deposits by increasing loans and investments so long as they keep enough currency on hand to redeem whatever amounts the holders of deposits want to convert into currency. This unique attribute of the banking business was discovered several centuries ago. At one time, bankers were merely middlemen. They made profit by accepting gold and coins brought to them for safekeeping and lending them to borrowers. But they soon found that the receipts they issued to depositors were being used as money since whoever held them could go to the banker and exchange them for metallic money.

"Then bankers discovered that they could make loans merely by giving borrowers their promise to pay (bank notes). In this way, banks began to create money. More notes could be issued than the gold and coin on hand because only a portion of the notes outstanding would be presented for payment at any one time. Enough metallic money had to be kept on hand, of course, to redeem whatever volume of notes was presented for payment.

"Transaction deposits are the modern counter-part of bank notes. It was a small step from printing notes to making book entries to the credit of borrowers which the borrowers, in turn, could 'spend' by writing checks, thereby, 'printing their own money.'" – *Modern Money Mechanics, A Workbook on Deposits, Currency and Bank Reserves,* 1982 Rev. Ed., Federal Reserve Bank of Chicago, P.O. box 834, Chicago, Illinois 60609, pages 3 and 4.)

An Old Cold War rages against the American people

Eighty-six years is in no way "temporary." It's a permanent state of "emergency" and was clearly instituted, formed, and engineered within the Union for the sole purpose of creating a constitutional dictatorship, all accomplished through gross usurpation and breach of legal duties and through the Presidents' use of Executive Orders, on demand, of the international financial institutions, organizations, corporations, and associations, including the Federal Reserve, their "fiscal and depository agent" (22 U.S.C.A. § 286 (d). This profligate practice has led to such "emergency" legislation as the "Public Debt Limit-Balance Budget And Emergency Deficit Control Act of 1985," Public Law 99-177, etc.

The government, by becoming a Corporation (22 U.S.C.A. §286 [e]), lays down its sovereignty and takes on the mantle of a private citizen. It can exercise no power which is not derived from the corporate charter. (*The Bank of the United States vs. Planters Bank of Georgia*, 6 L. Ed. [9 Wheat] 244, U.S. vs. Burr, 309 U.S. 242.) The real party in interest is not the de jure "United States of America" or "State," but "The Bank" and "The Fund", (22 U.S.C.A 286 et seq.). The acts committed under fraud, force, and seizures are many times done under "letters of marque and reprisal," i.e., "recapture," (31 U.S.C.A §5323). Such principles as "fraud and justice never dwell together" (*Wingate's Maxims* 680) and "a right of action cannot arise out of fraud" (*Broom's Maxims* 297, 729; Cowper Reports 343; 5 *Scott's New Reports* 558; 10 Mass. 276; 38 Fed. 800) are far too high a thought concept for these internationalists, as is "Due Process" or "Just Compensation" and Justice itself; forget about truth.

Will Rogers' old saying, "There are men running governments who shouldn't be allowed to play with matches," is just as astute and accurate today as it was then.

The contrived "emergency" has created numerous abuses, usurpations, and abridgments of delegated Powers and Authority. As stated in Senate Report 93-549:

"Since March 9, 1993, the United States has been in a state of declared national emergency. In fact, there are now in effect four presidential proclaimed states of national emergency. In addition to the national emergency declared by President Roosevelt in 1933, there are also the national emergency proclaimed by President Truman on December 16, 1950, during the Korean conflict, and the states of national emergency declared by President Nixon on March 23, 1970, and August 15, 1971.

"These proclamations give force to 470 provisions of Federal law. These hundreds of statues delegate to the President extraordinary powers, ordinarily exercised by the Congress, which affect the lives of American citizens in a host of all-encompassing manners. This vast range of powers, taken together, confers enough authority to rule the country without reference to normal constitutional process.

"Under the powers delegated by these statues, the president may: seize property; organize and control the means of production; seize commodities;

assign military forces abroad; institute martial law; seize and control all transportation and communication; regulate the operation of private enterprise; restrict travel; and in a plethora of particular ways, control the lives of all American citizens." (Foreword, Page III)

The "Introduction" on page 1 begins with a phenomenal declaration:

"A majority of the people of the United States have lived all of their lives under emergency rule. For 40 years, freedoms and governmental procedures guaranteed by the Constitution have in varying degrees been abridged by laws brought into force by states of national emergency ..."

According to all my research of 16 American Jurisprudence, 2nd Ed., Sections 71 and 82, no emergency justifies a violation of any constitutional provision. Arguing the "Supremacy Clause" and "Separation of Powers" is clearly admitted in Senate Report No. 93-549; that abridgement has clearly occurred. We have all heard, on numerous occasions, statements in federal and state tribunals that Constitutional arguments are "immaterial" or "frivolous." That is based upon the concealment, furtherance and compounding of fraud and "emergency" created and sustained by the "expatriated" aliens of the United Nations and its organizations, corporations, and associations. (Letter, *Insight Magazine*, February 18, 1991, page 7, Lowell L. Flanders, President, UN Staff Union, New York.) 8 U.S.C.A §1481 is one of the controlling statutes on expatriation, as is 22 U.S.C.A. §§§611, 612 and 613 and 50 USCA §781. This is where the Federal government gets jurisdiction over you because you have an invisible contract with the Secretary of the Treasury in the form of bank accounts, credit cards, Social Security participation, etc. Contract law is Equity/Admiralty jurisdiction, and the Constitution is of no use to you in those Courts.

CONSPIRACY THEORIES: DELUSIONAL OR REAL

Unlike the government, I permit my readership the right to determine for themselves whether or not there exists a conspiracy in this country. My views on the subject are totally irrelevant; you know on which side of the road I stand.

Where is the money?

Where does the money go that is paid into the IRS?

It spends at least a year in what is called a "quad zero" account under an Individual Master File, after which time the Director of the IRS Center can apparently do whatever he wants with the money. It is sometimes dispersed under Treasury Order 91 (Rev. 1), May 12, 1986, which is a service agreement between the IRS and the Agency for International Development, AID. (UNITED NATIONS)

CHAPTER NINE

HOW YOU ROB A REALLY BIG BANK

WHERE IS THE MONEY (GOLD) FROM FT. KNOX?

INVESTIGATION INTO THE ROBBERY OF FORT KNOX

My research uncovered the following information that was never intended by the government to be revealed, ever! What you are about to discover will shock and anger the average hard working, tax paying American. I know it did me!

The law requires that the Secretary of the Treasury submit to Congress a report on the amount and value of gold held in the vaults at Fort Knox each year. Yet, the Secretary has issued no report in the last twenty-five years. No person has been allowed to view the contents of the vaults at Fort Knox. And no audit of the gold supplies belonging to the United States Treasury can be found for at least the last twenty-five years.

The government is covering up the fact that Fort Knox has been systematically looted.

In 1933, Franklin D. Roosevelt penned executive orders that confiscated all privately held gold and that did so without compensation. The American people were forced to exchange their gold for valueless Federal Reserve Notes. The rate of exchange fixed by the government was about 40% below the market price. The total loss to the American economy was approximately $5 billion. All gold exchanged was added to the supply in the vaults at Fort Knox, Kentucky. Records show that the total gold supply in the vaults in 1935 was worth about $28 billion, or $350 billion in today's market.

World in debt to U.S.

Between 1935 and 1956 most of the nations of the world became indebted to the United States. Most of the indebtedness was incurred when the U.S. furnished aid to its allies during World Wars I and II. Debts between nations have been traditionally satisfied by payment in gold. Thus our gold supplies should have escalated exponentially. A few nations did make payments on their debt and one or two may have even paid the entire amount. Most, however, delayed payment, and eventually the United States Congress forgave their debt. In any event by 1956, our gold supplies should have been far in excess of $940 billion, but even if they were not, where is the $80 billion that should have been there?

U.S. News and World Report published the following in an article dated February 24, 1956:

"U.S. could get into a 'tight' gold supply position, if the countries were to decide to withdraw the gold reserves on which they hold claims. In 1953, our gold reserve was $23.3 Billions; in 1956 it is down to $21.8 Billions; but other nations hold claim against our gold totaling $13.8 billions; so in an emergency, available for our need is a gold reserve of only $8 billions; whereas we need $12 billions of gold reserve, to backup our currency."

How could this be when most of the nations in the world owed the United States billions of dollars? How could there have ever been a claim against our gold, $13.8 billions over the gold owed the U.S., by the allied nations and the defeated Germany and Japan? Is the U.S. government covering up the theft of U.S. gold by misinforming the public?

Let's support Communism

The answer can be found in a book entitled *From Major Jordan's Diaries*, by George Racey Jordan. There are several other sources which all agree upon basic facts. Major Jordan recounts in his diary that during a farewell talk with Russian Colonel Kotikov he was told that a "money plane" had crashed in Siberia and had to be replaced. Kotikov explained that the U.S. Treasury was shipping engraving plates, ink, paper, and other materials to Russia so that they could print the same occupation money for Germans as the United States was printing.

Colonel Kotikov insisted the equipment had been shipped through Great Falls, Montana, in May of 1944 in two shipments in five C-47s each. The shipments had been arranged on the highest level in Washington and the planes had been loaded at the Washington National Airport.

Years later a Senate investigation into the scandal found and confirmed the fact that in spite of widespread protests and warnings, Harry Hopkins, Secretary of the Treasury Henry Morgenthau, U.S. Ambassador to Russia Averell Harriman and Assistant Secretary of the Treasury Harry Dexter White were able to exert enough pressure to see that Russia got the plates. Later White was exposed as a Russian agent.

Occupation Money Printed in Leipzig, Germany

Official records show that the photographic plates and all the materials necessary for making high quality plates and high quality reproductions were shipped from Washington, D.C., on May 24, 1944. A second shipment to replace the equipment "lost" in the alleged crash was sent on June 7, 1944. The Red army set up shop in a former Nazi printing plant in Leipzig and started the presses rolling and rolling and rolling.

The Russians insisted upon printing the occupation currency in their own territory where there could be no accountability. They knew that the U.S. Army would convert such currency into dollars. As a result every Russian printed occupation Mark that fell into the hands of an American soldier or accredited civilian became a potential charge against the Treasury of the United States. The Russians paid their own occupation forces with these Marks, adding a two-year bonus for good measure.

The American taxpayer footed the bill. By using the occupation currency which cost them nothing, the Russians snapped up anything of value left in the German economy. When they could get purchases out of America, that was even better. By December 1946, the U.S. Military government found itself $250,000,000 or more in the red. It had redeemed in dollars at least 2,500,000,000 Marks in excess of the total Marks issued by its Finance Office. The deficit could have had no other origin than the Russian plant in Leipzig, Germany.

Harry Dexter White, Assistant Secretary of the Treasury, conspired with the Russians to give them the plates, ink, paper, formulas, and the correct serial numbers needed for Russia to print U.S. currency that could be redeemed in gold. This could not have been done without the full knowledge and approval of Secretary of the Treasury Morgenthau.

Morgenthau and White then traitorously sent five planeloads of money plates, paper and ink to Russia for the printing of $5,000 and $10,000 Federal Reserve Notes, which could be redeemed in gold. It is the responsibility of the Federal Reserve System to secure the plates. When I asked the Treasury Department to advise me of the whereabouts of those plates they replied, "We do not know."

The United States Treasury Department and the Federal Reserve are very sensitive, even threatening, on this issue. This information proves beyond any shadow of a doubt that Senator Joseph McCarthy was absolutely right about the infiltration and takeover of the United States government by communist agents.

When these bills printed in Russia were spent into circulation in foreign countries or used in trade, the result was an equivalent value of gold directly transferred from Fort Knox to an overseas destination. Over a period of years, the Treasury was emptied of its gold. The bills that reached the Federal Reserve or the Treasury Department were destroyed. The bills that fell into the hands of the American public and eventually the vaults of collectors have revealed the greatest gold theft in the history of the world.

Serial Numbers Tell the Tale

The proof may be found in the statistics of the U.S. Treasury. Check the Woods-Mellon, large letter in seal, denoting bank of issue, $5,000 Federal Reserve Notes, Series 1928. The record shows that for the Federal Reserve Bank in Boston, only 960 were printed, with the first note delivered on November 19th, 1929, and the last note delivered on July 26th, 1933. Mysteriously in 1977, the record shows that there are 1,320 of these notes known to exist. The record shows the same notes were printed at the Federal Reserve Bank in San Francisco in the number of 1,224 with the first note delivered on November 19th, 1929, and the last note delivered on July 23rd, 1930. Mysteriously in 1977 the record shows that there are 51,300 notes known to exist.

If you check the Julian-Morgenthau letter in seal, $10,000 Federal Reserve Notes, Series 1934, the record shows that the five Federal Reserve Banks in Cleveland, Richmond, Atlanta, Kansas City, and Dallas were never issued plates for these notes. No notes were printed and none were delivered. Mysteriously in 1977 the record shows that 1,480 exist from Cleveland, 1,200 exist from Richmond, 2,400 exist from Atlanta, 1,200 exist from Kansas City, and 1,200 exist from Dallas.

I have included the documentation the Treasury does not want you to see. Compare for yourself the number of notes authorized and the number of notes that were actually printed and redeemed in gold. Then you tell me whether the International Bankers and the Russians robbed Fort Knox in their plan to enslave the American people.

HEWITT - DONLON CATALOG OF UNITED STATES SMALL SIZE PAPER MONEY

10th ANNUAL EDITION - 1974 -

$5000 FEDERAL RESERVE NOTES - SERIES 1928

SECRETARY-TREASURER-MELLON-WOODS

Federal Reserve Bank	Number of Notes Authorized
Boston	960
New York	2,400
Philadelphia	None
Cleveland	2,400
Richmond	3,192
Atlanta	1,032
Chicago	4,440
St. Louis	None
Minneapolis	None
Kansas City	480
Dallas	240
San Francisco	1,224

$10,000 FEDERAL RESERVE NOTES-SERIES 1934

SECRETARY-TREASURER-MORGENTHAU-JULIAN

Federal Reserve Bank	Number of Notes Authorized
Boston	3,600
New York	7,800
Philadelphia	600
Cleveland	None
Richmond	None
Atlanta	None
Chicago	3,600
St. Louis	1,200
Minneapolis	None
Kansas City	None
Dallas	None
San Francisco	1,800

WHAT THE TREASURY PAID OUT FROM FORT KNOX

THE COMPREHENSIVE CATALOG OF U.S. PAPER MONEY

- 1977 -

$5,000 FEDERAL RESERVE NOTES - SERIES 1928

SECRETARY-TREASURER -MELLON-WOODS

Federal Reserve Bank	Number of Notes Printed
Boston	1,320
New York	2,640
Philadelphia	No Record
Cleveland	3,000
Richmond	3,984
Atlanta	1,440
Chicago	3,480
St. Louis	No Record
Minneapolis	No Record
Kansas City	720
Dallas	360
San Francisco	51,300

$10,000 FEDERAL RESERVE NOTES-SERIES 1934

SECRETARY-TREASURER-MORGENTHAU-JULIAN

Federal Reserve Bank	Number of Notes Printed
Boston	9,720
New York	11,520
Philadelphia	6,000
Cleveland	1,480
Richmond	1,200
Atlanta	2,400
Chicago	3,840
St. Louis	2,040
Minneapolis	No Record
Kansas City	1,200
Dallas	1,200
San Francisco	3,600

1938 Law Used to Hide Theft of Gold

I believe this Public Law was used to hide the statistics that would have revealed the transactions of foreign countries or corporations, including banks, which redeemed the notes for gold. The fact that this law was passed years before the transfer of printing technology to the Russians is of little significance, as the plans for the destruction of America's monetary system have been long in existence, at least since 1910, as evidenced by the banking collapse of 1933. Public Laws §11-13 Jan. 27, 29, 1938, Feb. 3, 1938 (52 §.]) (Chapter 11)

The money that was printed in Russia and laundered through the U.S. Army and the international banking circles was used to purchase technology. It funded the communist agenda in third world nations, financed wars of liberation, and promoted the cause of international socialism. This drained the U.S. Gold reserves, weakened the United States of America, and placed you and your future generations into perpetual bankruptcy and servitude.

We Financed Soviet Weapons

William Casey was Director of the Central Intelligence Agency during Iran-Contra. He was the head of AID, an Agency of the United Nations. He and the Federal Reserve Bank funneled hundreds of millions of dollars to the Soviet Union. The money being spent financed the Kama River Truck Factory, the largest military production facility for tanks, trucks, armored personnel carriers, and other wheeled vehicles in the world. The Kama River factory has a production capability larger than all combined automobile and truck manufacturing plants in the United States.

IRS/AID Service Agreement

The agreement states:

"Authority is hereby delegated to the Assistant Commissioner International to develop and enter into the service agreement between the Treasury Department and the Agency for International Development."

The Secretary of the Treasury is always appointed U.S. Governor of the International Monetary Fund in accordance with the international Bretton Woods agreement that created the IMF. The IMF pays the Secretary of the Treasury while serving as Governor, not the United States Treasury.

Agent of Foreign Powers

The Secretary of the Treasury holds the following positions, and at the same time he serves as the Secretary of the Treasury:

- U.S. Governor of the International Monetary Fund
- U.S. Governor of the International Bank for Reconstruction and Development
- U.S. Governor of the Inter-American Development Bank
- U.S. Governor of the African Development Bank
- U.S. Governor of the Asian Development Bank
- U.S. Governor of the African Development Fund
- U.S. Governor of the European Bank for Reconstruction and Development.

The Secretary of the Treasury received a salary from each of these organizations, which literally makes him an unregistered agent of several foreign powers, as are any personnel that serve under him. This includes the Internal Revenue Service.

A BETRAYAL OF TRUST

Those whom we trusted have betrayed the American people. We have been robbed of our dignity, our money, property, our freedom and life. By choice and consent it happened, because we trusted imperfect men to rule imperfect men and we failed in our duty as watchdog. It happened because we have been intellectually lazy, ignorant, apathetic, and mostly stupid; you choose your own adjective.

The following chapter demonstrates the enormous fraud foisted upon us without our detecting it. There must have been a perpetual fog of ignorance embracing the entire country during the early 1900s.

CHAPTER TEN

ALLODIAL TITLE

What is a Land Patent and Allodial Title? What is it and how does it affect my life or that of my children?

Essentially, a Land Patent is the first conveyance of title ownership to land, which the U.S. Government grants a citizen who applies for one. One of the earliest laws for granting Land Patents was passed by Congress on April 24, 1820. Among other things, Congress set up Government Land offices, now known as the Bureau of Land Management. Land was usually sold in parcels of 160 acres for $1.25 per acre. The law in 1820 prohibited the borrowing or use of "credit" for the purchase of government land. In the debates in Congress prior to passage of this act, Senator King of New York said on March 1820:

"...it was calculated to plant in the new country a population of independent unembarrassed freeholder, ...that it would place in every man, the Power to Purchase a freehold the price of which could be cleared in 3 years, ...that it would cut up speculation and monopoly, that it would prevent the accumulation of alarming debt which experience proved never would and never could be paid."

Later on, in 1862, a Homestead Act stated in Section 4: "That no lands acquired under the provisions of this act shall in any event become liable to the satisfaction of any debt or debts contracted prior to the issuing of the patent therefor."

It can be clearly seen that the intent of these early lawmakers was for the people of this country to be FREEMEN AND FREEHOLDERS of their land, never to be subject to nor to have it taken from them by any government, feudal authority or banker, or any other party who might have a claim against the person who owned the land.

In plain English, a Land Patent, which gave you an allodial freehold, was "judgment proof" and, yes, even immune from tax liens. In effect, the only authority over you or your land was GOD himself. In England, a man who owned free from authority of the king was known as a freeholder and his land was called a freehold or allodial freehold. Most land patents in the U.S. were issued prior to 1900. However, even today, new land patents continue to be issued, mostly for gas, oil and mineral rights on public lands. For this reason, there are several land offices that remain open in the United States.

MEMORANDUM OF LAW ON ALLODIAL v. FEUDAL TITLES

In America today, there is a phenomenon occurring that has not been experienced since the mid 1930s. That phenomenon is an increasing number of foreclosures, both in the rural sector and in the cities. This is occurring because of the inability of the debtor to pay the creditor the necessary interest and principal on a rising debt load that is expanding across the country. As a defense, the land patent title to the land and the congressional intent that accompanies the Land Patent Act is hereby being presented. For the Court to properly evaluate the Land Patent, in any given situation, it is necessary to understand what a Land Patent is, why it was created, what existed before the patent, particularly in common-law England. These questions must be answered to effectively understand the association between the government, the law, the land and the people.

First, what existed before land patents? Since it is imperative to understand what the land patent is and why it was created, the best method is a study of the converse, or the common-law English land titles. This method thus allows us to fully understand what "We the People" are presently supposed to have by way of actual ownership of land as envisioned by our founding fathers.

In England, at least until the mid-1600s and arguably until William Blackstone's time in the mid-1700s, the King exclusively owned property. In arbitrary governments the title is held by and springs from the supreme head, be he the emperor, king, potentate, or by whatever name he is known. *McConnell v. Wilcox*, I Seam (111.) 344, 367 (1837) The king was the true and complete owner, giving him the authority to take and grant the land from the people in his kingdom who either lost or gained his favor. The authority to take the land may have required a justifiable reason, but the king, leaving the dis-seised former holder of the land wondering what it was that had brought the King's wrath to bear upon him, could conceivably have fabricated such a reason. At the same time the beneficiary of such a gift, while undoubtedly knowing the circumstances behind the gift, may have been left to wonder if the same fate awaited him if ever he fell into disfavor with the king.

The King's gifts were called fiefs, a fief being the same as a feud, which is described as an estate in land held of a superior on condition of rendering him services. (*2 Blackstone's Commentaries*, p. 105.) It is also described as an inheritable right to the use and occupation of lands, held on condition of rendering services to the lord or proprietor, who himself retains the ownership in the lands, (*Black's Law Dictionary*, 4th Edition p. 748 [1968].) Thus, the people had land they occupied, devised, inherited, alienated, or disposed of as they saw fit, so long as they remained in favor with the King. (F. L. Ganshof, *Feudalism*, p. 113 (1964)).

This holding of lands under another was called a tenure and was not limited to the relation of the first or paramount lord and vassal. It extended to those to whom such vassal, within the rules of feudal law, may have parted out his own feud to his own vassals, whereby he became the mesne lord between his vassals and his own or lord paramount. Those who held directly to the king were called his "tenants in...chief." (I E. Washburn, Treatise on the American Law of Real Property, Ch. 11, Section 58, P. 42 [6th Ed. 1902].) In this manner, the lands, which had been granted to the barons principal lands were again subdivided, and granted by them to sub-feudatories to be held of themselves. (Id., Section 65, p.44.) The size of the gift of the land could vary from a few acres to thousands of acres, depending on the power and prestige of the lord. (See supra Ganshof at 113.)

The fiefs were built in the same manner as a pyramid, with the King, the true owner of the land, being at the top, and from the bottom up there existed a system of small to medium sized to large sized estates on which the persons directly beneath one estate owed homage to the lord of that estate as well as to the King. (Id. at 114)

At the lowest level of this pyramid through at least the 14th and 15th centuries existed serfs or villains, the class of people that had no rights and were recognized as nothing more than real property. (F. Goodwin, *Treatise on The Law of Real Property*, Ch. 1, p. 10. [1905]) This system of hierarchical land holdings required an elaborate system of payment. These fiefs to the land might be recompenses in any number of ways.

One of the more common types of fiefs, or the payment of a rent or obligation to perform rural labor upon the lord's lands known as "socage," were the crops from the field. (Id. at 8) Under this type of fief a certain portion of the grain harvested each year would immediately be turned over to the lord above that particular fief even before the shares from the lower lords and then serfs of the fief would be distributed. A more interesting type of fief for purposes of this memorandum was the money fief. In most cases, the source of money was not specified, and the payment was simply made from the fief holder's treasury. The fief might also consist of fixed revenue to be paid from a definite source in annual payments in order for the tenant owner of the fief to be able to remain on the property. (Gilsebert of Mons, Chronique, cc. 69 and 1 15, pp. 109, 175 ed. Vanderkindere)

The title held by such tenant-owners over their land was described as a fee simple absolute. "Fee simple, Fee commeth of the French fief, i.e., praedium beneficiarium, and legally signifieth inheritance as our author himself hereafter expoundeth it and simple is added, for that it is descendible to his heirs generally, that is, simply, without restraint to the heirs of his body, or the like, Feodum est quod quis tenet ex quacunque causa sive sit tenementum sive redditus, etc. In Domesday it is called feudom." (Littleton, Tenures, Sec. Ib, Fee Simple) In Section 11, fee simple is described as the largest form of inheritance. Id. In Modern English tenures, the term "fee" signifies an inheritable estate, being the highest and most extensive interest the common man or noble, other than the King, could have in the feudal system. (*2 Blackstone's Commentaries*, p. 106)

Thus, the term "fee simple absolute" in common-law England denotes the most and best title a person could have as long as the King allowed him to retain possession of (own) the land. It has been commented that the basis of English land law is the ownership of all realty by the sovereign. From the crown, all titles flow. The original and true meaning of the word "fee" and, therefore, "fee simple absolute" is the same as fief or feud, this being in contradiction to the term "allodium" which means or is defined as a man's own land, which he possesses merely in his own right, without owing any rent or service to any superior. *Wendell v Crandall*, 1 N. Y. 491 (1848). Therefore in common law England, practically everybody that was allowed to retain land had the type of fee simple absolute often used or defined by courts: a fee simple that grants or gives the occupier as much of a title as the "sovereign" allows such occupier to have at that time. The term became a synonym with the supposed ownership of land under the feudal system of England at common law. Thus, even though the word "absolute" was attached to the fee simple, it merely denoted the entire estate that could be assigned or passed to heirs, the "fee" being the operative word. Fee simple absolute dealt with the entire fief and its divisibility, alienability and inheritability. *Friedman v Steiner*, 107 Ill. 131 (1883). If a fee simple absolute in common-law England denoted or was synonymous with only as much title as the King allowed his barons to possess, then what did the King have by way of a title?

The King of England held ownership of land under a different title and with far greater powers than any of his subjects. Though the people of England held fee simple titles to their land, the King actually owned all the land in England through his Allodial title. And though all the land was in the feudal system, none of the fee simple titles were of equal weight and dignity with the King's title. The land always remained Allodial, in favor of the King. (Gilsbert of Mons, Chronique, Ch. 43, p. 75 [ed. Vanderkindere])

Thus, it is relatively easy to deduce that Allodial lands and titles are the highest form of lands and titles known to Common Law. An estate of inheritance without condition, belonging to the owner and alienable by him, transmissible to his heirs absolutely and simply, is an absolute estate in perpetuity and the largest possible estate a man can have, being in fact Allodial in its nature. *Stanton v Sullivan*, 63 R.I. 216, 7 A. 696 (1839) "The original meaning of a perpetuity is an inalienable, indestructible interest." *Bouvier's Law Dictionary*, Volume 111, p. 2570 (1914)

The King had such a title in land. As such, during the classical feudalistic period of common-law England, the King answered to no one concerning the land. Allodial titles, being held by sovereigns, and being full and complete titles, allowed the King of England to own and control the entire country in the form of one large estate belonging to the Crown. Allodial estates owned by individuals exercising full and complete ownership on the other hand existed only to a limited extent in the County of Kent.

In summary of Common-Law England:

1. The King was the only person (sovereign) to hold complete and full title to a land (Allodial title).

2. The people who maintained estates of land (either called manors or fiefs) held title by fee simple absolute.

3. This fee simple absolute provided the means by which the supposed owner could devise, alienate, or pass by inheritance the estates of land (manors or fiefs).

4. This fee simple absolute in feudal England, being not the full title, did not protect the "owner" if the King found disfavor with the "owner."

5. The "owner" therefore had to pay a type of homage to the King or a higher baron each year to discharge the obligation of his fief.

6. This homage of his fief could take the form of a revenue or tax, an amount of grain, or a set and permanent amount of money.

7. Therefore, as long as the "owner" of the fief in fee simple absolute paid homage to the king or sovereign who held the entire country under an Allodial title, then the "owner" could remain on the property with full rights to sell, devise or pass it by inheritance as if the property was really his.

LAND OWNERSHIP IN AMERICA TODAY

THE AMERICAN FEUDALISTIC SOCIETY

The private ownership of land in America is one of those rights people have proclaimed to be fundamental and essential in maintaining this republic. The necessary question in discussing this topic, however, is whether ownership of land in America today really is a true and complete ownership of land under an Allodial concept, or is it something much different. In other words, are we living in an actual Allodial freehold, or are we living in an updated version of feudalistic Common Law?

The answer is crucial in determining what rights we have in the protection of our reality against improper seizures and encumbrances by our government and creditors. The answer appears to be extremely clear upon proper reflection of our rights when payments are missed on mortgages or when taxes, for whatever reason, are not paid. If mortgage payments are missed or taxes are not paid, we actually fall into disfavor with the parties who have the power, and these powers, through court proceedings or otherwise, take the land as a penalty.

When one is unable to perform as the government or his creditors request, and for such failures of performance his land can be forfeited, then he can begin to understand exactly what type of land-ownership system controls his life, and should recognize the inherent unjustness of such constitutional violations. The American-based system of land ownership today consists of three key requirements. These three are:

1. Warranty deed or some other type of deed purporting to convey ownership of land.
2. Title abstracts to chronologically follow the development of these different types of deeds to a piece of property.
3. Title insurance to protect the ownership of that land.

These three ingredients must work together to ensure a systematic and orderly conveyance of a piece of property; none of these three by it can act to completely convey possession of the land from one person to another. At least two of the three are always deemed necessary to adequately satisfy the legal system and real estate agents that the titles to the property had been placed in the hands of the purchaser. Oftentimes, all three are necessary to properly pass the ownership of the land to the purchaser. Yet do the absolute title and, therefore, the ownership of the land really pass from the seller to purchaser with the use of any one of these three instruments or in any combination thereof? None of the three by itself passes the absolute or Allodial title to the land, the system of land ownership America originally operated under, and even all three combined can not convey this absolute type of ownership.

What then is the function of these three instruments that are used in land conveyances and what type of title do the three convey?

Since the abstract only traces the title and the title insurance only insures the title, the most important and, therefore, the first group examined are the deeds that purportedly convey the fee from seller to purchaser. These deeds include: warranty deed, quit claim deed, sheriff's deed, trustee's deed, judicial deed, tax deed, wig or any other instrument that purportedly conveys the title. Each of these documents state that it conveys the ownership to the land. Each of these, however, is actually a color of title. (G. Thompson, *Title to Real Property, Preparation and Examination of Abstracts*, Ch. 3, Section 73, p.93 [1919])

A color of title is that which in appearance is title, but which in reality is not title. *Wright v Mattison*, 18 How. (U.S.) 50 (1855) In fact, any instrument may constitute color of title when it purports to convey the title of the land, as well the land itself, although it is void as a muniment of title. *Joplin Brewing Co. v Payne*, 197 No. 422, 94 S.W. 896 (1906)

The Supreme Court of Missouri has stated "...that when we say a person has a color of title, whatever may be the meaning of the phrase, we express the idea, at least, that some act has been previously done... by which some title, good or bad, to a parcel of land of definite extent had been conveyed to him." *St. Louis v German,* 29 Mo. 593 (1860)

In other words, a color of title is an appearance or apparent title, and "image" of the true title, hence the phrase "color of," which, when coupled with possession, purports to convey the ownership of the land to the purchaser. This however does not say that the color of title is the actual and true title itself, nor does it say that the color of title itself actually conveys ownership. In fact, the claimant or holder of a color of title is not even required to trace the title through the chain down to his instrument. *Rawson v Fox*, 65 111. 200 (1872)

Rather it may be said that a color of title is *prima facie* evidence of ownership of and rights to possession of land until such time as that presumption of ownership is disproved by a better title or the actual title itself. If such cannot he proven to the contrary, then ownership of the land is assumed to have passed to the occupier of the land. To further strengthen a color title-holder's position, courts have held that the good faith of the holder to a color of title is presumed in the absence of evidence to the contrary. *David v Hall*, 92 R. 1. 85 (1879); see also *Morrison v Norman*, 47 Ill. 477 (1868); and *McConnell v Street*, 17 Ill. 253 (1855) With such knowledge of what a color of title is, it is interesting what constitutes colors of title. A warranty deed is like any other deed of conveyance.

Mahrenholz v County Board of School Trustees of Lawrence County, et. al., 93 Ill. app. 3d 366 (1981) A warranty deed or deed of conveyance is a color of title, as stated in *Dempsey v Bums,* 281 Ill. 644, 650 (1917) (Deeds constitute colors of title); see also *Dryden v Newman,* 116 Ill. 186 (1886) (A deed that purports to convey interest in the land is a color of title.) *Hinckley v Green* 52 Ill. 223 (1869) (A deed which, on its face, purports to convey a title, constitutes a claim and color of title.); *Busch v Huston,* 75 Ill. 343 (1874); *Chicking v Failes,* 26 Ill. 508 (1861) A quit claim deed is a color of title as stated in *Safford v Stubbs,* 1 17 Ill. 389 [1886); see also *Hooway v Clark,* 27 Ill. 483 (1861) and *McCellan v Kellogg,* 17 Ill. 498 (1855) Quit claim deeds can pass the title as effectively as a warrant with full covenants. *Grant v Bennett,* 96 Ill. 513, 525 (1880) See also *Morgan v Clayton,* 61 Ill. 35 (1871); *Brady v Spurck,* 27 Ill. 478 (1861); *Butterfield v Smith,* Ill. 11 1. 485 (1849) Sheriffs deeds also are colors of title. *Kendrick v Latham,* 25 Fla. 819 (1889); as is a judicial deed, *Huls v Buntin,* 47 Ill. 396 (1865).

The Illinois Supreme Court went into detail in its determination that a tax deed is only color of title: "...there the complainant seems to have relied upon the tax deed as conveying to him the fee, and to sustain such a bill, it was incumbent of him to show that all the requirements of the law had been complied with."

A simple tax deed by itself is only a color of title. Fee simple can be acquired only though adverse possession via payment of taxes, claim and color of title, plus seven years of payment of taxes. Thus any tax deed that purports, on its face, to convey title is a good color of title.

Walker v Converse, 148 Ill. 622, 629 (1894); see also *Peadro v Carriker,* 168 Ill. 570 (1897); *Chicago v Middlebrooke,* 143 Ill. 265 (1892); *Piatt County v Gooden,* 97 Ill. 84 (1880); *Stubblefield v Borders,* 92 Ill. 570 (1897); *Coleman v Billings,* 89 Ill. 183 (1878); *Whitney v Stevens,* 89 Ill. 53 (1878); *Holloway v Clarke,* 27 Ill. 483 (1861), *Thomas v Eckard,* 88 Ill. 593 (1878) color of title. *Baldwin v Ratcliff,* 125 Ill. 376 (1888); *Bradley v Rees,* 113 Ill. 327 (1885) (A wig can pass only so much as the testator owns; though it may attempt to pass more.) A trustee's deed, a mortgage and strict foreclosure, *Chickering v Failes,* 26 Ill. 508, 519 (1861), or any document defining the extent of a disseisor's claim or purported claim, *Cook v Norton,* 43 Ill. 391 (1867), all have been held to be colors of title. In fact, "If there is nothing here requiring a deed, to establish a color of title, and under the former decisions of this court, color or title may exist without a deed." *Baldwin v Ratcliff,* 125 Ill. 376, 383 (1882); *County of Piatt v Goodell,* 97 Ill. 84 (1880); *Smith v Ferguson,* 91 Ill. 304 (1878); *Hassett v Ridgely,* 49 Ill. 197 (1868); *Brooks v. Bruyn*, 35 Ill. 392 (1864); *McCagg v Heacock*, 34 Ill. 476 (1864); *Bride v Watt*, 23 Ill. 507 (1860); and *Woodward v Blanchard*, 16 Ill. 424 (1855).

All of the above cases being still valid and none being overruled, in effect the statements in these cases are settled law. All of the documents described in these cases are the main avenues of claimed land ownership in America today, yet none actually conveys the true and Allodial title. They in fact convey something quite different.

When it is stated that a color of title conveys only an appearance of or apparent title, such a statement is correct but perhaps too vague to be properly understood in its correct legal context. What are useful are the more pragmatic statements concerning titles. A title or color of title, in order to be effective in transferring the ownership or purported ownership of the land, must be a marketable or merchantable title.

A marketable or merchantable title is one that is reasonably free from doubt. *Austin v Bamum*, 52 Minn. 136 (1892). This title must be as reasonably free from doubts as necessary to not affect the marketability or salability of the property, and must be a title a reasonably prudent person would be willing to accept. *Robert v McFadden*, 32 Tex. Civ. App. 471 74 S.W. 105 (1903). Such a title is often described as one which would ensure to the purchaser a peaceful enjoyment of the property, *Barnard v Brown*, 112 Mich. 452, 70 N.W. 1038 (1897), and it is stated that such a title must be obvious, evident, apparent, certain, sure or indubitable. *Ormsby v Graham*, 123 La. 202, 98 N.W. 724 (1904).

Marketable Title Acts, which have been adopted in several of the states, generally do not lend themselves to an interpretation that they might operate to provide a new foundation of title based upon a stray, accidental, or interloping conveyance. Their object is to provide, for the recorded fee simple ownership, an exemption from the burdens of old conditions which at each transfer of the property interfere with its marketability. *Wichelman v Messner*, 83 N.W. 2d 800 (1957) What each of these legal statements in the various factual situations say is that the color of title is never described as the absolute or actual title. Rather, each says that it is one of the types of titles necessary to convey ownership or apparent ownership.

A marketable title, which a color of title must be in order to be effective, must be a title that is good of recent record, even if it may not be the actual title in fact. *Close v Stuyvesant*, 132 Ill. 607, 24 N.E. 868 (1890) "Authorities hold that to render a title marketable it is only necessary that it shall be free from reasonable doubt; in other words, that a purchaser is not entitled to demand a title absolutely free from every possible suspicion." *Cummings v Dolan*, 52 Wash. 496, 100 P. 989 (1909) The record being spoken of here is the title abstract and all documentary evidence pertaining to it. It is an axiom of hornbook law that a purchaser has notice only of recorded instruments that are within his "chain of title." I. R. Patton & C. Patton, Patton on Land Title, Section 69, at 230-233. (2nd ed. 1957); *Sabo v Horvath*, 559 P. 2d 1038, 1043 (Ak.1976). Title insurance then guarantees that a title is marketable, not absolutely free from doubt.

Thus, under the color or title system used most often in this country today, no individual operating has the absolute or allodial title. All that is really necessary to have a valid title is to have a relatively clean abstract with a recognizable color of title as the operative marketable title within the chain of title.

It therefore becomes necessarily difficult, if not impossible after a number of years, considering the inevitable contingencies that must arise and the title disputes that will occur, to ever properly guarantee an absolute title. This is not necessarily the fault of the seller, but it is the fault of the legal and real estate systems for allowing such a diluted form of title to be controlling in an area where it is imperative to have the absolute title. In order to correct this problem, it is important to return to those documents that the early leaders of the nation created to properly ensure that property remained one of the unalienable rights that the newly established sovereign freeholders could rely on to always exist.

This correction must be in the form of restricting or perhaps eliminating the widespread use of a marketable title and returning to the absolute title.

Other problems have developed because of the use of a color of title system for the conveyance of land. These problems arise in the area of terminology that succeeds only in confusing and clouding the title to an even greater extent than merely using terms like marketability, salability or merchantability. When a person must also determine whether a title is complete, perfect, good and clear, or whether it is a bad, defective, imperfect and doubtful, there is any obvious possibility of destroying a chain of title because of an inability to recognize what is acceptable to a reasonable purchaser.

A complete title means that a person has possession, the right of possession and the right of property. *Dingey v Paxton*, 60 Miss. 1038 (1883) and *Ehle v Quackenboss*, 6 Hill (N.Y.) 537 (1844). A perfect title is exactly the same as a complete title. *Donovan v Pitcher*, 53 Ala. 411 (1875) and *Converse v Kellogg*, 7 Barb. (N. Y.) 590 (1850). Each simply means the type of title that a well-informed, reasonable and prudent person would be willing to accept when paying full value for the property. *Birge v Beck*, 44 Mo. App. 69 (1890). In other words, a complete or perfect title is, in reality, a marketable or merchantable title and is usually represented by a color of title.

A good title does not necessarily mean one perfect of record but one which consists of both rightful ownership and rightful possession of the property. *Bloch v Ryan*, 4 App. Cas 283 (1894). It means a title free from litigation, palpable defects and grave doubts consisting of both legal and equitable titles and fairly deducible of record. *Reynolds v Borel*, 86 Cal. 538, 25 P. 67 (1890).

"A good title means not merely a title valid in fact, but a marketable title, which can again be sold to a reasonable purchaser or mortgaged to a person of reasonable prudence as security for a loan of money." *Moore v Williams*, 115 N.Y. 586, 22 N.E. 253 (1889)

A clear title means there are no encumbrances on the land. *Roberts v Bassett*, 105 Mass. 409 (1870). Thus when contracting to convey land, the use of the phrase "good and clear title" is surplusage, since the terms good title and clear title are in fact synonymous. *Oakley v Cook*, 41 N.J. Eq. 350, 7 A.2d 495 (1886).

The terms "good title" and "clear title," just like the terms "complete title" and "perfect title," describe nothing more than a marketable title or merchantable title, and as stated above, each can and almost always is represented in a transaction by a color of title. None of these types of title purports to be the absolute, or allodial title, and none of them are that type of title. None of these actually claims to be a fee simple absolute, and since these types of titles are almost always represented by a color of title, none represents that it passes the actual title. Each one does state that it passes what can be described as a title good enough to avoid the necessity of litigation to determine who actually has the title. If such litigation to determine titles is necessary, then the title has crossed the boundaries of usefulness and entered a different category of title descriptions and names.

This new category consists of titles that are bad, defective, imperfect or doubtful. A bad title conveys no property to the purchaser of the estate. *Heller v Cohen*, 15 Misc. 378, 36 N.Y.S. 668 (1895). A title is defective when the party claiming to own the land has not the whole title, but some other person has title to a part or portion of it. Such a title is the same as no title whatsoever. *Place v People*, 192 Ill. 160, 61 N.E. (1901); see also *Cospertini v Oppermann*, 76 Cal. 181, 18 P. 256 (1888). Imperfect title is one where something remains to be done by the granting power to pass the title to the land. *Raschel v Perez*, 7 Tex. 348 (1851). A doubtful title is also one which conveys no property to the purchaser of the estate. *Heller v Cohen*, 15 Misc. 378, 36 N.Y.S. 668 (1895). Every title is described as doubtful which invites or exposes the party holding it to litigation. *Herman v Somers*, 158 PA.ST. 424, 27 A. 1050 (1893)

Each of these types of titles describes exactly the same idea stated in many different ways: that because of some problem, defect, or question surrounding the title, no title can be conveyed since no title exists. Yet in all of these situations, some type of color of title was used as the operative instrument. What then makes one color of title complete, good or clear in one situation, and in another situation the same type of color of title can be described as bad, defective, imperfect or doubtful?

What is necessary to make a good title of what might otherwise be a doubtful title is the belief of others in the community, whether or not properly justified, that the title is a good one that they would be willing to purchase. *Moore v Williams*, 115 N.Y. 586, 22 N.E. 253 (1889) The methods presently used to determine whether a title or color of title is good enough to not be doubtful are the other two-thirds of the three possible requirements for the conveyance of a good or complete (marketable) title.

These two methods of properly ensuring that a title is a good or complete title are title abstracts, the complete documentary evidence of title, and title insurance. The legal title to land, based on a color of title, is made up of a series of documents that are required to be executed with the solemnities prescribed by law, and of facts not evidenced by documents which show the claimant a person to whom the law gives the estate.

Documentary evidences of title consist of voluntary grants by the sovereign, deeds of conveyances and wills by individuals, conveyances by statutory or judicial permission, deeds made in connection with the sale of land for delinquent taxes, proceedings under the power of eminent domain, and deeds executed by ministerial or fiduciary officers. The land patent and the colors of title represent these documentary evidences. (I.G. Thompson, *Commentaries on the Modem Law of Real Property*, pp. 99-100 [5th ed. 1980])

In compiling the abstract the abstractor must use these instruments, relied upon to evidence the title, coupled with the outward assertive acts that import dominion, and the attorney must examine to determine the true status of the title. The abstract is the recorded history of the land and the various types of titles, mortgages and other liens, claims and interests that have been placed on the property. The abstract can determine the number of times the patent has been re-declared, who owns the mineral rights, what color of title is operable at any particular point in time, and what lien holder is in first position, but it does not convey or even attempt to convey any form of the title itself.

As Thompson has stated, when operating with colors of title, it is necessary to have an abstract to determine the status of the operable title and to determine whether that title is good or doubtful. If the title is deemed to be good after this lengthy process, then the property may be transferred without doing anything more, since it is assumed that the seller was the owner of the property. This is not to say emphatically that the seller is the paramount or absolute owner. This does not even completely guarantee against any adverse claimants that he is the owner of the land. It is not even that difficult to claim that the title holder has a good title due to the leniency and attitude now evidenced by the judicial authorities toward maintaining a stable and uniform system of land ownership, whether or not that ownership is justified. This, however, does not explain the purpose and goal of a title abstract.

An abstract that has been properly brought up simply states that it is presumed that the seller is the owner of the land, making the title marketable and guaranteeing that he has a good title to sell. This is all an abstract can legally do since it is not the title itself and it does not state that the owner has an absolute title. Therefore, the abstract cannot guarantee unquestionably that the owner holds the title. All of this rhetoric is necessary if the title is good; if there is some question concerning the title without making it defective, then the owner must turn to the last of the three alternatives to help pass a good title – title insurance. (G. Thompson, *Title to Real Property, Preparation and Examination of Abstracts*, Ch.111, Section 79r pp. 99-100 [1919]) To ensure the validity of the title against any defects, title insurance companies issue title insurance against any encumbrances affecting the designated property and to protect the purchaser against any losses he may sustain from any subsequent determination that his title is actually unmarketable.

Title insurance extends to any defects of title. It protects against the existence of any encumbrances, provided only that a court of competent jurisdiction shall pronounce any judgments adverse to the title. It is not even necessary that a defect actually exist when the insurance policy was issued, but simply that there exists at the time of issuance of the policy an inchoate or potential defect which is rendered operative and substantial by some subsequent event. Since all one normally has is a color of title, the longer a title traverses history, the greater the possibility that the title will become defective.

The greater the need for insurance simply to keep the title marketable, the easier it is to determine that the title possessed is not the true, paramount and absolute title. If a person had the paramount title, there would be no need for title insurance, though an abstract might be useful for record keeping and historical purposes. Title insurance and abstract record keeping are useful, primarily because of extensive reliance on colors of title as the operative title for a piece of property.

This then supplies the necessary information concerning colors of title, title abstracts, and title insurance. This does not describe the relationship between the landowner and the government. As was stated in the introduction, in feudal England the King had the power, right and authority to take a person's land away from him if and when the King felt it necessary.

The question is whether most of the American system of land ownership and titles is in reality any different and whether therefore the American-based system of ownership is in reality nothing more than a feudal system of land ownership.

Land ownership in America presently is founded on colors of title, and though people believe they are the complete and total owners of their property, under a color of title system, this is far from the truth. When people state that they are free and own their land, in fact they own it exactly to the extent the English barons owned their land in common-law England: they own their land so long as some "sovereign" – the government or a creditor – states that they can own their land. If one recalls from the beginning of this memorandum, if the King felt it justified, he could take land from one person and give it to another prospective baron.

Today in American color-of-title property law, if the landowner does not pay income tax, estate tax, property tax, mortgages or even a security note on personal property, then the "sovereign" – the government or the creditor – can justify the taking of the property, then the sale of that same property to another prospective "baron," while leaving the owner with only limited defenses to such actions. The only real difference between this and common-law England is that now others besides the King can profit from the unwillingness or inability of the "landowner" to perform the socage or tenure required of every landowner of America.

No one is completely safe or protected on his property; no one can afford to make one mistake or the consequences will be forfeiture of the property. If this were what the people in the mid-1700s wanted, there would have been no need to have an American Revolution, since the taxes were secondary to having a sound monetary system and complete ownership of the land.

Why fight a Revolutionary War to escape sovereign control and virtual dictatorship over the land, when in the 2000s these exact problems are prevalent, with this one exception: private (fiat) tender now changes hands in order to give validity to the eventual and continuous takeover of the property between the parties?

This is hardly what the forefathers planned when creating the United States Constitution. What they did strive for is the next segment of the memorandum of law: allodial ownership of the land via the land patent. The next segment will analyze the history of this type of title so that the patent can be properly understood, making it possible to comprehend the patent's true role in property law today.

LAND PATENTS AND WHY THEY WERE CREATED

As was seen in the previous sections, when distressful economic or weather conditions make it impossible to perform on the debt, there is little to protect the landowner who holds title in the chain of title. Under the color-of-title system, the property, one of those "inalienable rights," can be taken for the nonperformance on loan obligations. This type of ownership is similar to the feudal ownership found in the Middle Ages.

Upon defeating the English in 1066 AD, William the Conqueror, pursuant to his 52nd and 58th laws, "effectually reduced the lands of England to feuds, which were declared to be inheritable. From that time the maxim prevailed there, that all lands in England are held from the King, and that all proceeded from his bounty." (I.E. Washburn, *Treatise on The American Land of Real Property*, Section 65, p.44 [6th ed. 1902])

Prior to the creation of the feudal system in France and Germany, all lands in Europe were Allodial. Most of these lands were voluntarily changed to feudal lands as protection from the neighboring barons or chieftains. Since no documents protected one's freedom over his land, once the lands were pledged for protection, the lands were lost forever. This was not the case in England.

England never voluntarily relinquished its land to William I. In fact, were it not for a tactical error by King Harold II's men in the Battle of Hastings, England might never have become feudal.

Prior to the Conquest of AD 1066, a large proportion of the Saxon lands were held as allodial, that is, by an absolute ownership without recognizing any superior to whom any duty was due. The conveyance of these allodial lands was most commonly done by a writing or charter called a land-bloc or land allodial charter which, for safekeeping between conveyances, was generally deposited in the monasteries. In fact one portion of England, the County of Kent, was allowed to retain this form of land ownership while the rest of England became feudal. Therefore, when William I established feudalism in England to maintain control over his barons, that control created animosity over the next two centuries. (F.L. Ganshof, *Feudalism*, p. 114 [1964])

As a result of such dictatorial control, some twenty-five barons joined forces to exert pressure on the then-ruling monarch, King John, to gain some rights, not all of which the common man would possess. The result of this pressure at Runnymede became known as the Magna Charta (1215).

The Magna Charta was the basis of modern common law – a series of judicial decisions and royal decrees interpreting and following that document. The Magna Charta protected the basic rights that gave all people more freedom and power, rights that would slowly erode. Among these rights was a particular section dealing with ownership of the land. The barons still recognized the king as the lord paramount, but the barons wanted some of the rights their ancestors had had prior to A.D. 1066. (F. Goodwin, *Treatise on The Law of Real Property*, Ch. 1, p. 3 [1905])

Under this theory, as the visible owners, the barons would have several rights and powers over the land that had not existed in England for 150 years. The most important section, § 62, gave the most powerful barons letters of patent, raising their land ownership close to the level found in the County of Kent. Other sections – 10, 11, 26, 27, 37, 43, 52, 56, 57, and 61 – were written to protect the right to "own" property, to illustrate how debts affected this fight to own property, and to secure the return of property that was unjustly taken. All of these paragraphs were written with the single goal of protecting the "landowner," helping him to retain possession of his land, acquired in the service of the King, from unjust seizures or improper debts. The barons attempted these goals with the intention of securing property to pass to their heirs.

Unfortunately goals are often not attained. Having re-pledged their loyalty to King John, the barons quickly disbanded their armies. King John died in 1216, one year after signing the Magna Charta. The new king did not wish to grant the privileges found in that document. When the barons who had forced the signing of the Magna Charta died, the driving force that created this great charter died with them. The Magna Charta may have still been alive, but the new kings had no armies at their door forcing them to follow policies, and the charter was to a great extent forced to lie dormant. Perhaps the barons who had received the letters of patent and other landholders should have enforced their rights, but their heirs were not in a position to do so and eventually the fiefs contained in the charter were forgotten. Increasingly, until the mid-1600s, the king's power waxed, abruptly ending with the execution of Charles I in 1649. By then, however, the original intent of the Magna Charta was in part lost and the descendants of the original barons never required property protected, free land ownership. To a great extent to this day, the freehold lands in England are still held upon the feudal tenures.

This lack of complete ownership in the land, as well as the most publicized search for religious freedom, drove the more adventurous Europeans to the Americas to be away from these restrictions. The American colonists, however, soon adopted many of the same land concepts used in the old-world. The kings of Europe still had the authority to exert influence, and the American version of barons sought to retain large tracts of land. As an example, the first patent granted in New York went to Killian Van Rensselaer, dated in 1630 and confirmed in 1685 and 1704. (A. Getman, *Title to Real Property, Principles and Sources of Titles – Compensation For Lands and Waters,* Part Ill, Ch. 17, p.229 [1921].)

The colonial charters of these American colonies, granted by the king of England, had references to the lands in the County of Kent, effectively denying the more barbaric aspects of feudalism from ever entering the continent, but feudalism with its tenures did exist for some time.

"It may be said that, at an early date, feudal tenures existed in this country to a limited extent." (C. Tiedeman, *An Elementary Treatise on the American Law of Real Property*, Ch. 11; *The Principles of the Feudal System*, Section 25, p. 22 [2nd ed. 1892].)

The result was a newly created form of feudal land ownership in America. As such, the feudal barons in the colonies could dictate who farmed their land, how their land was to be divided, and to a certain extent to whom the land should pass. But, just as the original barons discovered, this power was premised in part upon the performance of duties for the king. Upon the failure of performance, the king could order the grant revoked, and grant the land to another willing to acquiesce to the king's authority. This authority, however, was premised on the belief that people recently arrived and relatively independent would follow the authority of a king based 3000 miles away. Such a premise was ill founded.

The colonists came to America to avoid taxation without representation, to avoid persecution of religious freedom, and to acquire a small tract of land that could be owned completely. When the colonists were forced to pay taxes and to allow their homes to be occupied by soldiers; they revolted, fighting the British and declaring their Declaration of Independence.

The Supreme Court of the United States reflected on this in *Chisholm v Georgia*, 2 Dall. (U.S.) 419 (1793), stating:

"...the revolution or rather the Declaration of Independence, found the people already united for general purposes, and at the same time providing for their more domestic concerns by state conventions, and other temporary arrangements. From the crown of Great Britain, the sovereignty of their country passed to the people of it, and it was then not an uncommon opinion, that the unappropriated lands, which belonged to that crown, passed not to the people of the colony or states within those limits they were situated, but to the whole people; ...'We, the people of the United States, do ordain and establish this constitution.' Here we see the people acting as sovereigns of the whole country; and in the language of sovereignty, establishing a constitution by which it was their will, that the state governments should be bound, and to which the state constitutions should be made to conform. ...It will be sufficient to observe briefly, that the sovereignties in Europe, and particularly in England, exist on feudal principles. That system considers the Prince as the sovereign, and the people his subjects; it regards his person as the object of allegiance, and excludes the idea of his being on an equal footing with a subject, either in a Court of Justice or elsewhere. That system contemplates him as being the fountain of honor and authority; and from his grace and grant derives all franchises, immunities and privileges; it is easy to perceive that such a sovereign could not be amenable to a Court of Justice, or subjected to judicial control and actual constraint....

"The same feudal ideas run through all their jurisprudence, and constantly remind us of the distinction between the prince and the subject. No such ideas obtain here: at the revolution, the sovereignty devolved on the people; and they are truly the sovereigns of the country, but they are sovereigns without subjects and have none to govern but themselves; the citizens of America are equal as fellow-citizens, and as joint tenants in the sovereignty. From the differences existing between feudal sovereignties and governments founded on compacts, it necessarily follows that their respective prerogatives must differ. Sovereignty is the fight to govern; a nation or state sovereign is the person or persons in whom that resides. In Europe, the sovereignty is generally ascribed to the prince; here it rests with the people; there, the sovereign actually administers the government; here, never in a single instance; our governors are the agents of the people, and at most stand in the same relation to their sovereigns, in which the regents of Europe stand to their sovereigns. Their princes have personal powers, dignities, and pre-eminences, our rules have none but official; nor do they partake in the sovereignty otherwise, or in any other capacity, than as private citizens."

The Americans had a choice as to how they wanted their new government and country to be formed. Having broken away from English sovereignty and establishing themselves as their own sovereigns, they had their choice of types of taxation, freedom of religion and, equally important, ownership of land. The American founding fathers chose allodial ownership of land. In the opinion of Judge Kent, the question of tenure as an incident to the ownership of lands "has become wholly immaterial in this country, where every vestige of tenure has been annihilated. At the present day there is little, if any, trace of the feudal tenures remaining in the American law of property. Lands in this country are now held to be absolutely Allodial."

Upon the completion of the Revolutionary War, lands in the thirteen colonies were held under a different form of land ownership.

As stated in re Waltz et. al., *Barlow v Security Trust & Savings Bank,* 240 p.19 (1925), quoting *Matthews v Ward,* 10 Gill & J. (Md.) 443 (1839) "after the American Revolution, lands in this state (Maryland) became Allodial, subject to no tenure, nor to any services incident there to."

The tenure, as you will recall, was the feudal tenure and the services or taxes required to be paid to retain possession of the land under the feudal system. This new type of ownership was acquired in all thirteen states. *Wallace v Harmstead,* 44 Pa. 492 (1863)

The American people, before developing a properly functioning stable government, developed a stable system of land ownership, whereby the people owned their land absolutely and in a manner similar to the king in common-law England. As has been stated earlier, the original and true meaning of the word "fee" and, therefore, fee simple absolute is the same as fief or feud, this being in contradistinction to the term "allodium," which means or is defined as man's own land which he possesses merely in his own right, without owing any rent or service to any superior. *Wendell v Crandall,* 1 N. Y. 491 (1848) [27] Stated another way, the fee simple estate of early England was never considered as absolute, as were lands in allodium, but was subject to some superior on condition of rendering him services, and in which the such superior had the ultimate ownership of the land. In re Waltz, at page 20, quoting *I Cooley's Blackstone,* (4th ed.) p. 512.

"This type of fee simple is a Common-Law term and sometimes corresponds to what in civil law is a perfect title." *United States v Sunset Cemetery Co.,* 132 F. 2d 163 (1943).

It is unquestioned that the king held an allodial title that was different from the Common Law fee simple absolute. This type of superior title was bestowed upon the newly established American people by the founding fathers. The people were sovereigns by choice, and through this new type of land ownership, the people were sovereign freeholders or kings over their own land, beholden to no lord or superior. As stated in *Stanton v Sullivan,* 7 A-696 (1839), such an estate is an absolute estate in perpetuity and the largest possible estate a man can have, being, in fact allodial in its nature. This type of fee simple, as thus developed, has definite characteristics: (1) it is a present estate in land that is of indefinite duration; (2) it is freely alienable; (3) it carries with it the right of possession; and most importantly (4) the holder may make use of any portion of the freehold without being beholden to any person. (I. G. Thompson, *Commentaries on the Modern Law of Real Property,* Section 1856, p. 412 [1st ed. 1924]).

This fee simple estate means an absolute estate in lands wholly unqualmed by any reservation, reversion, condition or limitation, or possibility of any such thing present or future, precedent or subsequent. Id.; *Wichel'man v Messner*, 83 N.W. 2d 800, 806 (1957) It is the most extensive estate and interest one may possess in real property where an estate subject to an option is not in fee. In *Bradford v Martin*, [28] 201 N.W. 574 (1925), the Iowa Supreme Court went into a lengthy discussion on what the terms "fee simple" and "allodium" mean in American property law. The Court stated:

"The word 'absolutely' in law has a varied meaning, but when unqualifiedly used with reference to titles or interest in land, its meaning is fairly well settled. Originally the two titles most discussed were 'fee simple' and 'allodium.'" (Which meant *absolute.*) See *Bouvier's Law Dictionary.* (Rawle Ed.) 134; *Wallace v Harmstead*, 44 Pa. 492; *McCartee v Orphan's Asylum*, 9 Cow. (N.Y.) 437, 18 Am. Dec. 516.

Prior to Blackstone's time the allodial title was ordinarily called an "absolute title." An allodial title was superior to a "fee simple title," the latter being encumbered with feudal clogs, which were laid upon the first feudatory when it was granted, making it possible for the holder of a fee-simple title to lose his land in the event he failed to observe his feudatory oath. The allodial title was not so encumbered. Later, however, the term "fee simple" rose to the dignity of the allodial or absolute estate, and since the days of Blackstone the words of "absolute" and "fee simple" seem to have been generally used interchangeably; in fact, he so uses them.

The basis of English land law is the ownership of the realty by the sovereign: from the crown all titles flow. *People v. Richardson*, 269 M. 275, 109 N.E. 1033 (1914); see also *Matthew v. Ward*, 10 Gill & J (Md.) 443 (1844) *McConnell v. Wilcox*, I Seam. (IR.) 344 (1837), stated it this way:

"From what source does the title to the land derived from a government spring? In arbitrary governments, from the supreme head, be he the emperor, king, or potentate, or by whatever name he is known. In a republic, from the law, making or authorizing to be made the grant or sale. In the first case, the party looks alone to his letters patent; in the second, to the law and the evidence of the acts necessary to be done under the law, to a perfection of his grant, donation or purchase. The law alone must be the fountain from whence the authority is drawn; and there can be no other source."

The American people, newly established sovereigns in this republic after the victory achieved during the Revolutionary War, became complete owners in their land, beholden to no lord or superior; sovereign freeholders in the land themselves. These freeholders in the original thirteen states now held allodial the land they possessed before the war only feudally. This new and more powerful title protected the sovereigns from unwarranted intrusions or attempted takings of their land and, more importantly, it secured in them a right to own land absolutely in perpetuity.

By definition, the word perpetuity means: "Continuing forever. Legally, pertaining to real property, any condition extending the inalienability." *Black's Law Dictionary*, p.1027 (5th ed. 1980) In terms of an allodial title, it is to have the property of in-alienability forever. Nothing more need be done to establish the ownership of the sovereigns to their land, although confirmations were usually required to avoid possible future title confrontations. The states, even prior to the creation of our present constitutional government, were issuing titles to the unoccupied lands within their boundaries.

In New York, even before the war was won, the state issued the first land patent in 1781, and only a few weeks after the battle and victory at Yorktown in 1783, the state issued the first land patent to an individual. In fact, even before the United States was created, New York and other states had developed their own land offices with commissioners. New York was first established in 1784 and was revised in 1786 to further provide for a more definite procedure for the sale of un-appropriated State lands. Id. The state courts held:

"The validity of letters patent and the effectiveness to convey title depends on the proper execution and record. (It has) generally been the law that public grants to be valid must be recorded. The record is not for purposes of notice under recording acts but to make the transfer effectual."

Later, if there was deemed to be a problem with the title, the state grants could be confirmed by issuance of a confirmatory grant. This then, in part, explains the methods and techniques the original states used to pass title to their lands, lands that remained in the possession of the state unless purchased by the still yet uncreated federal government or by individuals in the respective states. To much this same extent Texas, having been a separate country and republic, controlled and still controls its lands. In each of these instances, the land was not originally owned by the federal government and then later passed to the people and states.

This, then, is a synopsis of the transition from colony to statehood and the rights to land ownership under each situation. This, however, has said nothing of the methods used by the states in the creation of the federal government and the eventual disposal of the federal lands.

The Constitution in its original form was ratified by a convention of the States on September 17, 1787. The Constitution and the government formed under it were declared in effect on the first Wednesday of March, 1789. Prior to this time, during the Constitutional Convention, there was serious debate on the disposal of what the convention called the "Western Territories," now the states of Ohio, Indiana, Illinois, Michigan, Wisconsin and part of Minnesota, more commonly known as the Northwest Territory. This tract of land was ceded to the new American republic in the treaty signed with Britain in 1783.

The attempts to determine how such a disposal of the Western territories should come about were the subject of much discussion in the records of the Continental Congress. Beginning in September 1783, there was continual discussion concerning the acquisition and later disposition of the lands east of the Mississippi River. Journals of Congress, Papers of the Continental Congress, No. 25, 11, folio 255, p. 544-557 (September 13, 1783):

"and whereas the United States have succeeded to the sovereignty over the Western territory, and are thereby vested as one undivided and independent nation, with all and every power and right exercised by the king of Great Britain, over the said territory, or the lands lying and situated without the boundaries of the several states, and within the limits above described; and whereas the western territory ceded by France and Spain to Great Britain, relinquished to the United States by Great Britain, and guarantied to the United States by France as aforesaid, if properly managed, will enable the United States to comply with their promises of land to their officers and soldiers; will relieve their citizens from much of the weight of taxation; ... and if cast into new states, will tend to increase the happiness of mankind, by rendering the purchase of land easy, and the possession of liberty permanent; therefore Resolved, that a committee be appointed to report the territory lying without the boundaries of the several states; ... and also to report an establishment for a land office."

Later the then technically nonexistent federal government acquired land originally held by the colonial governments. As the years progressed, the goal remained the same – a proper determination of a simple method of disposing of the western lands. "That an advantageous disposition of the western territory is an object worthy the deliberation of Congress." Id. February 14, 1786, at p. 68. In February 1787, the Continental Congress continued to hold discussions on how to dispose of all western territories. As part of the basis for such disposal, it was determined to divide the new northwestern territories into medians, ranges, townships, and sections, making for easy division of the land, and giving the new owners of such land a certain number of acres in fee. Journals of Congress, p. 21, February 1787, and Committee Book, Papers of the Continental Congress, No. 190, p. 132 (1788)

There were more discussions on the methods of disposing the land in September of that same year. Those discussions included debates about the validity and solemnity of the state patents that had been issued in the past. Only a week earlier the Constitution was ratified by the conventions of the states. Finally, the future Senate and House of Representatives, though not officially a government for another one and a half years, held discussions on the possible creation of documents that would pass the title of lands from the new government to the people. The first patents were created and ratified in these discussions, making the old land-bloc or land-allodial charters of the Saxon nobles, 750 years earlier, and the letters patent of the Magna Charta, guidelines by which the land would pass to the sovereign freeholders of America. Id., July 2, 1788, pp.77-286.

As part of the method by which the new United States decided to dispose of its territories, it created in the Constitution an article, section, and clause that specifically dealt with such disposal. Article IV, Section 111, Clause 11, states in part, "The Congress shall have Power to dispose of and make all needful Rules and Regulations respecting the Territory or other property belonging to the United States."

Thus, Congress was given the power to create a vehicle to divest the Federal Government of all its right and interest in the land. This vehicle, known as the land patent, was to forever divest the federal government of its land and place such total ownership in the hands of the sovereign freeholders who collectively created the government.

The members of Constitutional Congress ratified the land patents issued prior to the initial date of recognition of the United States Constitution. Those patents created by statute after March 1789 had only the power of the statutes and the Congressional intent behind such statutes as a reference and basis for the determination of their powers and operational effect originally and in the American system of land ownership today.

There have been dozens of statutes enacted pursuant to Article IV, §III, Clause II. Some of these statutes had very specific intents of aiding soldiers of wars, or dividing lands in a very small region of one state, but all had the main goal of creating in the sovereigns, freeholders on their lands, beholden to no lord or superior. Some of the statutes include:

12 Stat 392, 37th Congress, Sess. 11, Ch. 75, (1862) (the Homestead Act); 9 Stat. 520, 3 1st Congress, Sess. 1, Ch. 85 (1850) Military Bounty Service Act); 8 Stat. 123, 29th Congress, Sess. 11, Ch. 8, (1847) (Act to raise additional military force and for other purposes); 5 Stat 444, 21st Congress, Sess. 11, Ch. 30 (1831); 4 Stat 51, 18th Congress, Sess. 1, Ch. 174 (1824); 5 Stat 52, 18th Congress, Sess. 1, Ch. 173 (1824); 5 Stat 56, 18th Congress, Sess. 1, Ch. 172, (1824); 3 Stat. 566, 16th Congress, Sess. 1, Ch. 51, (1820) (the major land patent statute enacted to dispose of lands); 2 Stat 748, 12th Congress, Sess. 1. Ch. 99 (1812); 2 Stat. 728, 12th Congress, Sess. 1, Ch. 77, (1812); 2 Stat. 716, 12th Congress, Sess. 1, Ch. 68, (1812) (the act establishing the General Land-Office in the Department of Treasury); 2 Stat

590, 11th Congress, Sess. U, Ch. 3.5,(1810);2 Stat 437, 9th Congress, Sess. H, Ch. 34, (1807); and 2 Stat 437, 9th Congress, Sess. H, Ch. 31, (1807).

These, of course, are only a few of the statutes enacted to dispose of public lands to the sovereigns. One of these acts, however, was the main patent statute in reference to the intent Congress had when creating the patents. That statute is 3 Stat 566.

In order to understand the validity of a patent in today's property law, it is necessary to turn to other sources than the acts themselves. These sources include the congressional debates and case law citing such debates. For the best answer to this question, it is necessary to turn to the Abridgment of the Debates of Congress, Monday, March 6, 1820, in the Senate, considering the topic "The Public Lands." This abridgment and the actual debates found within it concern one of the most important of the land patent statutes, 3 Stat 566, 16th Congress, Sess. 1. Ch. 51, Stat. 1, (April 24, 1820).

In this important debate, the reason for such a particular act in general and the protection afforded by the patent in particular were discussed. As Senator Edwards states,

"It is not my purpose to discuss, at length, the merits of the proposed change. I will, at present, content myself with an effort merely to shield the present settlers upon public lands from merciless speculators, whose cupidity and avarice would unquestionably be tempted by the improvements which those settlers have made with the sweat of their brows, and to which they have been encouraged by the conduct of the government itself, for though they might be considered as embraced by the letter of the law which provides against intrusion on public lands, yet, that their case has not been considered by the Government as within the mischief's intended to be prevented is manifest, not only from the forbearance to enforce the law, but from the positive rewards which others, in their situation, have received, by the several laws which have heretofore been granted to them by the same right if preemption which I now wish extended to the present settlers."

Further, Senator King from New York considered the change as highly favorable to the poor man, and he argued at some length that it was calculated to plant in the new country a population of independent, unembarrassed freeholders; that it would cut up speculation and monopoly; that the money paid for the lands would be carried from the State or country from which the purchaser should remove; that it would prevent the accumulation of an alarming debt, which experience proved never would and never could be paid.

In other statutes, the Court recognized much of these same ideas. In *United States v. Reynes*, 9 How. (U.S.) 127 (1850), the Supreme Court stated:

"The object of the Legislature is manifest....[I]t was intended to prevent speculation by dealing for rights of preference before the public lands were in the market. The speculator acquired power over choice spots, by procuring occupants to seat themselves on them and who abandoned them as soon as the land was entered under their preemption right, and the speculation accomplished. Nothing could be more easily done than this, if contracts of this description could be enforced."

The act of 1830, however, proved to be of little avail, and then came the Act of 1835 (5 Stat 251) which compelled the preemptor to swear that he had not made an arrangement by which the title might inure to the benefit of anyone except himself, or that he would transfer it to another at any subsequent time. This was preliminary to the allowing of his entry, and it discloses the policy of Congress.

"It is always to be borne in mind, in construing a congressional grant that the act by which it is made is a law as well as a conveyance and that such effect must be given to it as will carry out the intent of Congress. That intent should not be defeated by applying to the grant the rules of the common law...words of present grant, are operative, if at all, only as contracts to convey. But the rules of common law must yield in this, as in other cases, to the legislative will." *Missouri, Kansas & Texas Railway Company v. Kansas Pacific Railway Company*, 97 US 49 1, 497 (1878).

"The administration of the land system in this country is vested in the Executive Department of the Government, first in the Treasury and now in the Interior Department, the officers charged with the disposal of the public domain under are required and empowered to determine so far as it relates to the extent and character of the rights claimed under them, and to be given, though their actions, to individuals. Government, and courts of justice must never interfere with it." *Marks v. Dickson*, 61 US (20 How) 501 (1857); see also *Cousin v. Blanc's ex.*, 19 How. US 206, 209 (1856). "The Power of the Congress to dispose of its land cannot be interfered with, or its exercise embarrassed by any State legislation; nor can such legislation deprive the grantees of the United States of the possession and enjoyment of the property granted by reason of any delay in the transfer of the title after the initiation of proceedings for its acquisition." *Gibsion v Chouteau*, 13 Wal. (U. S.) 92, 93 (1871)

State statutes that give lesser authoritative ownership of title than the patent cannot even be brought into federal court. *Langdon v. Sherwood*, 124 U.S. 74, 81 (1887) These acts of Congress making grants are not to be treated both law and grant, and the intent of Congress when ascertained is to control in the interpretation of the law. *Wisconsin C. R. Co. v. Forsythe*, 159 U.S. 46 (1895)

"The intent to be searched for by the courts in a government Patent is the intent which the government had as that time, and not what it would have been had no mistake been made. The true meaning of a binding expression in a patent must be applied, no matter where such expressions are found in the document. It should be construed as to effectuate the primary object Congress had in view; and obviously a construction that gives effect to a patent is to be preferred to one that renders it inoperative and void. A grant must be interpreted by the law of the country in force at the time when it was made. The construction of federal grant by a state court is necessarily controlled by the federal decisions on the same subject. The United States may dispose of the public lands of such terms and conditions, and subject to such restrictions and limitations as in its judgment will best promote the public welfare, even if the condition is to exempt the land from sale on execution issued or judgment recovered in a State Court for a debt contracted before the patent issues." *Miller v. Little*, 47 Cal. 348, 350 (1874)

Congress has the sole power to declare the dignity and effect of titles emanating from the United States and the whole legislation of the Government must be examined in the determination of such titles. *Bagneu v. Broderick*, 38 U.S. 436 (1839) It was clearly the policy of Congress, in passing the preemption and patent laws, to confer the benefits of those laws to actual settlers upon the land. *Close v. Stuyvesant*, 132 M. 607, 617.

"The intent of Congress is manifest in the determinations of meaning, force and power vested in the patent. These cases all illustrate the power and dignity given to the patent. It was created to divest the government of its lands, and to act as a means of conveying such lands to the generations of people that would occupy those lands. This formula, "or his legal representatives," embraces representatives of the original grantee in the land, the contract, such as assignees or grantees, as well as the operation of law, and leaves the question open to inquiry in a court of justice as to the party to whom the patent, or confirmation, should enure." *Hogan v. Page*, 69 US 605 (1864)

The patent was and is the document and law that protects the settler from the merciless speculators, from the people that use avarice to unjustly benefit themselves against an unsuspecting nation. The patent was created with these high and grand intentions for a sound reason.

"The settlers as a rule seem to have been poor persons, and presumably without the necessary funds to improve and pay for their land, but it appears that in every case where the settlement was made under the preemption law, the settler...entered and paid for the land at the expiration of the shortest period at which entry could be made." *Close v. Stuyvesant*, 132 HI. 607, 623 (1890).

"We must look to the benefit character of the acts that created these grants and patents and the peculiar objects they were intended to protect and secure. A class of enterprising, hardy and valuable citizens has become the pioneers in the settlement and improvement of the new and distant lands of the government." *McConnell v· Wilcox*, 1 Seam. (M.) 344, 367 (1837).

"In furtherance of what is deemed a wise policy, tending to encourage settlement, and to develop the resources of the country, it invites the heads of families to occupy small parcels of the public land.... To deny Congress the power to make a valid and effective contract of this character...would materially abridge its power of disposal, and seriously interfere with a favorite policy of the government, which fosters measures tending to a distribution of the lands to actual settlers at a nominal price." *Miller v. Little*, 47 Cal. 348, 351(1874)

The legislative acts, the Statutes at Large, enacted to divest the United States of its land and to sell that land to the true sovereigns of this republic, had very distinct intents. Congress recognized that the average settler of this nation would have little money. Therefore Congress built into the patent and its corresponding act the understanding that these lands were to be free from avarice and cupidity, free from the speculators who preyed on the unsuspecting nation, and forever under the control and ownership of the freeholder, who by the sweat of his brow made the land produce the food that would feed himself and eventually the nation.

Even today, the intent of Congress is to maintain a cheap food supply through the retention of the sovereign farmers on the land. *United States v. Kimball Foods, Inc.*, 440 U.S. 715 (1979); see also *Curry v. Block*, 541 F. Supp. 506 (1982). Originally the intent of Congress was to protect the sovereign freeholders and create a permanent system of land ownership in the country. Today, the intent of Congress is to retain the small family farm and utilize the cheap production of these situations. It has been necessary to protect the sovereign on his parcel of land, and ensure that he remain in that position. The land patent and the patent acts were created to accomplish these goals. In other words, the patent or title deed being regular in its form, the law will not presume that such was obtained through fraud of the public right.

This principle is not merely an arbitrary rule of law established by the courts; rather, it is a doctrine founded upon reason and the soundest principles of public policy. It is one which has been adopted in the interest of peace in the society and the permanent security of titles. Unless fraud is shown, this rule is held to apply to patents executed by the public authorities. *State v. Hewitt Land Co.*, 134 P. 474,479 (1913)

It is therefore necessary to determine exact power and authority contained in a patent. Legal titles to lands cannot be conveyed except in the form provided by law. *McGaffahan v. Mining Co.*, 96 U.S. 316 (1877) Legal title to property is contingent upon the patent issuing from the government. *Sabo v. Horvath*, 559 P.2d 1038, 1040 (Aka. 1976)

"That the patent carries the fee and is the best title known to a court of law is the settled doctrine of this court." *Marshall v. Ladd*, 7 Wall. (74 U.S.) 106 (1869) "A patent issued by the government of the United States is legal and conclusive evidence of title to the land described therein. No equitable interest, however strong, to land described in such a patent, can prevail at law, against the patent" (Land Patents, Opinions of the United States Attorney General's office, [September, 1969])

"A patent is the highest evidence of title, and is conclusive against the government and all claiming under junior patents or titles, until it is set aside or annulled by some judicial tribunal." *Stone v. United States*, 2 Wall. (67 U.S.) 765 (1865)

The patent is the instrument which, under the laws of Congress, passes title from the United States, and the patent, when regular on its face, is conclusive evidence of title in the patentee. When there is a confrontation between two parties as to the superior legal title, the patent is conclusive evidence of title in the patentee. When there is a confrontation between two parties as to the superior legal title, the patent is conclusive evidence as to ownership. *Gibson v. Chouteau*, 13 Wall. 912 (1871)

Congress having the sole power to declare the dignity and effect of its titles has declared the patent to be the superior and conclusive evidence of the legal title. *Bagnefl v. Brodrick*, 38 US 438 (1839)

"Issuance of a government patent granting title to land is the most accredited type of conveyance known to our Law." *United States v. Creek Nation*, 295 US 103, 111 (1935); see also *United States v. Cherokee Nation*, 474 F.2d 628,634 91973). The patent is prima facie conclusive evidence of the title. *Marsh v. Brooks*, 49 U.S. 223, 233 (1850). A patent, once issued, is the highest evidence of title, and is a final determination of the existence of all facts. *Walton v. United States*, 415 F. 2d 121, 123 (I0th Cir. 1969); see also *United States v. Beaman*, 242 F. 876 (1917) *File v. Alaska*, 593 P. 268, 270 (1979)

When the federal government grants land via a patent, the patent is the highest evidence of title. Patent rights to the land is the title in fee, *City of Los Angeles v. Board of Supervisors of Mono County*, 292 P.2d 539 (1956), the patent of the fee simple, *Squire v. Capoeman*, 351 U.S. 1,6 (1956), and the patent is required to carry the fee. *Carter v. Rubby*, 166 U.S. 493, 496 (1896); see also *Klais v. Danowski*, 129 N.W.2d 414, 422 (1964) 1423 (Interposition of the patent or interposition of the fee title).

The land patent is the muniment of title, such title being absolute in its nature, making the sovereigns absolute freeholders on their lands.

Finally, the patent is the only evidence of the legal fee simple title. *McConnell v. Wilcox*, I Scam (ILL.) 381, 396 (1837)

All of these various cases and quotes illustrate one statement that should be thoroughly understood at this time: the patent is the highest evidence of title and is conclusive of the ownership of land in courts of competent jurisdiction. This, however, does not examine the methods or possibilities of challenging a land patent.

In *Hooper et al. v. Scheimer*,,64 U.S. (23 How.) 235 (1859), the United States Supreme Court stated: "I affirm that a patent is unimpeachable at law, except, perhaps, when it appears on its own face to be void; and the authorities on this point are so uniform and unbroken in the courts, Federal and State, that little else will be necessary beyond a reference to them." Id. at 240 (1859)

A patent cannot be declared void at law, nor can a party travel behind the patent to avoid it. Id. A patent cannot be avoided at law in a collateral proceeding unless it is declared void by statute, or its nullity indicated by some equally explicit statutory denunciations. One perfect on its face is not to be avoided in a trial at law by anything save an elder patent. It is not to be affected by evidence or circumstances, which might show that the impeaching party might prevail in a court of equity. A patent is evidence, in a court of law, of the regularity of all previous steps to it, and no facts behind it can be investigated. A patent cannot be collaterally avoided at law, even for fraud. A patent, being a superior title, must of course, prevail over colors of title; nor is it proper for any state legislation to give such titles, which are only equitable in nature with a recognized legal status in equity courts, precedence over the legal title in a court of law.

The Hooper case has many of the maxims that apply to the powers and possible disabilities of a land patent; however, there is extensive case law in this area.

The presumptions arise from the existence of a patent evidencing a grant of land from the United States that all acts have been performed and all facts have been shown which are prerequisites to its issuance, and that the right of the party, grantee therein, to have it issued, has been presented and passed upon by the proper authorities. *Green v. Barber*, 66 N.W. 1032 (1896) As stated in *Bouvier's Law Dictionary*, Vol. H, p. 1834 (1914):

Misrepresentations knowingly made by the application for a patent will justify the government in proceedings to set it aside, as it has a right to demand a cancellation of a patent obtained by false and fraudulent misrepresentations. *United States v. Manufacturing Co.*, 128 U.S. 673 (1888). But courts of equity cannot set aside, annul, or correct patents or other evidence of title obtained from the United States by fraud or mistake, unless on specific averment of the mistake or fraud, supported by clear and satisfactory proof. *Maxelli Land Grant Cancellation*, 11 How. (U.S.) 552 (1850) A patent fraudulently obtained by one knowing at the time that another person has a prior right to the land may be set aside by an information in the nature of a bill in equity filed by the attorney of the United States for the district in which the land lies. Id. A court of equity, upon a bill filed for that purpose, will vacate a patent of the United States for a tract of land obtained by mistake from the officers of the land office, in order that a clear title may be transferred to the previous purchaser *Hughes v. United States*, 4 Wall. (U.S.) 232 (1866); but a patent for land of the United States will not be declared void merely because the evidence to authorize its issue is deemed insufficient by the court. *Milliken v·Starling's Lessee*, 16 Ohio 61·A state can impeach the title conveyed by it to a grantee only by a bill in chancery to cancel it, either for fraud on the part of the grantee or mistake of law; and until so canceled it cannot issue to any other party a valid patent for the same land. *Chandler v. Manufacturing Co.*, 149 U.S. 79 (1893)

Other cases espouse these and other rules of law. A patentee can be deprived of his rights only by direct proceedings instituted by the government or by parties acting in its name, or by persons having a superior title to that acquired through the government. *Putnum v. Ickes*, 78 F.2d 233, denied 296 U.S. 612 (1935)

It is not sufficient for the one challenging a patent to show that the patentee should not have received the patent; he must also show that he as the challenger is entitled to it. *Kale v. United States*, 489 F.2d 449, 454 (1973) A United States patent is protected from easy third party attacks. *Fisher v· Rule*, 248 U.S. 314, 318 (1919); see also *Hooffiagle v· Anderson*, 20 U.S. (7 Wheat.) 212 (1822)

A Patent issued by the United States of America so vests the title in the lands covered thereby that it is the further general rule that such patents are not open to collateral attack. *Thomas v. Union pacific Railroad Company*,588, 596 i1956) See also *State v. Crawford*, 475 P.2d 515 (Ariz. App. 1970) (A patent is prima facie valid, and if its validity can be attacked at all, the burden of proof is upon the defendant); *State v. Crawford*, 441 P.2d 586,590 (Ariz. APP· 1968) (A patent to land is the highest evidence of title and may not be collaterally attacked); and *Dredge v. Husite Company* 369 P.2d 676,682 (1962) (A Patent is the act of legally instituted tribunal, done within its jurisdiction, and passes the title. Such a patent is a final judgment as well as a conveyance and is conclusive upon a collateral attack) absent some facial invalidity, the patents are presumed valid. *Murray v. State*, 596 P.2d 805, 816 (1979)

The government retains no power to nullify a patent except through a direct court proceeding. *United States v. Reimann*, 504 F.2d 135 (1974) See also *Green v. Barker*, 66 N.W. 1032, 1034 (1896) (The doctrine announced was that the deed upon its face purported to have been issued in pursuance of the law, and was therefore assailable only in a direct proceeding by aggrieved parties to set it aside.)

Through these cases, it can be shown that the patent, which passes the title from the United States to the sovereigns, was created to keep the speculators from the land. It is assailable only in a direct proceeding for fraud or mistake. In no other situation may the courts eliminate the patent.

One question that may arise is what do the courts mean by a collateral attack and what can be done by courts of equity if a collateral attack is presented?

Perhaps the easiest means of defining a collateral attack is to show the converse corollary, a direct attack on a patent. As was stated in the previous paragraphs, a direct attack upon a land patent is an action for fraud or mistake brought by the government or a party acting in its place. Therefore, a collateral attack, by definition, is any attack upon a patent that is not covered within the direct attack list.

Perhaps the most prevalent collateral attack in property law today is a mortgage or deed of trust foreclosure on a color of title. In these instances it is determined that the mortgagee or another purchases the complete title and interest in the land in his place. Such a determination displaces the patentee's ownership of the title without the court ever ruling that the patent was acquired through fraud or mistake.

This is against public policy, legislative intent, and the overwhelming majority of case law. Therefore, to see what powers the courts of equity have in protecting the rights of the challengers of patents, it is now necessary to determine the patent's role in American property law today.

The attitude of the courts is to promote simplicity and certainty in title transactions, thereby they follow what is in the chain of title and not what is outside. *Sabo v. Horvath*, 559 p.2d 1038, 1044 (1976) However, in equity courts, title under a patent from the government is subject to control to protect the rights of parties acting in a fiduciary capacity. *Sanford v. Sanford*, 139 U.S. 290 (1891). This protection, however, does not include the invalidation of the patent.

The determination of the land department in matters cognizable by it in the alienation of lands and the validity of patents cannot be collaterally attacked or impeached. Therefore the courts have had to devise another means to control the patentee, if not the patent itself, as stated in *Raestle v. Whitson*, 582 P.2d 170, 172 (1978): "The land patent is the highest evidence of title and is immune from collateral attack. This does not preclude a court from imposing a constructive trust upon the patentee for the benefit of the owners of an equitable interest." This then explains the most equitable way a court may effectively restrict the sometimes harsh justice handed down by a strict court of law. Equity courts will impose a trust upon the patentee until the debt has been paid.

As has been stated, a patent cannot be collaterally attacked; therefore, the land cannot be sold or taken by the courts unless there is strong evidence of fraud or mistake. However, the courts can require the patentee to pay a certain amount at regular intervals until the debt is paid unless, of course, there is a problem with the validity of the debt itself. This is the main purpose of the patent in this growing epidemic of farm foreclosures that defy the public policy of Congress, the legislative intent of the Statutes at large, and the legal authority as to the type of land ownership possessed in America. Why then is the rate of foreclosures on the rise?

Titles to land today, as was stated earlier in this memorandum, are normally in the form of colors of title. This is because of the trend in recent property law to maintain the status quo. The rule in most jurisdictions, in particular those that have adopted a grantor-grantee index, is that a deed outside the chain of title does not act as a valid conveyance and does not serve notice of a defect of title on a subsequent purchaser. These deeds outside the chain of title are known as "wild deeds." *Sabo v. Horvath*, 559 P.2d 1038, 1043 (1976); See also *Porter v Buck*, 335 So.2d 369, 371 (1976); *The Exchange National Bank v Lawndale National Bank*, 41 ILL.2d 316, 243 N.E.2d 193, 195-96 (1968) (The chain of title for purposes of the marketable title act, may not be founded on a wild deed. These stray, accidental, or interloping conveyances are contrary to the intent of the marketable title act, which is to simplify and facilitate land title transactions); and *Manson v. Berkman*, 356 ILL. 20, 190 N. E. 77, 79 (1934). This liberal construction of what constitutes a valid conveyance has led to a thinning of the title to a point where the absolute and paramount title is almost impossible to guarantee.

This thinning can be directly attributed to the constant use of the colors of title. Under the guise of being the fee simple absolute, these titles have operated freely, but in reality, they evidence something much different. It was said in common-law England that when a title was not completely alienable and not the complete title, it was not a fee simple absolute. Rather it was some type of contingent conveyance that depended on the performance of certain tasks before the title was considered to be absolute. In fact, normally the title never did develop into a fee simple absolute. These types of conveyance were evidenced in part by the operable word "conveyance" and in part by the manner in which the granter could reclaim the property. If the title automatically reverted to the grantor upon the happening of a contingent action, then the title was by a fee simple determinable. *Scheller v. Trustees of Schools of Township* 41 North, 67 ILL. App.3d 857, 863 (1978).

This is evidenced most closely today by deeds of trust in some states. If it required a court's ruling to reacquire the land and title, then the transaction and title were held by a fee simple with a condition subsequent. *Mahrenholz v. Country Board of Trustees of Lawrence County*, 93 III.App.3d 366, 370-74 (1981) This is most closely evidenced by a mortgage in a lien or intermediate-theory state.

These analogies may be somewhat startling and new to some, but the analogies are accurate. When a mortgage is acquired on property, the mortgagee steps into the position of a grantor with the authority to create the contingent estate as required by the particular facts. This is exactly what the grantor in Common Law property law could acquire. All the grantor had to do was choose a particular type of contingency and use the necessary catchwords, and almost invariably the land would one day be refused due to a violation of the contingency.

In today's property law, the color of title has little power to protect the landowner. When the sovereign is unable to pay the necessary principal and interest on the debt load, then the catchwords and phrases found in the deed of trust or mortgage become operational. Upon that occurrence, the mortgagee or speculator, having through a legal maneuver acquired the position of a grantor, is in a position to either automatically receive the property simply by advertising and selling it, or can acquire the position of the grantor and eventually the possession of the property by a court proceeding.

In Common Law, the grantor of a fee simple determinable could automatically take the land from the grantee holder, by force if necessary, where the contingency was broken or violated. If, however, the grant was a fee simple upon condition subsequent, when the contingency was broken, the grantor, to declare the grantee in violation and to order the grantee to vacate the premises, had to bring a legal proceeding to declare the contingence broken.

These situations, though under different names and proceedings, occur every day in America. Is there really any serious debate, therefore, that the colors of title used today with the creation of a lien upon the property, become fee simple determinable and fee simples upon condition subsequent? Is this a legitimate method of ensuring a stable and permanent system of land ownership? If the color of title is weak, then how strong is a mortgage or deed of trust placed on the property?

Fee simple estates may be either legal or equitable. In each situation it is the largest estate in the land that the law will recognize. *Hughes v. Miller's*

Mutual Fire Insurance Co., 246 S.W.23 (1922) If a mortgagee, upon the creation of a mortgage or deed of trust, steps into the shoes of the grantor upon a conditional fee simple, does it then mean that the mortgagee has acquired one of the two halves of a fee simple, when cases have shown the fee simple is only evidenced by a patent?

Actually, courts have held in many states that a mortgage is only a lien. *United States v. Certain Interests in Property in Champaign County, State of Illinois*, 165 F.Supp.474, 480 (1958) (In Illinois and other lien theory states, the mortgagee has only a lien and not a vested interest in the leasehold.) See also *Federal Farm Mortgage Corp. v. Ganswer*, 146 Neb. 635, 20 N.W.2d 689 (1945) Even after a condition is broken or there is a default on a mortgage, a mortgagee has only an equitable lien that can be enforced in proper proceedings. *South Omaha Bank v. Levy*, 95 N.W.603 (1902). (Strict foreclosure will not lie when mortgagor holds the legal title.) *First National Bank v. Sergeant*, 65 Neb. 394, 91 N.W. 595 (1902) (Mortgagee cannot demand more than is legally due.) *Morrill v. Skinner*, 57 Neb. 164, 77 N.W. 375 (1898) (Mortgage conveys no estate but merely creates a lien.) *Barber v. Crowell*, 55 Neb. 571, 75 N. W. 1 109 (1898)

(Mortgage is mere security in form of conditional conveyance.) *Speer v. Hadduck*, 31 Freeman (HI) 439, 443 (1863). (Assignments or conveyances of mortgages do not convey the fee simple; rather they hold only security interests.) In lien and intermediate-theory states, these cases amply illustrate that a mortgage or deed of trust is only a lien. Even in title theory of mortgage states, courts of equity have determined that the fee simple title is not really conveyed, either in its equitable or legal state. See Barber, supra, at 1110.

A fee simple estate still exists even though the property is mortgaged or encumbered. *Hughes v. Miller's Mutual Fire Insurance Co.*, 246 S.W. 23, 24 (1922) In fact, a creditor asserting a lien (mortgage) must introduce evidence or proof that will clearly demonstrate the basis of his lien. *United States v. United States Chain Company*, 212 F. Supp. 171 (N. D. If a mortgagee, even in the title theory states, has only a lien, yet when the mortgage or deed of trust is created he has a fee simple determinable or condition subsequent, then obviously the color of title used as the operative title has little force or power to protect the sovereign Freeholder. Nor can it be said that such a color of title is useful in the intenance of stable and permanent titles.

The patent, in almost all cases, has been originally issued to the first purchaser from the government. Theoretically, then, the public policy, Congressional intent from the 1930s through the last few decades should protect the sovereign in the enjoyment and possession of his freehold.

This, however, is not the case. Instead, vast mortgaging of the land has occurred. The agriculture debt alone has risen to over $220 billion in the past three decades. This is in part due to the vast expansion of mortgaged holdings and in part due to the rural sector's inability to repay existing loans, requiring the increased mortgaging of the land. This is in exact contradiction to public policy and legislative intent if maintaining stable and simplistic land records; yet marketable titles (colors of title) were supposed to guarantee such records. *Wichelman v. Messner*, 83 N.W.2d 800, 805 357.

Colors of title are ineffective against mortgages and promote the instability and complexity of the records of land titles by requiring abstracts and title insurance simply to guarantee a marketable title. Worse, in some of the states an injustice has prevailed that permits actions to determine titles to be maintained upon warrants for land (warranty deeds) and other titles not complete or legal in their character. This practice is against the intent of the Constitution and the Acts of Congress. *Bagnell v. Broderick*, 38 U.S. 438 (1839). Such lesser titles have no value in actions brought in federal courts, notwithstanding a State legislature that may have provided otherwise. *Hooper et. al. v. Scheimer*, 64 U.S. (23 How.) 235 (1859)

It is, in fact, possible that the state legislatures have even violated the Supremacy Clause of the United States Constitution.

These actions are against the intent of the founding fathers and against the legislative intent of the Congressman who enacted the statutes at large, creating the land patent or land grant. This patent or grant, since the "land grant" is in some states another name for the patent, the terms being synonymous, *Northern Pacific Railroad Co. v. Barden*, 46 F. 592, 617 (1891), prevented every problem that was created by the advent of colors of title, marketable titles, and mortgages. Therefore, it is necessary to determine the validity of returning to the patent as the operative title.

Patents are issued (and theoretically passed) between sovereigns; deeds are executed by persons and private corporations without these sovereign powers. *Leading Fighter v. County of Gregory*, 230 N.W.2d 114, 116 (1975) As was stated earlier, the American people, in creating the Constitution and the government formed under it, made such a document and government as sovereigns, retaining that status even after the creation of the government. *Chisholm v. Georgia*, 2 Dall. (U.S.) 419 (1793)

The government, as sovereign, passes the title to the American people, creating in them sovereign Freeholders. Therefore, it follows that the American people, as sovereigns, should also have this authority to transfer the fee simple title, through the patent, to others. Cases have been somewhat scarce in this area, but there is some case law to reinforce this idea. In *Wilcox v. Calloway*, I Wash. (Va.) 38, 38-41 (1823), the Virginia Court of Appeals heard a case where the patent was brought up or reissued to the parties four separate times. Some patents were issued before the creation of the constitutional

United States government, and some occurred during the creation of that government.

The courts determined the validity of those patents, recognizing each actual acquisition as being valid, but reconciling the differences by finding that the first patent, properly secured with all the necessary requisite acts fulfilled, carried the title. The other patents and the necessary requisition, a new patent each time, yielded the phrase "lapsed patent," a lapsed patent being one that must be required to perfect the title. Id. Subsequent patentees take subject to any reservations in the original patent. *State v. Crawford*, 441 P.2d 586,590 (1968).

A patent regularly issued by the government is the best and only evidence of a perfect title. The actual patent should be secured to place at rest any question as to validity of entries (possession under a claim and color of title). *Young v. Miller*, 125 So.2d 257, 258 (1960). Under the color of title act, the Secretary of Interior may be required to issue a patent if certain conditions have been met, and the freeholder and his predecessors in title are in peaceful, adverse possession under claim and color of title for more than a specified period. *Beaver v. United States*, 350 F.2d 4, cert. denied, 387 U.S. 937 (1965).

A description that will identify the lands (and possession) is all that is necessary for the validity of the patent, *Lossing v. Shull*, 173 S.W.2d 1, 1 Mo. 342 (1943). A patent to two or more persons creates presumptively a tenancy in common in the patentees. *Stoll v. Gottbreht*, 176 N.W. 932, 45 N.D. 158 (1920). A patent to be the original grantee or his legal representatives embrace the representatives by contract as well as by law. *Reichert v. Jerome H. Sheip, Inc.*, 131 So. 229, 222 Ala. 133 (1930).

A patent has a double operation. In the first place, it is documentary evidence having the dignity of a record of the evidence of the title or such equities respecting the claim as to justify its recognition and later confirmation. In the second place, it is a deed of the United States or a title deed. As a deed, its operation is that of a quitclaim or rather of a conveyance of such interest as the United States possess in the land, such interest in the land passing to the people or sovereign freeholders. 63 Am. Jur. 2d Section 97, p. 566.

Finally, the United States Supreme Court, in *Summa Corporation v. California ex rel. State Lands Commission*, etc., 80 L.Ed.2d 237 (1984), made determinations as to the validity of a patent confirmed by the United States through the Treaty of Guadalupe Hidalgo, 9 Stat. 631 (1951). The State of California attempted to acquire land that belonged to the corporation. The State maintained that there was a public trust easement granting to the State authority to take the land without compensation for public use. The corporation relied in part on the intent of the treaty, in part on the intent of the patent and the statute creating it, and in part in the requisite challenge date of the patent expiring.

The *Summa* Court followed the lengthy dissertation of the dissenting judge on the California Supreme Court (see 31 Cal. 3d 288, dissenting opinion), in determining that the patent, which had been the apparent operative title throughout the years, was paramount and that the actions by the State were against the manifest weight of the Treaty and the legislative intent of the patent statutes. According to each of these cases, the patent, through possession, or claim and color of title, or through the term "his heirs and assigns forever," or through the necessary passage of title at the death of a joint tenant or tenant in common, is still the operable title and is required to secure the peaceful control of the land.

These same ideas can also apply to state patents for lands that went to the state or remained in the hands of the state upon admission into the Union. *Oliphant v. Frazho*, 146 N.W.2d 685, 686,687 (1966); *Fiedier v. Pipers*, 107 So.2d 409, 411-412 (1958) (Not even the State could be heard to question the validity of a patent signed by the Governor and the Register of the State Land Office.)

"No government can object to the intent and creation of a patent after such is issued, unless issued through fraud or mistake. The patent, either federal or state, has an intent to create sovereign freeholders in the land protected from the speculators (any lending institution speculates upon land), and a public policy to maintain a simplistic, stable and permanent system of land records. Land patents were designed to effectively insure that this intent and policy were retained. Colors of title cannot provide this type of stability since such titles are powerless against liens, mortgages, when the freeholder is unable to repay principle and interest on the accompanying promissory note. Equity will entertain jurisdiction at the instance of the owner of fee of lands to remove a cloud upon his title created by the sale of the premises and a deed issued thereto under a decree of foreclosure of a mortgage thereon." *Hodgen v. Guttery*, 58 Free. (i 1.) 431, 438 (1871) (Though this case dealt with an improper sale of land covered by a patent, any forced sales of lands covered by a patent is improper in view of the policy and intent of the Congress.)

Equity, however, will protect the mortgagee who stands to lose his interest in the property, thereby requiring a trust to be created until the debt is erased, making partners of the creditor and debtor. What then exists is a situation where the patent should be declared (confirmed or reissued) to protect the sovereign freeholder and to re-institute the policy and intent of Congress.

The patent as the paramount title, fee simple absolute, cannot be collaterally attacked, but when a debt cannot be paid, immediately placing the creditor in jeopardy, the courts will impose a constructive trust until the new "partners" can mutually eliminate the debt. If the debt cannot be satisfactorily removed, it is still possible, considering the present intent of the government, to maintain sovereign freeholders on the property, immune from the loss of the land, since it is Congress' intent to keep the family farm in place.

The use of colors of title to act as the operative title is inappropriate, considering the rising number of foreclosures and the inability of the colors of title to restrain a mortgage or lien. However, the lending institutions, speculators on the land, maintain that the public policy of the country includes the eradication of the sovereign freeholders in the rural sector in an effort to implant large corporate holdings upon the country. This last area must be effectively met and eliminated.

To those who framed the Constitution, the rights of the States and the rights of the people were two distinct and different things. Throughout their debates, they had two objects foremost in their minds. First, create a strong and effective national government, and, second, protect the people and their rights from usurpation and tyranny by government.

The people's liberties and individual rights and safeguards were to be kept forever beyond the control and dominion of the legislatures of the States, whom they distrusted, and against whom they so carefully guarded themselves. If such control and domination and unlimited powers were given to a few legislatures, they could override every one of the reserved rights covered by the first ten Amendments (the Bill of Rights); they could change the government of limited powers to one of unlimited powers; they could declare themselves hereditary rulers; they could abolish religious freedoms; they could abolish free speech and the right of the people to petition for redress; they could not only abolish trial by jury, but even the rights to a day in court; and most importantly they could abolish free sovereign ownership of the land.

The whole literature of the period of the adoption of the Constitution and the first ten amendments is one of great testimony to the insistence that the Constitution must be so amended as to safeguard unquestionably the rights and freedoms of the people so as to secure from any future interference by the new government matters the people had not already given into its control, unless by their own consent. *United States v. Sprague*, 282 U.S. 716, 723-726 (1930)

The problem has not been in the lending institutions that simply practice good business on their part. The problem in the loss of freedoms by this present interference with allodial sovereign ownership lies with the state legislatures that created law or marketable title acts, that claimed to enact new simplistic, stable land titles and actually created a watered-down version of the fee simple absolute that requires complicated tracing and protection, and is ineffective against mortgage foreclosures.

None of these problems would occur if the patent were the operable title again, as long as the sovereigns recognized the powers and disabilities of their fee simple title. The patent was meant to keep the sovereign freeholder on the land, but the land was also to be kept free of debt, since that debt was recognized in 1820 as un-repayable and today is un-repayable.

The re-declaration of the patent is essential in the protection of the rural sector of sovereign freeholders, but also essential is the need to impress the state legislatures that have strayed from their enumerated powers with the knowledge that they have enacted laws that have defeated the intent and goal of man since the Middle Ages. That intent, of course, is to own a small tract of land absolutely, whether by land-bloc or patent, on which the freeholder is beholden to no lord or superior. The patent makes sovereign freeholders of each person who own his/her land. A return to the patent must occur if those sovereign freeholders wish to protect that land from the encroachment of the state legislatures and the speculators that benefit from such legislation.

CONCLUSION

As has been seen, man is always striving to protect his rights, the most dear being the absolute right to ownership of the land. This right was guaranteed by the land patent, the public policy of the Congress, and the legislative intent behind the Statutes at Large. Such rights must be reacquired through the re-declaration of the patent in the color of title claimant's name, based on his color of title and possession. With such re-born rights, the land is protected from the forced sale because of delinquency on a promissory note and foreclosure on the mortgage.

This protected land will not eliminate the debt; a trust must be created whereby "partners" will work together to repay it. These rights must be recaptured from the state legislated laws, or the freedoms guaranteed in the Bill of Rights and Constitution will be lost. Once lost, those rights will be exceedingly hard if not impossible to reclaim, and quite possibly, as Thomas Jefferson said, the children of this generation may someday wake up homeless on the land their forefathers founded. There can be no higher duty for a court than to embrace the opportunity – nay, the obligation – to uphold the original intent of the founding fathers and the Constitution of the United States and the Congress in the protection of the peoples' most valued unalienable right – the right to Allodial Freehold Property.

CHAPTER ELEVEN

MIRRORS OF ILLUSION BROKEN

The IRS con game is exposed

For a good many years, I have heard Patriots and tax evaders of all stripes argue that they were not subject to tax for as many reasons as I have hairs on my head. Not many truly understand the proper argument and most invariably loose their valiant fights, winding up in federal prison, primarily because their arguments were not focused and were in most part devoid of logic.

This chapter, titled "Mirrors of Illusion Broken," concerns the taxing power of the UNITED STATES and the average citizen's relationship to the federal government. Read carefully and follow the logic as well as the supporting statutes and case law; they all have the same reoccurring theme and all are supportive of the American people.

If this is the only chapter in the book that you remember, your life will be changed forever.

The following chapter is a Memorandum of Law. I did not make many changes, so it may not fit your particular situation to a tee, but in general the sum and substance is the same for us all.

NONRESIDENT ALIEN

Plaintiffs in the above entitled action are nonresident aliens with respect to the "United States" as those terms are defined in Title 26 U.S.C., and have had no income effectively connected to a trade or business within the "United States" or any source income derived from any excise taxable event. Plaintiffs are not withholding agents, government employees or elected officials.

Defendant's Revenue Officer (Name), District Director (Name), are Internal Revenue employees. It appears from documentary evidence that the Internal Revenue Service Agents, etc., are "agents of a foreign principal" within the meaning and intent of the Foreign Agents Registration Act of 1938. They are directed and controlled by the corporate "Governor" of "The Fund," a.k.a., "Secretary of Treasury"[c] and the corporate "Governor" of "The Bank,"[d] said agents acting as "information-service employees"[e] and have been, and do now, solicit, collect, disburse, or dispense contribution, tax-pecuniary contribution, loan money or other things of value, for, or in interest of such foreign principal,[f] and they entered into agreements with a foreign principal pursuant to Treasury Delegation Order No. 91, i.e., the "Agency For International Development"[g]. (Exhibit #) The Internal Revenue

Service is also an agency of the International Criminal Police Organization and solicits and collects information for 150 Foreign Powers.[h]

The Defendant UNITED STATES believes or wants We the People of the fifty States to believe that the "united States of America" is the same as the "UNITED STATES." Nothing could be further from the truth. The "*united*" States of America is an adjective, describing a continent consisting of connecting sovereign States plus two other landmasses (States) that are not connected to the American continent. These united States of America consist of the fifty States, all of which have been admitted to the Union of the united States of America. This is clearly designated by the fifty Stars on the flag of the united States of America.

The "UNITED STATES," on the other hand, is a noun, a "federal corporation" that is defined in 18 USC §5 by the "places" where it has political jurisdiction. That jurisdiction is clearly and unambiguously granted pursuant to Article 1, §8, Clause 17, of the Constitution for the United States. That jurisdiction is limited to the District (not exceeding ten square miles) for the seat of government (District of Columbia), along with other "federal areas," "federal enclaves," and "federal islands" that may sit within the exterior boundaries of one of the fifty American States of the Union. If the Congress does not have exclusive legislative jurisdiction over an area, then the Executive Branch of the government would have little or nothing to enforce, other than some related defense matters and inter-state commerce issues within the fifty Union states.

It is this District of Columbia that has obtained territories over the years that include the District of Columbia, Commonwealth of Puerto Rico, Guam, American Samoa, Northern Mariana Islands and the Virgin Islands, etc. These are the *several states* of the UNITED STATES.[i] It is these areas and these areas only that are within the exclusive political jurisdiction of the UNITED STATES (District of Columbia). All jurisdictions of the UNITED STATES (District of Columbia) exist "without" the jurisdiction of a particular State of the Union. These federal states of the UNITED STATES have not been admitted to the Union of fifty American states of the united States of America. Each of the above definitions is unambiguous and cannot be challenged for ambiguity. Since the words "fifty States" are not used in Title 26 U.S.C. §7701(A)(9), it appears that the "fifty States" are excluded from that definition of UNITED STATES.

The statutory construction becomes crystal clear when we consider the language used by the Supreme Court in *Hooven & Allison Co. v. Evatt*:[j]

"This term has several meanings. It may be merely the name of a sovereign occupying the position analogous to that of other sovereigns in the family of nations, it may designate territory over which sovereignty of the United

States extends, or it may be the collective name of the states which are united by and under the Constitution."

Thus, in *Hooven*, supra, it is readily discernible that there are two literal UNITED STATES consisting of definitive landmasses or geographical areas. The third definition in *Hooven*, supra, consists of the fifty States united under the Constitution. The second definition designates the geographical area consisting of the District of Columbia and all territory over which the political sovereignty of the UNITED STATES extends. Congress expresses the sovereignty of this second UNITED STATES under authority of Article 1, §8, Clauses 17 and 18, and Article 4, §3, Clause 2 of the Constitution with no constitutional restrictions placed on said powers. In legislating for the District and its territories, Congress always defines the words "State" and "United States" in its Public Laws to only include such geographical areas.

The issue as to whether there are different meanings for the term "United States" and whether there are three different and distinct "United States" operating within the same geographical areas and one "United States" operating outside the Constitution over its own territory in which it has citizens belonging to said "United States" was settled in 1901 by the Supreme Court in the cases of *De Lima v. Bidwell*[k] and *Downes v. Bidwell*[l]. In *Downes*, supra, at page 380, Justice Harlan dissented as follows:

"The idea prevails with some – indeed, it found expression in arguments at the bar – that we have in this country substantially or practically two national governments; one, to be maintained under the Constitution, with all its restrictions; the other to be maintained by Congress outside and independently of that instrument, by exercising such powers as other nations of the earth are accustomed to exercise."

He went on to say, on page 382: "It will be an evil day for American liberty if the theory of a government outside of the supreme law of the land finds lodgment in our constitutional jurisprudence. No higher duty rests upon this court than to exert its full authority to prevent all violation of the principles of the Constitution."

This theory of a government operating outside the Constitution over its own territory with citizens of the "United States" belonging thereto under Article 4, Section 3, Clause 2, of the Constitution has been long understood. In 1922 in *Balzac v. Porto Rico*,[m] the Supreme Court further affirmed the proposition that the Constitution does not apply outside the limits of the fifty States of the Union. The Court, quoting *Downes* and *De Lima*, supra, held that, under Article IV, §3, Clause 2, the "United States" was given exclusive power over the territories.

The issue arose again in 1944, in the case of *Hooven & Allison Co. v. Evatt,*[n] wherein the United States Supreme Court stated as follows at page 671-672.

"The term "United States" may be used in any one of several senses. [1] It may be merely the name of a sovereign occupying the position analogous to that of other sovereigns in the family of nations. [2] It may designate the territory over which the sovereignty of the United States extends, [3] or it may be the collective name of the states which are united by and under the Constitution." [Brackets, numbers and emphasis added]

Quoting *Fourteen Diamond Rings v. United; States*, 183 U.S. 176; cf. *De Lima v. Bidwell*, 182 U.S. 1; *Dooley v. United States*, 182 U.S. 222; *Faber v. United States*, 221 U.S, 649; cf. *Huus v. New York & P.R.S.S. Co.*, 182 U.S. 392; *Gonzales v. Williams*, 192 U.S. 1; *West India Oil Co. v. Domenech*, 311 U.S. 20., also see; Langdell, "The Status of our New Territories," 12 Harvard Law Review 365, 371; see also Thayer, "Our New Possessions," 12 Harvard Law Review 464; Thayer, "The Insular Tariff Cases in the Supreme Court," 15 Harvard Law Review 164; Littlefield, "The Insular Cases," 15 Harvard Law Review 169, 281.

The Court in *Hooven*, supra, indicated that this was the last time it would address the issue; it would just be judicially noticed.

The issue arose in *Brushaber v. Union Pacific Railroad Company,*[o] In that case, the high Court affirmed that the "United States" could levy a tax on the income of a nonresident alien when that income was derived from sources WITHIN the "United States" (i.e., its territorial or political jurisdiction).

Affirming the decision in *Brushaber*, supra, the Commissioner of Internal Revenue, with the approval of the Secretary of the Treasury, promulgated the Court's decision as Treasury Decision ("T.D.") 2313.

T.D. 2313 declared that Frank R. Brushaber was a "Nonresident Alien" with respect to the "United States." In addition, T.D. 2313 declared, as did the Court, that the Union Pacific Railroad Company was a "Domestic Corporation" with respect to the "United States" (i.e. its territorial jurisdiction).

The Complaint filed by Mr. Brushaber demonstrated that he was a nonresident of the "United States," residing instead in the State of New York, in the borough of Brooklyn and a Citizen thereof, his principal place of business being in the borough of Manhattan. He owned stocks and bonds issued by the Union Pacific Railroad Company, upon which a cash dividend was declared to him by said company, a domestic corporation of the "United States." Union Pacific was chartered by an Act of Congress for the territory of the federal state of Utah, in order to build a railroad and telegraph line and other purposes. It is a matter of public record that the Union Pacific Railroad

Company was a domestic "United States" corporation, of the federal state of Utah, residing in the District of Columbia, with its principal place of business in Manhattan, New York. The Corporation was created by an Act of the "United States" Senate and House of Representatives under the exclusive authority granted by the Constitution for the United States at Article 1, §8, Clause17 on July 1, 1862 by the 37th Congress.[p] Considering the foregoing res judicata on the matter of the diversity of citizenship of the two parties, it is clear that Mr. Brushaber was a "nonresident alien with respect to the United States." Brushaber had income from sources within said "United States." His income derived from the Union Pacific Railroad Company, a corporate citizen created by Congress and residing WITHIN the "United States" i.e. the District of Columbia.

"[A] domestic corporation is an artificial person whose residence or domicile is fixed by law within the territorial jurisdiction of the state which created it. That residence cannot be changed temporarily or permanently by the migrations of its officers or agents to other jurisdictions. So long as it is an existing corporation, its residence, citizenship, domicile, or place of abode is within the state which created it. It cannot reside or have its domicile elsewhere; neither can it in legal contemplation be absent from the state of its creation." [q]

Related cases are *Hylton v. United States*, 3 U.S. (3 Dall.) 171 (1796): Hylton was a Congressman; his salary was income from sources WITHIN the "United States." See also *Springer v. U.S.*, 102 U.S. 586 (1881): Springer, a Virginia Citizen, operated a carriage business in the District of Columbia.

The first paragraph of the Secretary's Treasury Decision is quoted here as follows:

(T.D. 2313)

Income Tax

Taxability of interest from bonds and dividends on stock of domestic corporations owned by nonresident aliens, and the liabilities of nonresident aliens under Section 2 of the act of October 3rd 1913.

To collectors of internal revenue:

Under the decision of the Supreme Court of the United States in the case of *Brushaber v. Union Pacific Railway [sic] Co.*, decided January 24, 1916, it is hereby held that *income accruing to nonresident aliens in the form of interest from the bonds and dividends on the stock of domestic corporations is subject to the income tax* imposed by the act of October 3, 1913. [Emphasis added]

The above decision by the Secretary of the Treasury determined that a tax on income derived from rents, sales of property, wages, professions, or a trade or business WITHIN the "United States" was applicable to such "income" when payable to a nonresident alien, i.e. a Union States Citizen.

"Domestic" in the "United States" statutes means inside the District of Columbia, possessions, territories and enclaves of the "United States," i.e. federal states of which there are 14. All income tax provisions under 26 U.S.C. Subtitle A (an excise tax on "income"), are divided between sources WITHIN and WITHOUT the "United States." They are taxes imposed upon the worldwide income of citizens of the "United States" and aliens residing therein. This provision of the code applies to nonresident aliens of all species, receiving income from sources WITHIN said "United States," as well as WITHIN the other parts of the American Empire that fall WITHIN the exclusive legislative jurisdiction of the Congress of the "United States" pursuant to Article 1, §8, Clause 17 and Article 4, §3, Clause2.

CONSTITUTIONAL AUTHORITY GRANTED TO CONGRESS

The Constitution, in Article 1, § 8, and Clauses l thru 16, grants to Congress the power to act for the fifty Union States as an international representative and to do so without (outside) the boundaries of each of those fifty States.

The Constitution specified to Congress the seat of government, subsequently known as the District of Columbia. In time, Congress created a government for the "District" and this "District" became a federal state by definition. However, this "state" (District of Columbia) is not "united" by or under the Constitution for the United States of America. The District has never joined the Union although several unsuccessful attempts have been made to achieve this end.

Furthermore, the Constitution granted to Congress the authority to govern the "District," just as the Legislatures of each of the several States of the Union govern their States within the geographical limits of those States. As Congress began to legislate for the "District" under authority of Article 1, §8, Clauses 17 and 18, the difference between the citizens of the "District" and the Citizens of the Union became apparent. The citizens of the "District" did not possess the right of suffrage or other rights retained by the Citizens of the Republic States (see *Balzac, De Lima* and *Downes*, supra,) and were therefore not recognized as a part of the Sovereign Body of "We the People." The Constitution for the United States of America provided no means of taxing these "District" citizens of the "United States." A method was found by forming municipal governments and exercising taxing power over these citizens within the territories of the "United States" as was decided by "*The Insular Cases*" (see *Bidwell*, supra.)

"The Constitution was made for States, not territories," wrote Daniel Webster. "[T]he Constitution of the United States as such does not under it extend beyond the limits of the States which are united by and under it." wrote author Langdell in "The Status of Our New Territories," 12 Harvard Law Review 365, 371.

Judicial note should be taken that the United States Constitution, prior to the 14th Amendment, always denoted "Citizen" and "Person" in capital letters; thereafter, "citizen" and "person" were not capitalized. The distinction between "citizens of the United States" and "Union State Citizens" has been fully recognized by the Congress and the Courts as follows:

"We have in our political system a government of the United States and a government of each of the several States. Each one of these governments is distinct from the others, and each has citizens of its own who owe it allegiance, and whose rights, within its jurisdiction, it must protect."[r] [Emphasis added]

The Federal Government is a "state."[s]

Foreign State. A foreign country or nation. The several United States are considered "foreign" to each other except as regards their relations as common members of the Union. [*Black's Law Dictionary*, Sixth Edition, page 1407]

Congress identifies these citizens of the "District" as "individuals" or citizens who reside in the "United States" and who are subject to the direct control of Congress in its local taxing and other municipal laws.

In *De Lima*, supra, the U.S. Attorney defined federal taxes with the following words, at page 99-108:

"Federal taxation is either general or local. Local taxes are levied under Article 1, Section 8, Paragraph 1; local taxes are for the support of territorial or non-state governments."

Congress imposed a federal excise tax on the "income" of these citizens or "individuals," at 26 U.S.C., § 1, as a local municipal tax. Such taxes are not for the common welfare of the United States of America but are to defray the expense of the government of the locality. In the dual position which Congress occupies in our system of federal government and as local municipal government for the territory of the United States not ceded by the States of the Union, Congress has the power to tax only for local purposes in the latter role [*De Lima*, supra, page 99], hence the term "from sources WITHIN the United States." General taxes are of two kinds: "direct" and what for brevity may be called "indirect," meaning duties, imposts, and excises. Direct taxes must be laid on all the States alike. [*De Lima*, supra, page 100]

A Citizen of one of the fifty States, residing therein, is a nonresident alien with respect to this local taxing power of Congress (see *Brushaber*, supra). Outside the geographical area of the "United States" as that term is defined,[r] Congress lacks power to support the local municipal government of the District by imposing a tax on the incomes of nonresident aliens (ones outside the locality, i.e. Citizens of the fifty States), UNLESS they reside within that jurisdiction by residence, or UNLESS the source of their income is situated WITHIN that geographical territory. The "withholding agent" must withhold any income arising from sources therein at the source,[u] unless the recipient is engaged in a trade or business WITHIN. For a full understanding of this local taxation, see pages 55 and 99-108 of *De Lima*, supra. For confirmation of the domestic municipal jurisdiction of the "United States," see *Downes*, supra, at pages 383-388.

Congress has control of these "individuals," whether they "reside" WITHIN the "United States" territorial states or WITHOUT the "United States." These "individuals," i.e., born within the jurisdiction of Congress, such as citizens born in the District of Columbia or in one of the territories, whether they reside within "United States" territories or without the "United states "in the "foreign countries" as defined[v] or abroad, are still liable for the federal income tax unless they abrogate that citizenship by naturalization or otherwise.[w] However,[x] Congress has exempted from taxation all "foreign earned income" of these citizen individuals except for Puerto Ricans.[y]

Another species of nonresident alien is those citizens of contiguous countries such as Mexico, Canada and other foreign sovereign nations. These foreigners, residents or nonresidents, as the case may be, are subject to the tax on incomes received from any place within the American Empire, i.e. in these united States of America and in the "United States." A Union State Citizen previously nonresident may lose his nonresident status by residing within the territorial sovereignty of the "United States" for 183 days,[z] thereby becoming subject to the local municipal tax on incomes received from sources within and without the "United States" (i.e. worldwide income). The income tax is a Municipal Local Tax imposed within the "United States." Plaintiffs are strangers to this locality.

DEFINITIONS IN 26 U.S.C.

THE INTERNAL REVENUE CODE

The definitions used in 26 U.S.C. are very clear in defining "State" and "United States." In every definition that uses the word "include" or "including," only the words that follow are defining of the term. For example:

The term "State" includes the District of Columbia, the Commonwealth of Puerto Rico, the Virgin Islands, Guam, and American Samoa.[aa]

United States. – The term "United States," when used in a geographical sense, includes only the States and the District of Columbia.[ab]

The federal government has used these definitions correctly, but its agents of the Internal Revenue Service and the Department of Justice seem to erroneously assume that the definitions mean the fifty States of the Union (America) when they look at the word "States" in 26 U.S.C. 7701(a)(9). It would be disingenuous to use the common everyday meaning of the terms "United States" or "State" when talking about the tax laws and many other laws that are enacted under the local municipal authority of the "United States" government within and for the District of Columbia.

The following congressional Acts reveal the crafty illusory way in which the federal government uses correct English and how Congress changes the meanings of words by using "congressional" definitions. For example, all the United States Code definitions had to be changed to allow Alaska and Hawaii to join the Union of States united under the Constitution. When Alaska joined the Union, Congress added a new definition of "States of the United States."[ac] This definition had never appeared before, to wit:

Sec. 48. Whenever the phrase "continental United States" is used in any law of the United States enacted after the date of enactment of this Act, it shall mean the 49 States on the North American Continent and the District of Columbia, unless *otherwise expressly provided.*[ad] [Emphasis added]

Where is it otherwise expressly provided?

Answer:

Sec. 22. (a) Section 2202 of the Internal Revenue Code of 1954 (relating to missionaries in foreign service), and sections 3121(e)(1), 3306(j), 4221(d)(4), and 4233 (b) of such code (each relating to a special definition of "State") are amended by striking out "Alaska".

(b) Section 4262 (c) (1) of the Internal Revenue Code of 1954 (definition of "continental United States") is amended to read as follows: "(1) Continental United States. – The term 'continental United States' means the District of Columbia and the States other than Alaska."

When Hawaii was admitted to the Union, Congress again changed the above definition, to wit:

Sec. 18. (a) Section 4262 (c)(l) of the Internal Revenue Code of 1954 (relating to the definition of "continental United States" for purposes of the tax on transportation of persons) is amended to read as follows:

"(1) Continental United States. – The term 'continental United States' means the District of Columbia and the States other than Alaska and Hawaii."

WHAT ARE THE STATES OTHER THAN ALASKA AND HAWAII?

They certainly cannot be the other forty-eight States united by and under the Constitution, because Alaska and Hawaii at that point in time had just joined the Union, right? The same definitions apply to the Social Security Act. So, what is left? Answer: the District of Columbia, Puerto Rico, Guam, Virgin Islands, Northern Mariana Islands, etc. These are the States of (i.e. belonging to) the "United States" and which are under its sovereignty and exclusive political jurisdiction. Do not confuse this term with States of the Union, because the word "of" means "belonging to" in this context.

Congress can also change the definition of "United States" for two sentences and then revert back to the definition it used before these two sentences. This is proven in Public Law 86-624, page 414, under School Operation Assistance in Federally Affected Areas.

Affected Areas, section (d)(2): "The fourth sentence of such subsection is amended by striking out 'in the continental United States (including Alaska)' and inserting in lieu thereof '(other than Puerto Rico, Wake Island, Guam, or the Virgin Islands)' and by striking out 'continental United States' in clause (ii) of such sentence and inserting in lieu thereof 'United States' (which for purposes of this sentence and the next sentence means the fifty States and the District of Columbia). The fifth sentence of such subsection is amended by striking out 'continental' before 'United States' each time it appears therein and by striking out 'including Alaska.'"

This one section, standing alone and by the words of its construction, contains all the evidence needed to prove that the term "United States" on either side of these sentences do not mean the fifty States united by and under the Constitution. If that is not convincing, then see the following:

26 C.F.R. 31.3121(e) -1 State, United States, and citizen.

(a) When used in the regulations in this subpart, the term "State" includes [in its restrictive form] the District of Columbia, the Commonwealth of Puerto Rico, the Virgin Islands, the Territories of Alaska and Hawaii before their admission as States, and (when used with respect to services performed after 1960) Guam and American Samoa.

(b) When used in the regulations in this subpart, the term "United States", when used in a geographical sense, means the several states, (including the Territories of Alaska and Hawaii before their admission as States), the District of Columbia, the Commonwealth of Puerto Rico, and the Virgin Islands. When used in the regulations in this subpart with respect to services performed after 1960, the term "United States" also includes [in its expansive form] Guam and American Samoa when the term is used in a geographical sense. The term "citizen of the United States" includes [in its restrictive form] a citizen of the Commonwealth of Puerto Rico or the Virgin Islands, and, effective January 1, 1961, a citizen of Guam or American Samoa. [Emphasis added]

Alaska and Hawaii fit the definition of "State" only before joining the Union. That means that the definition of "State" was never meant to be the forty-eight, now fifty, States of the Union unless distinctly expressed.

If paragraph (b) clouds men's mind, the following is submitted:

The word "geographical" was never used in tax law until Alaska and Hawaii joined the Union, and it is not defined in the Internal Revenue Code. So, we must use the definition found in the *Standard Random House Dictionary*:

ge.o.graph.i.cal 1. of or pertaining to geography 2. or pertaining to the natural features, population, industries, etc., of a region or regions.

Were you born in the "United States"? The preposition "in" shows that the "United States" in this question is a place, a geographical place named "United States." It is singular, even though it ends in "s." It also can be plural when referring to the Union States, which are places that exist by agreement.

Every human in a nation is a natural Citizen of a place called a nation if he was born in that nation. Those same people must be naturalized (born again) if they want to become a citizen of another nation. Original citizenship exists because of places, not agreements. This is what is referred to as *Jus soli*, the law of the place of one's birth.[ae] Here are two questions, your own answers to which will prove the status distinction. In a geographical sense, where is the State of Minnesota located on the American Continent? In a geographical sense, where is the "United States" (Congress) located on the American Continent?

Additional supporting argument is found in legislation written by Congress to solve a problem caused by the admission of Alaska and Hawaii to the Union. Since typewriters were purchased by the government from the areas that had just joined the Union, namely Alaska and Hawaii, according to Title 1 USC, Congress was required to use a term that is NOT used in the

Internal Revenue Code, in order to buy the same typewriters from the same geographical area:

Sec. 45. Title 1 of the Independent Offices Appropriation Act, 1960, is amended by striking out the words "for the purchase within the continental limits of the United States of any typewriting machines" and inserting in lieu thereof "for the purchase within the STATES OF THE UNION AND THE DISTRICT OF COLUMBIA OF ANY TYPEWRITING MACHINES." [Emphasis added]

The Supreme Court obviously understands the distinction of citizenship for purposes of declarations made under penalties of perjury. The Court approved the statute[af] which separately defines declarations to be made by citizens made WITHIN and WITHOUT the "United States" as follow:

If executed WITHOUT the United States: I declare ... under the laws of the United States of America that the foregoing is true and correct. [Emphasis added]

If executed WITHIN the United States, its territories, possessions, or commonwealths: I declare ...that the foregoing is true and correct. [Emphasis added]

The latter declaration above is the declaration found on IRS Form 1040 and similar IRS forms.

And, 28 USC 1603(a)(3) states as follows:

(3) which is neither a citizen of a State of the United States as defined in section 1332(c] and (d) of this title ...

Section 1332 (d). The word "States" as used in this section, includes the Territories, the District of Columbia, and the Commonwealth of Puerto Rico.

Examples of Two Definitions of the term "United States" in 26 U.S.C.

First Definition:

Title 26 U.S.C. 7701(a) (9):

(9) United States. – The term "United States" when used in a geographical sense includes only the States and the District of Columbia.

Second Definition:

Title 26 U.S.C. 4612(a) (4) (A):

(A) In general. – The term "United States" means the fifty States, the District of Columbia, the Commonwealth of Puerto Rico, any possession of the United States, the Commonwealth of the Northern Mariana Islands, and the Trust Territory of the Pacific Islands. [Emphasis added]

The Supreme Court clarified the issue in *Hepburn & Dundas v. Ellsey*,[ag] stating that the District of Columbia is not a "State" within the meaning of the Constitution. Therefore it is apparent that the meaning of the term "States" in the first definition above can mean only the territories and possessions belonging to the "United States" because of the specific mention of the District of Columbia and the specific omission of the fifty States.[ah] The District of Columbia is not a "State" within the meaning of the Constitution; therefore, the fifty States are specifically excluded from this first definition of the term "United States."

Congress has no problem naming the "fifty States" when it is legislating for them, so, in the second definition of the term "United States" above, Congress expressly mentions them and there is no misunderstanding. If a statute in 26 U.S.C. does not have a special "word of art" definition for the term "United States," then the first Definition of the term "United States" is always used (see above) because of the general nature of that term as defined by Congress. English Grammar is inflexible and any use of the language in violation of the law of grammar is a fraudulent use of the English language. The total abandonment of grammatical discipline may be found in many of the Internal Revenue Services Forms.[ai]

When citizens or residents of the first "United States" are without the geographical area of this first "United States," their "compensation for personal services actually rendered" is defined as "foreign earned income."[aj]

911(b) Foreign Earned Income.

(d) (2) Earned Income.

(A) In general. – The term "earned income" means wages, salaries, or professional fees, and other amounts received as compensation for personal services actually rendered, but does not include that part of the compensation derived by the taxpayer for personal services rendered by him to a corporation which represents a distribution of earnings or profits rather than a reasonable allowance as compensation for the personal services actually rendered.

A citizen or resident of the first "United States" does not pay a tax on his "compensation for personal services actually rendered" while residing outside of the first "United States" because Congress has exempted all such compensation from taxation under 26 U.S.C., Section 911(a)(1), which reads as follows:

911(a) Exclusion from Gross Income. – ... [T]here shall be excluded from the gross income of such individual, and exempt from taxation ... [1] the foreign earned income of such individual...

When residing without (outside) this "United States," the citizen or resident of this "United States" pays no tax on "foreign earned income" but is required to file a return, claiming the exemption.[ak] (Exhibit #)

Title 26 C.F.R., Section 871-13 (c) permits the District citizen to abandon his citizenship or residence in the "United States" by residing elsewhere.

Title 26 C.F.R. Section 1.911-2(g) defines the term "United States" as follows:

(g) United States. The term "United States," when used in a geographical sense, includes any territory under the sovereignty of the United States. It includes the states [Puerto Rico, Guam, Mariana Islands, etc.], the District of Columbia, the possessions and territories of the United States, the territorial waters of the United States, the airspace over the United States, and the seabed and subsoil of those submarine areas which are adjacent to the territorial waters of the United States and over which the United States has exclusive rights, in accordance with international law."

This term "state" evidently does not embrace one of the fifty States of which Plaintiff is a free inhabitant, united by the Constitution, because they are separate governments or foreign states with respect to the "United States," District of Columbia, its territories, possessions and enclaves. None of the fifty united States comes under the sovereignty of the "United States" and subsection (h) defines the fifty States united by the Constitution as "foreign countries":

(h) Foreign country. The term "foreign country," when used in a geographical sense, includes any territory under the sovereignty of a government other than that of the United States.[al]

All of the fifty States are foreign with respect to each other and are under the sovereignty of their respective Legislatures, except where a power has been expressly delegated to Congress. The Citizens of each Union State are foreigners and aliens with respect to another Union State unless they establish a residence therein under the laws of that Union State. Otherwise, they are nonresident aliens with respect to all the other Union States.

The regulations at 26 C.F.R. Section 1.1-1 (a) state, in pertinent part:

(a) General Rule. (1) Section 1 of the Code imposes an income tax on the income of every individual who is a citizen or resident of the United States and, to the extent provided by Section 871(b) or 877(b), on the income of a nonresident alien individual.

Title 26 U.S.C. § 1 imposes a tax on "taxable income" as follows, in pertinent part:

There is hereby imposed on the taxable income of ... every married individual ... who makes a single return jointly with his spouse under section 6013...

The regulations promulgated to explain 26 U.S.C. Section 1 are found in 26 C.F.R., Section 1.1-1, and state in pertinent part:

(a) General Rule. (1) Section 1 of the Code imposes an income tax on the income of every individual who is a citizen or resident of the United States and, to the extent provided by Section 871(b) or 877(b), on the income of a nonresident alien individual.

Please note that the term "taxable income" is not used as such in the above statute because the "income" of those classes of individuals mentioned is taxable as "taxable income".

Section 1.871 Classification and manner of taxing alien individuals

(a) Classes of aliens. For purposes of the income tax, alien individuals are divided generally into two classes, namely, resident aliens and nonresident aliens.

(b) Classes of nonresident aliens.

(1) In general. For purposes of the income tax, nonresident alien individuals are divided into the following three classes:

(i) Nonresident alien individuals who at no time during the taxable year are engaged in a trade or business in the United States,

(ii) Nonresident alien individuals who at any time during the taxable year are, or are deemed under Section 1.871-9 to be engaged in a trade or business in the United States, and

(iii) NOT APPLICABLE (concerns residents of Puerto Rico)

Title 26 C.F.R., Section 871-13 states as follows:

(a) In general. (1) An individual who is a citizen or resident of the United States at the beginning of the taxable year but a nonresident alien at the end of the taxable year, or a nonresident alien at the beginning of the taxable year but a citizen or resident of the United States at the end of the taxable year, is taxable for such year as though his taxable year were comprised of two separate periods, one consisting of the time during which he is a citizen or resident of the United States and the other consisting of the time during which he is not a citizen or resident of the United States.

NONRESIDENT ALIEN

The federal Income tax is a local municipal tax for the "United States" designed to support local government. In order for an individual, a State Citizen of the Union States, to become liable for this tax, he/she must be a resident therein (i.e. a resident alien). Or receive income from sources therein, or be engaged in a trade or business therein or receive income from a source of an excise taxable event.

In 26 U.S.C., Section 7701(b) (1) (A) and (B), Congress defined the statutory difference between "resident alien" and "nonresident alien" as follows:

(b) Definitions of Resident Alien and Nonresident Alien.

(1) In general. – For purposes of this title

(A) Resident Alien. – An alien individual shall be treated as a resident of the United States with respect to any calendar year if (and only if) such individual meets the requirements of clause (i), (ii), or (iii):

(i) Lawfully admitted for permanent residence. – Such individual is a lawful permanent resident of the United States at any time during such calendar year.

(ii) Substantial presence. – Such individual meets the substantial presence test of paragraph (3)

(iii) First year election. – Such individual makes the election provided in subparagraph (4)

(B) Nonresident Alien. – An individual is a nonresident alien if such individual is neither a citizen of the United States nor a resident of the United States (within the meaning of subparagraph (A))

Plaintiffs are not "residents" (as that term is defined in the above statutes) nor are they citizens of this "United States." They are nonresident aliens as that term is defined in subsections (B) and (A)(i), (ii), and (iii), and they have the same status as the Plaintiff in Brushaber, supra.

INDIVIDUALS REQUIRED TO MAKE RETURNS OF INCOME

The following individuals are required to make returns of income:

26 CFR Section 1.6012-1. Individuals are required to make returns of income.

(a) Individual citizen or resident. –

(1) In general. ...an income tax return must be filed by every individual... if such individual is...

(i) A citizen of the United States, whether residing at home or abroad,

(ii) A resident of the United States even though not a citizen thereof, or

(iii) An alien bona fide resident of Puerto Rico during the entire taxable year.

(Plaintiff's name and wife's) clearly are not defined in the above statutes, but are defined in the following statute as ones that are not required to make a return.

Title 26 C.F.R., Section 1.6013-1 states:

(b) Nonresident Alien. A joint return shall not be made if either the husband or wife at any time during the taxable year is a nonresident alien.

Mr. (Plaintiff's name) and Mrs. (wife's name) are nonresident aliens with respect to the "United States," with no income derived from sources within the "United States" and with no source income derived from excise taxable events.

Title 26 C.F.R., § 871-7 states, in pertinent part, as follows:

Except as otherwise provided in Section 1.871-12, a nonresident alien individual to whom this section applies *is not subject to the tax imposed by section 1 or section 1201(b) 5,* but, pursuant to the provision of section 871(a), is liable to a flat tax of 30 percent upon the aggregate of the amounts determined under paragraphs (b), (c), and (d) of this section which are received during the taxable year *from sources within the United States.* [Emphasis added]

Please note 26 C.F.R., Section 1.871-4(b), proof of residence of aliens, which establishes a key legal presumption:

(b) Nonresidence presumed. An alien by reason of this alienage is presumed to be a nonresident alien.

Further facts are illustrated by the definition of "withholding agent" at 26 U.S.C. Section 7701(a)(16):

Withholding agent. – The term "withholding agent" means any person required to deduct and withhold any tax under the provisions of section 1441, 1442, 1443, or 1461.

Title 26 U.S.C. Section 1441 refers to nonresident aliens who receive income from sources within the "United States" as set forth in Section 871(a)(1). The other sections do not apply to the Plaintiffs.

Your attention is invited to 26 C.F.R., Section 31.3401(a)(6)-l (b), which states as follows:

Remuneration for services performed outside the United States. Remuneration paid to a nonresident alien individual for services performed outside the United States is excepted from wages and hence is NOT SUBJECT TO WITHHOLDING. [Emphasis added]

As a rule, military retirement pay of a nonresident alien individual is exempted from the income tax at 26 C.F.R., Section 31.3401(a)-l(b)(l)(ii), with the following exception:

Where such retirement pay or disability annuity ... is paid to a nonresident alien individual, withholding is required only in the case of such amounts paid to a nonresident alien individual who is a resident of Puerto Rico.

and at 26 C.F.R., Section 935-1(a)(3):

[F]or special rules for determining the residence for tax purposes of individuals under military or naval orders, see section 514 of the Soldiers' and Sailors' Civil Relief Act of 1946, 50 App. U.S.C. 574. The residence of an individual and, therefore, the jurisdiction with which he is required to file an income tax return under paragraph (b) of this section, may change from year to year.

Section 574(1) of The Soldiers' and Sailors' Relief Act states that:

For the purposes of taxation in respect of the personal property, income, or gross income of any such person by any State, Territory, possession, or political subdivision of any of the foregoing, or the District of Columbia, of *which such person is not a resident or in which he is not domiciled* ... personal property shall not be deemed to be located or present in or to have a situs for taxation in such State, Territory, possession or political subdivision, or district. [Emphasis added]

AUTHORITY FOR THE COURT TO ISSUE THE INJUNCTION

In *Botta v. Scanlon*,[am] the Court set forth the general exceptions to the bar,[an] stating:

"[I]t has long been settled that this general prohibition is subject to exception in the case of an individual taxpayer against a particular collector where the tax is clearly illegal or other special circumstances of an unusual character make an appeal to equitable remedies appropriate."[ao]

The Court then gave a number of examples as follow:

"(a) Suits to enjoin collection of taxes which are not due from the plaintiff but, in fact, are due from others. For example, see *Rafael v. Granger*, 3 Cir. 1952, 196 F.2d 620, 622....

"(b) Cases in which plaintiff definitely showed that the taxes sought to be collected were 'probably' not validly due. For example, *Midwest Haulers Inc. v. Brady*, 6 Cir. 1942, 128 F.2d 496, and *John M. Hirst & Co. v. Gentsch*, 6 Cir. 1943, 133 F.2d 247.

"(c) Cases in which a penalty was involved. For example, *Hill v. Wallace*, 259 U.S. 44, 42 S.Ct 453, 66 L.Ed, 822; *Lipke v. Lederer*, 259 U.S. 557, 42 S.Ct. 549, 66 L.Ed. 1061; *Regal Drug Corporation v. Wardell*, 260 U.S. 386, 43 S.Ct 152, 67 L.Ed 318; *Alien v. Regents of the University System of Georgia*, 304 U.S. 439, 58 S.Ct 980, 82 L.Ed 1148.

"(e) Cases based upon tax assessment fraudulently obtained by the tax Collector by coercion. For example, *Mitsukiyo Yoshimura v. Alsup*, 9 Cir. 1948, 167 F.2d 104 "(141 F.Supp. at page 338)."

[4] In the present case, if any of the plaintiffs are not subject to any tax liability, such plaintiff might well be within the exception stated in 9 Mertens, law of Federal Income Taxation, Section 49.213, Chapter 49, page 226, as follows:

"[2] It is equally well settled [sic] that the Revenue laws relate only to taxpayers. No procedure is prescribed for a nontaxpayer where the Government seeks to levy on property belonging to him for the collection of another's tax, and no attempt has been made to annul the ordinary rights or remedies of a non-taxpayer in such cases. If the Government sought to levy on the property of A for a tax liability owing to B, A could not and would not be required to pay the tax under protest and then institute an action to recover the amount so paid. His remedy would be to go into a court of competent jurisdiction and enjoin the Government from proceeding against his property." In Tomlinson v. Smith, 7 Cir, 1942, 128 F.2d 808 ... the Court affirmed an order granting interlocutory injunction and noted the "distinction between suits instituted by taxpayers and non-taxpayers." (at page 811)

CONCLUSION

Plaintiffs are in no way subjected to any derivative liability for the District's local municipal tax. The procedures set forth in 26 C.F.R. do not authorize the Secretary or his delegate to manufacture income and tax it where a Person is without the taxable class. Title 26 C.F.R., § 871 is unclouded in that where there is no income from sources within the "United States" by a nonresident alien; the choice is delegated to that person by Congress as to whether a return is to be filed or not.[ap] This is why the system is repeatedly referred to as a voluntary compliance system. Where the Secretary determines the existence of taxable income when there has been no return, he should sign the substitute return and assume the responsibility for the determination.[aq]

Treasury Decision 2313 explains that the withholding agent is responsible for withholding the tax from sources within the "United States," for filing a Form 1040NR and for paying over the tax withheld from said nonresident alien.[ar] Therefore, no penalties should accrue to the Plaintiffs.

Plaintiffs were not aware of the information contained in this Memorandum of Law during the early years of their lives and reported "earned income" from their labor in the foreign States of the Union, and paid a local municipal tax of the "United States." This fact in no way subjects them to liability to the present day, nor does that fact in anyway change their status as Citizens of one of the Republic Union States. Nor does it change their status from nonresident aliens to the "individual" defined in 26 C.F.R., Section 1.1-1. Nor does it justify the Secretary's actions taken when the Plaintiffs, knowing their true status, repeatedly informed him through his agents, the Internal Revenue Service, of said status. The Secretary is *presumed to function in good faith*, much as is a criminal defendant *presumed innocent.* The Secretary is required to know the law he is administering. He is to administer said laws with justice and equality within the parameters mandated by Congress. By the Secretary's action in ignoring the law, once administratively noticed by the plaintiff, the mantel of presumed "good faith" wears perilously thin and any *good faith immunity, lost.* The Executive branch of government, the Congress and the Courts, all discourage arbitrary and malicious actions of their agents; to do otherwise would sanction tyranny. Pursuant to Federal Rule of Evidence 301, the burden now rests with the Defendants to bring forward evidence in rebuttal of any facts stated by the Plaintiffs herein.

CHAPTER TWELVE

WAR POWERS

If ye love wealth better than liberty, the tranquility of servitude better than the animating contest of freedom, go home from us in peace. We ask not your counsels or arms. Crouch down and lick the hands, which feed you. May your chains set lightly upon you, and may posterity forget that ye were our countryman. – Samuel Adams, August 1, 1776

How can the President and Congress do what they were prohibited from doing by the Constitution with complete impunity from the law?

Every chapter of this book has covered a topic that addresses a violation of some constitutional provision and deprivation of the rights of "We the People" by the de facto government. The question I am always asked is, "How can they get away with it?" Try as I may, I cannot find any legal theory that makes sense to me with the exception of the following.

This is my theory. It may be valid or not; you decide.

Is the Constitution alive and well ... or did it ever really exist?

There are those who believe there never existed a Constitution, in that it was never signed by any principal to the agreement; it was merely witnessed. That argument may have some legal currency under Contract Law; however, for our purposes, let us assume that there was and is a Constitution.

To understand our present day court system, we must examine first causes – the general nature of Emergency War Powers, martial law, and martial rule – to see how they operate, if in fact they do operate in our judiciary and why. Notice I didn't say "justice system," because if you want justice, go to church; you will not find it in our courts of law.

Characteristics of Emergency Powers

"Emergency Powers" means any form of military style government, martial law, or martial rule. Martial law and martial rule are not the same, as will be covered in greater detail.

NOTE: The term "emergency powers" is generic, as used herein.

Nations declare emergency powers under the Doctrine of Necessity when a crisis like war, riots, rebellion, financial collapse, possibly Y2K type crises, etc., occur, – crises that cannot be dealt with in a normal, peaceful manner. This has been the traditional manner of dealing with these emergency situations for several hundred years. Emergency powers are theoretically a temporary measure to deal with the specific event. When the crisis ends, emergency powers usually end as well. Only such has not been the case with the good ole United States.

Franklin Roosevelt declared emergency power in 1933 to deal with an alleged banking crisis in progress when he assumed the Presidency. In fact, the crisis was a figment of the Federal Reserve bankers' imagination. They had embezzled most of the gold on deposit in their banks and were running scared when they could not redeem the certificates for depositors, and they believed that by claiming the American people were hoarding gold, precipitating a banking crisis, they would then be off the hook. It suited Roosevelt's plans as a socialist to implement his "New Deal" agenda. The crisis permitted him to seize control of the nation and maintain it by Executive Order (Martial Rule). So he accepted the Federal Reserve Board's request, which amended the 1917 Wars Powers Act, giving the President license over all of the citizens of this country, rather than just an enemy. We became the enemy of our country under the language of the 1933 amended version of the 1917 War Powers Act, and as far as the federal government is concerned, we remain so to this day. It fits their purpose.

Congress returned from its annual recess and rubber-stamped Roosevelt's Executive Orders, and the Federal power grab began. From that day to the present, the United States of America has been under emergency war. Presidents and the Congress, to maintain and justify the enormous growth in the power and socialist spending of the Federal government, have systematically exploited powers and its people.

The States cooperated with the Federal government because they benefited, right down to the County level, from a massive increase in their tax revenues and powers which were available to them only under these conditions. The real property of the individual citizenry could be taxed, as well as all personal property owned by the individual.

The gold or lawful coin of the United States having been removed from circulation set the stage for the fiat money of the Federal Reserve and the resultant income generated from its use in the form of tax on the people's labor for the use of private money lenders. There being no constitutional currency, Congress made law embracing the notion that the Federal Reserve Notes were legal tender for all debts public and private, another violation of their duty to protect and defend the Constitution, as no Amendment has ever been passed permitting the use of anything other than Gold or Silver Coin as lawful currency.

Tendering a debt however, is not the same as paying the debt. The debt remains; it is merely tendered.

The area over which Emergency powers may be declared can cover part of a state (city or county), several states, or an entire nation, as is the case today.

The single most dominant feature of all emergency powers government is civil authority. Civil courts cease to exist, being replaced by courts with an appearance of legitimacy, but without the substance in the form of equity and admiralty.

Court process and procedures are a mix of rules from previous lawful courts and military courts. Traffic courts, for example, are courts of summary court martial using military rules as applied to civilians. An example of this is seen when defining so-called "traffic infractions." "Infraction" is not defined in most state codes, but is defined in "The Manual of Courts Martial" (1994) Section (4) along with the terms "contempt," "appeal," etc., and in other military source manuals. This by itself should tell us all something.

Emergency powers government varies in the degree of the emergency declared. The most extreme form is called Martial Law. The benign, less restrictive form is Martial Rule. Currently the U.S. is under the less restrictive form called Martial Rule.

Martial law puts all major resources in an emergency power jurisdiction – transportation, food, minerals, metals, communications, etc. – under direct control of the nation's armed forces and its Commander-in-Chief, the President. A blizzard of Executive Orders have been issued, so that in the event the President declares a National Emergency, all resources and citizens come under the direct control of the Federal Emergency Management Agency (FEMA) and the severe Martial Law form of governance.

In its raw sense martial law governs via a democracy, never in a republic. "Military law" uses municipal law. Courts are draped with quasi-civil/military forms of law, evidenced by draped military standards in courtrooms, i.e., the gold-fringed flag of the United States, mounted on a pole. Lawful civil authority never flies flags, only banners, which are always hung from the back of the flag with the red and white stripes hanging vertically. Banners are never hung on a pole. Banners on a pole never represent civil authority, only military authority on the march.

Evidences of Emergency Powers

First, under emergency powers, there must be an active and visible occupation of the land by armed troops of the entity that declares emergency powers. This is called "open and notorious, armed and hostile, occupation of the land." Is there an armed occupation of America? The answer, of course, is, Yes!

Under the guise of national emergencies (hurricanes, floods, earthquakes, etc.), all National Guard units were federalized, and all policemen, firemen, highway patrol, state marshals and county sheriffs have been placed under control of the Guard since 1972. They are all under the control of Federal Emergency Management Agency, called the Multi-Jurisdictional Task Force, which centralizes military and law enforcement power under the Federal government and the Commander-in-Chief, the President.

Though law enforcement officers may not know it, they are in fact a force occupying the land for the Federal government. Our own neighbors hold us the people hostage.

The reason why active duty Federal forces are stationed in all National Guard Armories is obvious – to sustain the emergency powers control of the states and counties by the Federal government and to maintain martial rule in the hands of the President as Commander in Chief. By these means the Federal martial rule government maintains "open, notorious, and hostile, armed occupation of the land."

Military law recognizes only municipal law. So, states had to create municipal courts to punish "infractions" of Motor Vehicle Codes. Such courts fly the flag of the Commander-in-Chief (solid fringed flag), as they are really an arm or an extension of the power of the President. Their primary function is to collect war reparations through fines, penalties, etc. They all operate as quasi-military courts using summary court martial proceedings. This is why such courts try only matters of fact and why judges make and declare law on a case-by-case basis, without the controls of precedent or constitutional restrictions.

Municipal Court judges do this because they act for the Commander-in-Chief in the field under emergency conditions. Judges make any decision to resolve the case under Doctrines of Necessity. In such courts, the Constitution, Supreme Court decisions, and civil stare decisis are not permitted.

Under emergency powers the final authority is always the chief military commander, who in this nation is the Commander-in-Chief, i.e., the military office of the President of the United States. This accounts for Executive Order landslides since F.D.R., who first declared – openly – his seizure of Emergency Powers in March 1933, again, by Executive Orders. Executive Orders have the force and effect of law when published in the Federal Register, and by this means they become "Public Policy."

Since under emergency powers there is no *lawful*, civil, or constitutional authority nor any *lawful* civil courts, neither can there be any lawful civil or administrative process. All emergency power process MUST BE DEFECTIVE in form, content, and authority when such process is compared to lawful Process and, defective as it is, it is valid in all cases except when abated.

Thus, all court appearances are VOLUNTARY, because the Process Rule is: ALL DEFECTS OF PROCESS ARE CURED BY "VOLUNTARY" APPEARANCE. Lawful or constitutional process has no bearing on the case. In other words, it does not matter how many errors one finds in process from emergency powers courts. If you appear, you inform the court that you have waived defects of process. Submission to defects in process waves the protection of fundamental rights.

There are many that believe that "special appearances" (by paper work, motions, etc.) nullify a court jurisdiction. Under emergency powers this is false doctrine. There is no remedy in challenging a court's jurisdiction except by abating its process first.

Abatements are not a challenge to a court jurisdiction but merely a good faith attempt to correct errors in process: "Clear up the errors, Judge, and I'll appear." Special appearances fail when a judge knows what he's doing. Under martial rule, judges do whatever they want, whenever they want, so long as they do not alarm the public or disturb the peace. Jurisdiction is always granted to try jurisdictional questions even if one goes to higher courts. Defendants grant jurisdiction without knowing it because they never challenge the process that creates the jurisdiction in the first place. Process is perfected by appearance, special or otherwise. Also, remember, the court is not the building, the judge, or anyone else; it's the paperwork. If the court paperwork is defective, there is no court and it ceases to exist.

By necessity, field officers (judges, highway patrol, sheriffs, etc.) exercise powers of life and death to maintain authority given them by International Law that prohibits lawful civil authority or constitutional mandates. Such procedures are too timely and clumsy for military or quasi-military operations. In sum, constitutional and common law precedents are too restrictive of Federal, State, County, and City power. Further, military courts exercise "benefit of discussion" that gives a court jurisdiction as soon as a defendant answers a question or demands any response or action of a military court, such as Motion practice or Petitions for writ.

Arrest warrants and procedures do not conform to Constitutional law because they don't have to if a defendant appears in person or by "special appearance" paperwork. Arrest warrants with a judge's signature (black ink) and proper affidavits with true court seals are instruments of lawful process and cannot be used in emergency powers courts. Federal, State, County, and City emergency powers courts and other entities manipulate the English grammar to protect their own International law status. Thus, a state either writes its name as The State of Florida, (instead of Florida State) or in caps (instead of proper upper and lower case), or uses abbreviations such as FL, CA, TX, MT, KS, NY, NJ, and so on, all of which are misnomers and no names at all. International Law requires that neither party to a case, the State nor the person, can appear in their own name, but only under the nom de guerre (war name), as indicated by a name in all caps or one name with an abbreviation. This creates a "juristic personality" which grants jurisdiction to the Equity, Admiralty/Maritime courts.

Again, emergency powers courts have no lawful process because they have no lawful authority. All process by such courts is, therefore, defective because courts are forbidden to use lawful process unless and until voluntarily given to them.

The real irony is that the U.S. government, in cooperation with the States, created emergency powers courts to expand their power and increase revenue. But by doing so, they have themselves become vulnerable to lawful process.

Further, there is little they can do about it now without coming directly into conflict with International Law. This is why the United States government will never pull out of the United Nations, because the U.N. is the source of the United States' authority to protect itself under International Law.

The point is that one who brings properly written lawful process against unlawful process must prevail.

Attorneys-at-law

One who hires an attorney-at-law cannot bring lawful process against an emergency powers court. Remember that attorneys are agents of the court and use only process allowed by the court that admitted the attorney to practice. All bar members are agents of emergency power courts, and most don't even know it. One must therefore never hire an attorney to appear on a case in an emergency powers court because doing so makes one "non compos mentis" – i.e., not mentally competent – and automatically gives the court jurisdiction over ones' self.

Arrest warrants with a judge's signature (black ink), proper affidavits, and proper court seals, are lawful processes and cannot be used in emergency powers courts. That's why such warrants as are being issued today are never proper.

What about the Constitution of the united States of America in all this? Without lawful process or authority, the Constitution is a dead letter, a façade manipulated at the Federal government's whim, because lawful process itself is based on the Constitution and they are, thus, inter-dependent. In short, if one is gone, so must be the other. The government permits a defendant to raise constitutional defenses only when it suits their purposes and will not permit the defense when it is not in their best interest. For all intents and purposes, the Constitution is an illusion, kept by the government only as a pacifier for we the people, nothing more.

Lincoln set precedence for the subversion of the Constitution in the War Between the States in 1860 when he had printed non-interest money to support his declaration of war. His was the first "War Powers," resurrected in 1917 and then again in 1933, and it has never been repealed since. The Federal government's use of the Constitution comes down to this: if Constitutional cites fit a Federal need, they are used; if the Constitution or precedent does not fit, it is ignored. In other words, the Constitution is optional to the Federal government, because after all, you answer to the "Juristic Personality" name, spelled in all capital letters, placing you in Equity jurisdiction without the protection of the Constitution.

This is why so many Supreme Court decisions ("Right to Privacy" cases, abortion rights, Social Security, etc.), for which there are no Constitutional precedents, are made under the Doctrine of Necessity.

A "social agenda" is impossible without Doctrines of Necessity and International Law to justify the imposition of emergency powers as a first priority.

Remember that there was no Federal Social Security before passage of the International Labor Organizations Treaty (1935). This Treaty mandated a social consciousness and enfranchisement of the masses. This process of Socialism began with the massive entitlements programs the people are burdened with today.

A hidden Constitutional problem for Americans under emergency powers is that all Constitutional Rights become "privileges" that, by necessity and International law, can be given or taken away at whim.

Thus, in *California v. Simpson*, when Mark Fuhrman was called to testify about the infamous tapes, etc., he replied to all questions with: "I wish to assert my Fifth Amendment 'privilege.'" Note that Furhman asserted no right, only a privilege, using words given him by his attorney/agent of an emergency power court. Privileges, being removable at the whim of the Commander-in-Chiefs, tells us why Congress feels so free to modify Constitutional Rights such as those in the Second Amendment, i.e., gun ownership, etc.

The remaining question is how are emergency powers and martial law, or martial rule, terminated?

Emergency powers are terminated in only three ways:

1. A Commander-in-Chief can terminate emergencies by Executive Orders. The emergency then ends on a specific date and time. But a lawful civil authority must exist (UN?) to which he may cede authority. The past ten Presidents have not seen the need to return the country back to the people, and I don't hold out much hope of there ever being a President of that caliber who would do his duty.

2. If conquered by another, the conquering power can terminate emergency powers by its own Executive Order or decree. This point deserves some expanded discussion for reasons that will become clear below. Remember, the U.S. is, by International Law and Supreme Court decisions,

a "foreign principal" with respect to the States. Further, Title II of the United States Code, the Congress, is not positive law, only Resolution. This means that a Title (USC) stands only until it is successfully challenged in the courts. Why is this? Did not the Congress abandon without proper recess the first Session during Lincoln's administration in 1860? Does this not tell us why the U.S. flag flies over all state flags since F.D.R.'s Executive Orders on September 9, 1933? And is this not a sign of conquest over the states and the people when taken in conjunction with the changes in the "Trading with the Enemy Act" (1917) as amended 1933, language supplied him by the Federal Reserve Inc.?

3. The people, if they restore lawful civil courts, processes, and procedures under authority of "inherent political powers" and re-establish proper, civil and "de jure" government, can terminate the emergency.

Abatements are a primary tool in achieving a peaceful and lawful restoration of godly authority to this nation. You can see why abatements are one of the most important tools the people have. If the people lawfully resist any submission to emergency power courts, process and procedure, and respond to unlawful paperwork with lawful process, emergency powers are nullified, and become null and void, ab initio.

A question that may occur is: if the people restore lawful process and procedure, how do they restore lawful authority in the courts?

The answer is, by re-forming lawful jural societies, using remedies provided in the Bible, Christianity, common law, and assizing courts/juries in conjunction with the grand jury where necessary.

On the subject of Biblical Law, we cannot forget that it is still law and adopted as such by many states of the union. In Old Testament law we find not just our moral law but also God's rules of restitution and the standard of law on which the common law is based. Common law grew out of English, medieval ecclesiastical courts, where the people had no access to the Kings' Bench. In the Christian churches the people found true justice based on the Bible. More importantly, common law connects the Bible with the Constitution of the United States of America and We the People.

CAUTION

Federal, State, County, and City governments will not – repeat, *not* – assist the people in restoring common law and the Constitution. It is not in their best interest to do so. The entire system of welfare, income and property taxes, codes, ordinances, rules, regulations, and bureaucracy, would cease to exist in the blink of an eye within the States.

The People and Citizens of this Nation were forewarned against the formation of democracies. "Democracies have ever been the spectacles of turbulence and contention; have ever been found incompatible with personal security or the rights of property; and have in general been as short in their lives as they have been violent in their deaths." (*Federalist Papers* No. 10; also see: *The Fredrick Bastiat: Code Of Professional Responsibility*, Preamble.)

This alien constitution financed and engineered by Rockefeller, however, has nothing to do with democracy in reality, but is the basis of and for the development of a despotic and tyrannical oligarchy.

The "Constitution for the New States of the United States," Article I, "Rights and Responsibilities," Sections 1 and 15, is evidence of their knowledge of the "emergency." The Rights of expression, communication, movement, assembly, petition, and Habeas Corpus are all excepted from being exercised under and in a "declared emergency." The Constitution for the New states of America openly declares, among other seditious things and delusions, that "Until each indicated change in the government shall have been completed, the provisions of the existing constitution and the organs of government shall be in effect." (Article XII, Section 3) "All operations of the national government shall cease as they are replaced by those authorized under this constitution." (Article XII, Section 4)

This is apparently what former Justice Warren Burger was promoting in 1976 after he resigned as a Supreme Court Justice and took up the promotion of a "constitutional convention." No trial by jury is mentioned, "just" compensation has been removed along with being informed of the "nature and cause of the accusation," etc., etc., and every one will participate in the "democracy." This constitution is but a reiteration of communist doctrines, ideology, intents and purposes and clearly establishes a "police power" state, under the direction and control of a self-appointed oligarchy.

The present operation of the de facto government in the United States is under foreign/alien constitutions, laws, rules and regulations. The plan to overthrow the "essential engine" declared in and by the ordained and established Constitution for the United States of America (1787) and by and under the "Bill of Rights" (1791) is obvious. The covert procedure used to implement and enforce these foreign constitutions, laws, procedures, rules, regulations, etc., have been and continue to be collected, assimilated and acted upon. The overwhelming body of evidence establishes seditious collusion and conspiracy of its actors.

The Government is supposed to set the example that we the Citizens are required to emulate. When the Government breaks the law, then there exists no law; we have anarchy. That, I am afraid, is the state of the Union as of today. In the famous case *Elkins Et Al v. United States* (364 U.S. 206), the Supreme Court, in reinforcing judicial integrity, stated:

"In a government of laws, existence of the government will be imperiled if it fails to observe the law scrupulously. Our Government is the potent, the omnipresent teacher. For good or ill, it teaches the whole people by its example. Crime is contagious. If the Government becomes a lawbreaker, it breeds contempt for law, it invites every man to become a law unto himself, and it invites anarchy."

Perhaps the words "invites anarchy," used by Justice Brandeis, should say, "invokes the responsibility of the people," by whatever steps necessary, to force its agent, the government, into compliance with the law. It is possible that in Justice Brandeis' day he was correct, but that was a simpler time and the government had not loosed the chains that the Constitution bound it down with. Unfortunately the federal judiciary has opted out of the separation of powers requirement of the Constitution and now has become self-regulating. It has not worked and it never will.

The courts do not maintain their independence as a judiciary. The system elevates judges above the law. Our courts are no longer courts of justice or a bastion of freedom. They became the Executive's tools with the passage of the War Powers Act of 1933. The judges are little more than organized crime families who have invaded the people's court and now only impersonate judges and give lip service to justice by exchanging obfuscation and sophistry in place of a justice system, void of any form of judicial integrity. Enforcing judicial standards on judges under this system is impossible. Even though the court has rules, the judges make up their own rules as they go or break the rules with impunity whenever it is convenient for them to do so. There is much ado about trying alleged terrorists in a Military Tribunal or a Civil Court system. I can assure you that today's federal court is in fact a military tribunal (Admiralty) and the way or method the "terrorists" will be treated is substantially the same in both venues. In fact they probably have more due process than we do because of media scrutiny.

Our patience and tolerance as the body politic of America for those who pervert the fundamentally necessary and basic foundations of society has been pushed to insufferable levels. These acts have fundamentally changed the form and substance of the guaranteed republican form of government envisioned by the framers of the Constitution. These individuals and organizations have exhibited a willful and wanton disregard for the rights, safety and property of others.

They have evinced a despotic design to reduce the American people to slavery, peonage, and involuntary servitude, under a fraudulent, tyrannical, seditious foreign oligarchy, whose intent and purpose is to institute, erect, and form a dictatorship over the Citizens and our posterity.

When the founding fathers of our Republic decided to sever their relationship with the English Crown, they felt it important that the world community of nations understand the reasons for their declaration of independence. If we were to list our reasons today, they would be very similar to those of our forefathers.

Statement of Grievances

They have completely debauched the lawful monetary system, destroyed the livelihood and lives of thousands, aided and abetted our enemies by trading atomic secrets for campaign contributions, declared war upon us and our posterity, destroyed untold families and embraced the destruction of our unborn through legalized abortion. They have afflicted widows and orphans; peopled sodomites loose among our young and in public office; and implemented foreign laws, rules, regulations, and procedures by the treaties of the United Nations, North American Free Trade Agreement and General Agreement on Trade and Tariff, within the body of the country. They have incited insurrection of the races, rebellion, sedition, and anarchy within the de jure society; illegally entered our land; taken false oaths; entered into seditious foreign constitutions, agreements, confederations, and alliances, all under pretense of "emergency" which they themselves created, promoted; and, further, they have formed a multitude of administrative offices and filled them with those of alien allegiance to execute their frauds and to eat out the sustenance of the good and productive people of this land. They have arbitrarily dismissed charges against or held mock trials for those who trespassed upon our Life, Liberty and Property. They have engineered and profited from drug trafficking, which has had the effect of destabilizing the American family and endangered our Peace, Safety, Welfare, and Dignity as a people. Amendment V of the Constitution for the United States of America (1787), is consistently and arrogantly ignored in one form or another. Numerous High Crimes and misdemeanors have been committed under the Constitution for the United States of America and our Laws made in Pursuance thereof, against the Peace and Dignity of the People.

The federal government has become to "We the People" of today what the British crown was to our forefathers. The damage, injury and costs have been higher than mere money can ever repay. They have done what they were commanded by the Constitution never to do, and the time for reckoning is fast approaching. The body of evidence is overwhelming to support any criminal indictment if we had control of our courts and certainly sufficient as cause for revolution.

"That whenever any Form of Government becomes destructive of these ends, it is the Right of the People to alter or to abolish it, and to institute new Government, having its foundations on such principles and organizing its powers in such form, as to them shall most likely to effect their Safety and Happiness." – Declaration of Independence, 1776

My hope is that you now understand the gravity of our present situation as a Nation. We are in deep trouble, and the only way out is to fight this "New World Order." We must not support those in favor of its creation. We must fight their laws in court whenever we see evidence that it is rearing its ugly head and as a last resort, if the Courts are so corrupted, in the streets.

If we permit these stooges of the internationalists, like senators Schumer and Clinton of New York, to ban guns in this country, then what happened in Nazi Germany and most recently in Kosovo will surely happen in America. The fact that there exist over 200 million guns in this country scares the daylight out of them. The only gun control we need is to hit what we shoot at, and I think I have illuminated for you a target-rich environment. We, as the guardians of our Republic, must in very short order take back from this de facto government our Court of Common Law by the creation of jural societies. The balance of our freedoms will follow once we again control the courts and justice is available to us all without purchase. If we cannot achieve our freedom by the rule of law, then the alternative is force of arms. That is the way it has always been. I prefer the rule of law, but what will be, will be.

CHAPTER THIRTEEN

ANOTHER PERSPECTIVE

Recently I reviewed a program in which a different strategy was being used in order to cancel out the legal fiction. It was an interesting concept, but one with which I personally have no experience. Some of what was said, I could subscribe to, but not the entire strategy. Not that it is wrong; rather that I do not have enough knowledge to verify it. This may work, and it may not. I thought it merited the light of day, in order that those who have failed in other attempts or in using different strategies may follow a fresh approach.

I do not endorse this strategy nor do I detract from it; to me the true test will be if it is repeatable each and every time. That is the only true test.

ANOTHER PERSPECTIVE

Beginning in 1933 the federal and state governments switched from common law into Equity/Admiralty, because the country was bankrupt, as we have no more gold.

Being that the sovereign, the natural person with the Christian appellation written in upper and lowercase letters, was distinct and separate from the citizen subject of the government, they had to give the natural person the same benefit or the same privilege or right on the other side in equity as given to legal fictions. And that person was described in statute as a non-resident alien, someone who is not subject to the jurisdiction.

These are terms out of *Black's Law Dictionary*. So when the person reads the law, he must read it in terms of *Black's* or another law dictionary and not in terms of *Webster's*, because the words mean something totally different.

The legal fiction is the person whose name is spelled in all capital letters, and that person is described as a vessel of the United States. You will locate that in the *United States Government Printing Office Style Manual*, available in most law libraries. In section 11.7 of the *Manual*, it says, "Names of vessels are quoted in matters printed in other than lowercase roman." It examples a vessel written in all capital letters.

A vessel of the United States has been defined in Title 18, §9:

Vessels of the United States defined.

"The term vessel of the United States as used in this title means a vessel belonging in whole or in part to the United States or any citizen thereof or any corporation created by or under the laws of the United States or any State or Territory or district or possession."

Insurance, which is social security, is under admiralty law jurisdiction.

Benedict on Admiralty, Admiralty Law, Title 22 - Foreign Relations, Sub-chapter I, Shipping and Seamen, Part 81 - General, 22 C.F.R. A7 81.1, Definitions.

"(b) 'American vessel' means any United States-owned vessel, which is not registered under the laws of a foreign government, vessels of the United States, and American undocumented vessels.

(c) 'American public vessel' means any vessel owned or operated by a United States Government department or agency and engaged exclusively in official business on a non-commercial basis.

(d) 'Vessel of the United States' means any vessel documented under the laws of the United States.

(e) 'American undocumented vessel' means any American vessel, other than an American public vessel, which is not documented under the laws of the United States... .

(f) 'Foreign vessel' means any foreign-owned vessel, or any vessel regardless of ownership, which is documented under the laws of a foreign country.

(i) 'Seaman' means any person employed as a member of the crew of a vessel.

(k) 'Alien seaman' means a seaman of foreign nationality who does not have status as an American seaman."

22 C.F.R. A7 81.3, Status of Vessels of the United States. Vessels documented under the laws of the United States are entitled to privileges and subject to the obligations prescribed by the laws of the United States for merchant vessels. The type of privileges and obligations appertaining to such vessels depends upon the form and the purpose of their documentation.

22 C.F.R. A7 81.4, Status of American Undocumented Vessels. American undocumented vessels are not under the jurisdiction of the United States, and consequently are not subject to the obligations nor entitled to the protection accorded vessels of the United States abroad. However, such vessels are entitled to the same degree of protection accorded any other property abroad owned by United States citizens.

This typically describes a vessel that is registered, enrolled or licensed. So anyone who is licensed, or registered, is considered a vessel, belonging in whole or in part to the United States. All would be under Admiralty Jurisdiction.

When a person signs up for social security, he is creating a vessel in all capital letters. When you walk into the social security office, you have to have a birth certificate.

The *History and System of the Common Law* states in pertinent part regarding persons:

"In law, PERSONALITY means capacity of having, acquiring and exercising rights, using the term in its widest sense. A legal person is an entity having interests which the law recognizes and secures, or, as it is commonly put, a subject of rights. The type is the individual human being as a natural person and in modern law every human being as a natural person has also a legal personality.

"A Juristic personality begins when the legal requirements for recognition of a group of associates as a legal person have been fulfilled, and the law in consequence clothes the association with the capacity of exercising a legal control over or influence upon the acts of others. Natural personality, the legal personality of the individual human being, begins upon birth and survival of birth."

When you get your birth certificate that is when the person with the three names comes into existence; that is your remedy in equity.

If a person were to put all of his property under the name on the birth certificate, that is written in upper and lowercase letters, that person's property would be protected and, if he doesn't use a social security number, he and his property will be protected from the government, because that is considered in law as a foreign situs trust.

In *Black's*, under "trust," a subsection describes "foreign situs trust" as: "A trust which owes its existence to foreign law. It is treated for tax purposes as a non-resident alien individual."

Many of us in this movement have heard that expression. But what we didn't know is that it is a trust, because all of equity is a trust.

Two types of birth certificates are issued. One is titled a "Certificate of Live Birth." It has the name written in upper and lowercase letters. Another is titled a "Certification of Vital Records." It is written in all upper case letters. So when babies are born and get social security numbers, they very seldom get Certificates of Live Birth, they get Certifications of Vital Records, and the person identified on it in all capital letters is considered a vessel of the United States owned in whole or in part by the United States. That is the Juristic Personality or legal fiction created by the government.

The 14th Amendment to the Constitution for the United States created the status of "person." There are two constitutions. One is based upon law, and one is based on equity. They re-wrote the Constitution shortly after the Civil War, creating our constitution under equity.

There are many who go around arguing that a lot of the laws of the United States are unconstitutional; however, that is patriot mythology.

Constitution, Article III, section 2, says:

"The judicial powers shall extend to all cases in law and equity arising under this Constitution, the laws of the United States and the treaties made or which shall be made under their authority, to all cases affecting ambassadors, other public ministers and consuls, to all cases of admiralty and maritime jurisdiction."

The social security is under admiralty law, so that is constitutional. Equity is constitutional as well. They can operate in equity, and equity is voluntary and by contract.

The following explains the agency relationship that we have with all these government agencies. It says they are all contractual.

3 American Jurisprudence 2d, under agency, section one.

"The term 'agency' means a fiduciary relationship by which a party confides to another the management of some business to be transacted in the former name or on his account, and by which such other assumes to do the business and render an account of it. It has also been defined as a fiduciary relationship, which results from the manifestation of consent by one person to another that the other shall act on his behalf and subject to his control and consent by the other so to act. Thus the term agency in its legal sense always imports commercial or contractual dealings between two parties by and through a medium of another."

Hence, the commerce clause has been used in regulating peoples' activities, since all these arrangements of agency are contractual or commercial in nature.

The 14th amendment refers to a person being born subject to the jurisdiction. When you look up the word "born" you will find that it describes "delivery" – when the res is transferred constructively over to another party (the "res" meaning the thing or the person, the property or future rights to property).

We are looking at some very fundamental relationships in the law which are crucial to our understanding if we want to be free, and you are convinced that the law still embodies freedom and that it can still be exercised. I guess that remains to be seen.

The problem remains that, if you don't know your proper status or rights, you don't have any. When legislative bodies pass a statute, they always must create a remedy to that statute in law, because this is still a free country.

Don't worry too much about the laws that are being passed; just concern yourself with the remedy because the majority of the laws being passed pertain to persons or entities *in personam*. It doesn't refer to the natural person. You will discover that *in personam* is always in capital letters, and that is the way they always invite you – your name written in all capital letters. You will see that on your driver's license, your credit cards, when you do business with corporations, and in any court actions.

Patriot mythology says that if you cross the bar in the courtroom you granted jurisdiction. You actually granted jurisdiction when you signed up for social security. That is when *you changed your name.* Trust law states that whenever title is transferred, a trust is created by operation of law, or whenever money is transferred, it is the operation of law. A trust is automatically created. That is stated in Am. Jur. under trusts.

The 13th amendment states, "...neither slavery nor involuntary servitude...." Those are prohibitions; there is no option. It says nothing regarding *voluntary* servitude: that is your choice. If you contract to be in voluntary servitude, that is your choice.

Then the 14th amendment, following immediately on the tail of the 13th amendment, reads – "...born or naturalized and subject to the jurisdiction..."

When you fill out forms, they always ask if you are a citizen of the United States and subject to the jurisdiction thereof. Jurisdiction is the modern word for allegiance, which is a feudal term meaning relationship to the land or the liege.

So are you subject to the jurisdiction of the United States as a citizen of the United States and of the state in which you reside?

The term "residence in a state" is not citizenship of a state. It is something less, usually commercial in nature. So on government applications, job applications, etc., they ask if you are a U.S. citizen and they ask for a residence address.

The combination of being a citizen of the United States and a resident in a state means you are volunteering to be treated as though you are a second-class citizen – property of the United States.

When the term "United States" is used in the US Code, it usually refers to territories and possessions such as Guam, Puerto Rico, etc. "Citizen of the United States" is defined in the Code as being someone from Guam, American Samoa, and the Virgin Islands. You can find that at 20 CFR Section 404.1004, Part 4, "Citizens of the United States includes citizens of the Commonwealth of Puerto Rico, Virgin Islands, Guam and American Samoa."

When one person delivers money to another for a specific purpose, the transaction becomes a trust. So it is axiomatic that whenever title is transferred, a trust is automatically created. It is by operation of law, and it is an express trust because you went requesting to have it done. You walked in with your birth certificate, the one in upper and lowercase letters and you transferred title, and from then on you were known, not as the named person on the birth certificate, but as the person in all capital letters.

That "person" comes into existence with signing the SS-5 application for the social security account which states, "Your card will show your full middle and last name unless you show otherwise." So however you write it on the application – if you use three names, two names or initial – that is the way it will show on your card in all capital letters. So now you have asked the government to step in and take a fiduciary responsibility over the property of the trust. The property of the trust is you.

You will find in 26 CFR, §301.7701-6, Definitions, Persons, Fiduciary.

You are the corpus of the trust that you created by the signing of the SS-5 application, and you authorized the government to be the Trustee of the Trust. That is why when people go into court, they can not understand why they are not being treated as a sovereign citizen in common law under an Article III court and they do not get any justice – because they are in *equity*, not in *law*, and *they* are the property that is being administered.

26 CFR, section 301.7701-6, Definitions, Persons, Fiduciary. Fiduciary distinguished from an agent. There may be a fiduciary relationship between an agent and a principal ...

The principal is the person who walks in and signs up with the government. The agent or the representative is the IRS, so forth.

But the word "agent" does not denote a fiduciary. An agent having an entire charge of property with authority to effect and execute leases and tenants ...

Remember, we are *tenants* on our own property and we are leasing it.

Entirely on his own responsibility and without consulting the principal (you), merely turning over the net proceeds from the property periodically to the principal by virtue of the authority conferred upon him by a power of attorney.

People need to realize the power of attorney is the 1040 form.

26 CFR §601.503 gives the description of a power of attorney:

"Requirements of a Power of Attorney, Signatures, Fiduciary's and Commissioner's authority to substitute other requirements."

This describes what a power of attorney consists of. The 1040 fits the description. It has everything the power of attorney must have; that is where we gave them the power of attorney.

One of the reasons we can not get any remedy is because we do not address the issue of the power of attorney. Where others have revoked it, they have not done it on the proper form. The Paper Reduction Act states you have to use their form when a remedy is provided.

The United States District Court is not a true United States court established under Article III of the constitution to administer the judicial powers of the United States therein conferred. It is created by virtue of the sovereign congressional faculty granted under Article IV, § 3, of that compact. *Balzac v. Porto Rico*, 258 US. 298.

That is the reason people do not get justice; they are in the wrong court. The proper court to go into is the "district court of the United States," small "d," small "c," and that is the law side of the court. However, to get into that court your status must be correct.

26 CFR 1.676A-1, Power to re-vest title to portions of the trust property in grantor; general rule. If a power to re-vest in the grantor title to any portion of a trust is exercisable by the grantor or non-adverse party or both, without the approval or consent of an adverse party ...

That is the government. So you have the power to revoke the power of attorney and re-vest and to terminate. You must do this on a government form.

Summary

The name in all capital letters, however it is written, is the vessel of the United States, and that is the trust. That is created where the government owns that in part and you own part of it. What they always come after is their part. That puts you in a fiduciary relationship for their part of this trust.

Your first and last name is written in upper and lowercase letters, the way a proper noun is supposed to be written. That consists of two names. You will find that under "name" in *Black's Law Dictionary*, 6th Edition, page1023.

The name on the birth certificate with the three names written in upper and lowercase letters is the foreign situs trust because equity deals only with trusts. Trusts came out of equity. You do not put periods, comas, colons, semi-colons or anything else, because every time you do something like that, it is not the way it is written on the original birth certificate you change the meaning of it. That is what they mean by title or appellation. Whenever you do something that is distinctive and different, you change the meaning of it.

The next name is the name written in upper and lowercase letters with an initial. That person comes into being on the W-4 form. The W-4 form says, "Write your first name, middle initial and last name." That is the trustee who turns over the res to the federal government, because a trust is created whenever property or money or title is transferred, and that is automatic.

There is another name, which is a corporate name, but we are not dealing with corporations. You can have a corporation named after yourself, and that is a separate entity, too. That is in all capital letters. Most corporations are vessels of the United States, and that is why whenever you see "in personam," in personam is contractual, and the contract that got you into this was the SS-5 SSA application.

Statutes at Large, Volume 48, 73rd Congress, Session 2, Chapter 756, June 26, 1934. Under that section you will find that the trust is called #62

Puerto Rico Special Fund Internal Revenue. So Title 26 contains the laws of the trust. In fact, all the titles are the laws of the trust.

"The funds appearing on the books of the government and listed in subsection (b) and (c) of this section, shall be classified on the books of the Treasury as trust funds. All monies accruing to these funds are hereby appropriated and shall be disbursed in compliance with the terms of the trust. Hereafter, monies received by the government as trustee analogous to these funds named in section (b) and (c) of this section and not otherwise herein provided for ..."

It gives the names of quite a few of the trusts, and #62 is the Puerto Rican Trust.

Another section people want to look at is Title 31 Money and Finance, sub-chapter 2, Administrative, §321, General Authority of the Secretary, and #2 under that says:

"For the purposes of the federal income, estate, and gift taxes, property accepted under paragraph 1 shall be considered as a gift or bequest to or for the use of the United States."

So all the monies that are given to the United States are from the trust and they are gifts, because the trust that is created on the social security account is a charitable trust, and the government is not taxing the individual; they are taxing the trust because they cannot tax the flesh and blood person without apportionment. So they are obeying the law, but we don't know what the law says.

Legal name. Under common law, consists of one Christian name and one surname, and the insertion, omission, or mistake in middle name or initial is immaterial. The legal name of an individual consists of a given or baptismal name usually assumed at birth and a surname deriving from the common name of the parents. – *Black's Law Dictionary* on page 896.

A person who is the nonresident alien, or the person who is neither a citizen nor resident of the United States, sui juris, is the Christian appellation or the legal name (legal as opposed to equity).

The reason why I believe that is because it is that individual who is not under a legal incapacity. The common law person is sui juris, outside of equity, so he is the only one that can do this procedure. Another thing is the address must be written in a foreign address because it is the law of domicile which determines what laws are going to be applicable.

Most people, unfortunately, don't know how they were born subject to the jurisdiction of the federal government. Look up "born" in the dictionary. We are thinking in terms of *Webster's Dictionary*, not in terms of the legal definitions, which mean something totally different. When you look up "born," you find the word "deliver." When you look up "delivery," it is when the res of your trust, the birth certificate (written in upper and lowercase letters, not the one that is now in capital letters on the bank paper), is transferred constructively to the Federal government.

In *Am Jur*, under "trust," it says that whenever title or property is transferred, a trust is automatically created by operation of law, regardless of the intent of the parties. So, when you applied for a Social Security Card and signed an SS-5 application with your birth certificate in upper and lowercase letters, you transferred title, you created this new entity in all capital letters, the Straw Man, Juristic Personality or legal fiction.

The proper designation in law for the straw man is found in *Black's Law Dictionary*, 6th Ed., on page 1142, definitions of "persons." To understand this even further, *Black's* uses the word "entity." When you look up "entity," it is defined on page 532 as "a real being, existence, an organization or being that possesses separate existence for tax purposes." So they got you to create this separate being, this so-called straw man, person, entity, corporation, trust, partnership, whatever, so they could tax that. That is the entity they are taxing because they have no legal authority to tax the individual. The 16th Amendment gave them no new authority to tax anybody.

The law says that when you do this, you are responsible for that vessel or entity – the legal fiction. As an example, if you own a car, that is considered in their law to be a vessel. That is because they brought the admiralty law on shore so the government could get jurisdiction, because the government is in admiralty jurisdiction. So if you have a car and it slips out of gear and hits another car, they are not going to drag the vessel in, which is in all capital letters; they are going to drag you in because you are responsible for that and you own it.

Some people seem to think we do not own this thing, and we do own it. The government owns it only constructively, not actually.

Title 26 U.S.C. 676(a), A grantor [that's the guy who created this trust] shall be treated as the owner of any portion of a trust, whether or not he is treated as such owner under any other provision of this part, where, at any time, the power to re-vest in the grantor title to such portion is exercisable by the grantor or non-adverse party, or both.

So the law says you have the power to change this situation and to revoke that situation at any time.

National Law Library, Volume IV, Business Law, by Nathan Isaac, talks about the different kinds of law that must be dealt with: contract, agency, corporation, and trusteeship. One not mentioned here is admiralty, which is insurance. That is where the Social Security comes in that puts us in admiralty. It says each one of those things must be dealt with, if you have contracts, on each level.

There is an agency relationship. If you look up "agency" in *Black's* you'll find that you hired the IRS to handle this account for you, and it is a power of attorney. If you do not revoke the power of attorney, then the attorney can come around your back and undo everything you have done.

Rocky Mountain News, November 13, 1995, in Colorado:

"The power of attorney should not be given to another person lightly. It depends on the scope of the document. ... If it is financial [the power of attorney], it can give the agent [the person who gets the power of attorney] the ability to rob you blind."

And that is what these guys are doing to us: they are robbing us blind.

Many patriots seem to be under the impression that you revoke the signature, but that is not correct. You revoke the instrument.

The UCC covers only two things: orders to pay and promises to pay. Murder does not come under that. It has been said that commerce is defined in Title 27 and that all crimes are commercial. That may be, but they are commercial because they are admiralty. What puts you in admiralty is the insurance program of social security. Insurance is under admiralty law. That is what gets us into commercial activity with the government, across state lines. All the crimes in Title 27 are under admiralty law because there are no common law crimes in the federal jurisdiction, so they all must be commercial. That is why they are commercial crimes, and what puts you in that jurisdiction is the contract.

20 CFR 404.1004, part 3, American vessel means a vessel documented or numbered under the laws of the United States.

So that is what a vessel is. Remember, the vessel is the straw man. You will see that in the *Government Style Manual* (which you can get when you go to a law library, usually at the reference desk) which will tell you what a vessel of the United States is. On Benedict on Admiralty, and I already quoted where that is found, it says:

Status of vessels of the United States. Vessels documented under the laws of the United States are entitled to privileges and subject to the obligations described by the laws of the United States for merchant vessels.

Section 81.4 under Regulations, Appendix B-13, Status of American undocumented vessels. American undocumented vessels are not under the jurisdiction of the United States and, consequently, are not subject to the obligations nor entitled to protections.

Here it is saying it is the documentation that gets you in trouble. Then if you want to find out what the number does, you go to section 783.41, which talks about the number of the vessels, and it says you are required to have a number if you are going to operate in admiralty waters, which is on their highways and their business and contracts – that it is not the number that gets you in trouble; it is the documentation.

Oddly enough, the government has a form to cancel the documentation or the SS-5 application. They think it is very important to cancel the application. It says nothing about the number. When you apply for Social Security, it does not say on the SS-5 that you are applying for a number; it says you are applying for a card, or the documentation..

So unless you get rid of the documentation, and there is a form to do that (however, it must be done in the correct way), then you are subject to the obligations. And if anyone wants to see what the documentation is, they even define what documentation is, and here it is. You will find it in the same thing, Benedict on Admiralty, section 783.41: "Numbered vessels." And in it, it says it is not the number that does you in; you need a number to operate in admiralty.

So the straw man is a person, corporation, trust, and all those things, which are considered vessels or entities – real beings possessing separate existence for tax purposes. And you create that entity when you sign up for Social Security. That is when you created the straw man. You created it, they did not, and the law says you created this when you walked in and you transferred title. Another thing about the document of title: I believe there are two birth certificates. There is the one they give now, which is on the bank note paper. I believe that one you actually transfer title. The previous ones written in upper and lowercase letters are certificates of live birth, versus those new ones you get now, which are documents of title that you still hold, but what it says is you transferred it constructively. When you look up "delivery," it says it is not actual transfer; it is constructive delivery of the trust. It is constructive, not actual, so you still have title. And at all times you have the power to revoke. Oddly enough, there is a law that says you can revoke this fiduciary relationship of principal and agent that you got yourself into.

You now have much of the story of the treason, which has been foisted upon you. It is now up to you.

THE END

EPILOGUE

The primary reason for the existence of any government is the protection of its citizens with all of their alienable rights intact. After the events of September 11, 2001, a Johnny-come-lately federal government now wants to furnish us the protections we should have enjoyed before the tragic reality of the thousands of dead in New York, Pennsylvania and Washington, D.C.

I have some concern with regard to the plane that crashed into the Pentagon. During my stint as a pilot, I must say I was rather hard on military equipment. After several crashes (none of which were my fault, mind you), I can say that I have some experience in reviewing a crash site for evidence of the event. In reviewing hundreds of photos of the scene, I could not locate any of the fuselage, wings, tail section or landing gear of the doomed aircraft. I know there was a fire, but there is always a fire at crash sites and still there are remnants of the aircraft, but not this time. Strange.

The Congress was quick to grant the President sweeping power in his war against Terrorists around the world via their overwhelming adoption of the "Patriot Act." If the provisions contained within the act were applied only against aliens suspected of terrorist activity in this country, then there *might* be some justification for some of the incomprehensible authority now permitted law enforcement. That act can and will most likely be used by all agencies of government to invade all citizens' constitutional protections, not just foreign terrorists. Anyone who dares to exercise the 1st Amendment right of free speech in speaking out against government policy can be denigrated by the government and labeled a terrorist. If you seek privacy protection in the form of a trust, you can be labeled a terrorist hiding his money. Any attempt to question the fairness of a tax can get you labeled a terrorist. That is the way it has always worked in fascist societies; ours is no exception.

The Constitution for the United States has been a dead letter ever since the 1933 passage of the War Powers Act. But the federal beast has permitted its use by defendants in court when it suited their purpose; it is otherwise optional to them. Now, however, even the pretense of constitutional protection is lost under the Patriot Act. Telephones can now be monitored, homes can be searched and property seized, all without a warrant or without judicial inquiry. The definitions of "terrorist" are left up to the Attorney General, the President, or the corner cop on the beat.

When, not *if*, there is another catastrophic event, be it terrorist-related, economic, or manufactured by the government, the President will impose a national emergency and Martial Law will be imposed on us all. All of the Executive Orders beginning with Jimmy Carter will be put into motion; the Federal Emergency Management Agency (FEMA) will be, in-fact, the rulers of this country, and we will all obey their every command or we will be either imprisoned or executed.

The newly formed Agency of Homeland Security will assume the role of the Gestapo of WW II in Germany and will undoubtedly employ many of the same tactics. With our military off fighting in all corners of the world, they won't be able to help us if the President declares Martial Law and enforces it with UN troops and Homeland Security personnel. Those soldiers from mostly Eastern European countries hate the United States and our way of life and would not hesitate to put a bullet between the eyes of anyone who does not follow their orders to the letter.

Upon review of some of the Executive Orders already in place, control of food and food processing and its distribution is one that stands out in my mind as the most perplexing. It is a well-known maxim of warfare that if you can deny your enemy food, the battle is won. A hungry soldier or a hungry patriot will do what ever his captor demands if he is promised food. It is amusing to me that there is federal law prohibiting the hoarding of food. It is a felony. I wonder why Congress ever thought a law of that type was needed in a land of bounty where all are free? I will let you ponder that question also.

I will list a few of the Executive Orders already issued which, as public policy have the force and effect of law, so that you can submit Freedom of Information Requests to confirm what I write.

EO 10995 provides for the takeover of the communication media.

EO 10997 provides for the takeover of all electrical power, petroleum, gas, fuels and minerals.

EO 10998 provides for the takeover of all food resources and farms.

EO 10999 provides for the takeover of all modes of transportation, control of highways and seaports.

EO 11000 provides for mobilization of all civilians into work brigades under government supervision.

EO 11001 provides for the takeover of all health, education and welfare functions.

EO 11002 designates the Postmaster General to operate a national registration of all persons.

EO 11003 provides for the takeover of all airports and aircraft.

EO 11004 provides for the housing and finance authority to relocate entire communities, designate areas to be abandoned and establish new locations for populations.

EO 11005 provides for government to take over railroads, inland waterways and public storage facilities.

Richard Nixon in Executive Order 11490 combined all of these listed orders into one neat little package. In that order, FEMA, the "Federal Emergency Management Agency," would be responsible for carrying out all of these orders against the American people.

President Reagan signed EO 12656, further eroding the rights of Americans under guise of a national emergency. Reagan's order defined such an emergency as any occurrence including natural disaster, military attack, technological emergency or OTHER EMERGENCY that seriously degrades or seriously threatens the national security of the United States.

President Clinton signed EO 12919 on June 3, 1994, streamlining the organizational control by his cabinet members and redefining FEMA's role in such a takeover. The EO, as I received it, does not contain the entire Order. The substantive portions of the Act (Sections 700 and 800) have been omitted from the public view. MY inquiry into the missing sections resulted in a refusal as it is considered Top Secret and a National Security interest. These sections outline what may be done to us, WE, THE PEOPLE, if we are in violation of the Order.

Now we have President Bush with a different agenda or another path to the same objective as his father – one world government. This time the excuse given for the nefarious legislation known as the Patriot Act is that the terrorists must be stopped at all costs, even the cost of our liberty. Why does the rest of the World believe that America is wrong in its foreign policy? Is it possible they are right and the reason for the terrorists is that misguided foreign policy?

NOTE

Following are four (4) facsimile section reproductions taken from a 156-page book officially compiled and issued by the U.S. War Department, November 30, 1928, setting forth exact and truthful definitions of a Democracy and of a Republic, explaining the difference between both. These definitions were published by the authority of the United States Government and must be accepted as authentic in any court of proper jurisdiction. The Chief of Staff of the United States Army carefully considered these precise and scholarly definitions of a Democracy and a Republic as a proper guide for U.S. soldiers and U.S. citizens. Such definitions take precedence over any "definition" that may be found in the present commercial dictionaries, which have suffered periodical "modification" to please "the powers in office." Shortly after the "bank holiday" in 1933, hush-hush orders from the White House suddenly demanded that all copies of this book be withdrawn from the Government Printing Office and the Army posts, to be suppressed and destroyed without explanation. This was the beginning of the complete Communist control of the Government from within, not from without.

Prepared under the direction of the Chief of Staff.

Official Definition of DEMOCRACY

Copied from Training Manual No. 2000-25 that was published by the then War Department, Washington, D.C., November 30, 1928.

CITIZENSHIP

This manual supersedes Manual of Citizenship Training. The use of the publication "*The Constitution of the United States,*" by Harry Atwood, is by permission and courtesy of the author.

CITIZENSHIP Democracy:

A government of the masses. Authority derived through mass meeting or any other form of "direct" expression. Results in mobocracy. Attitude toward property is communistic – negating property rights. Attitude toward law is that the will of the majority shall regulate, whether it be based upon deliberation or governed by passion, prejudice, and impulse, without restraint or regard to consequences. Results in demagogism, license, agitation, discontent, anarchy.

CITIZENSHIP Republic:

Authority is derived through the election by the people of public officials best fitted to represent them. Attitude toward law is the administration of justice in accord with fixed principles and established evidence, with a strict regard to consequences. A greater number of citizens and extent of territory may be brought within its compass. Avoids the dangerous extreme of either tyranny or mobocracy. Results in statesmanship, liberty, reason, justice, contentment, and progress. Is the "standard form" of government throughout the World. A republic is a form of government under a Constitution, which provides for the election of:

(1) an executive and (2) a legislative body, who working together in a representative capacity, have all the power of appointment, all power of legislation, all power to raise revenue and appropriate expenditures, and are required to create (3) a judiciary to pass upon the justice and legality of their government acts and to recognize (4) certain inherent individual rights.

Take away any one or more of those four elements and you are drifting into autocracy. Add one or more to those four elements and you are drifting into democracy.

Atwood. Superior to all others. – Autocracy declares the divine right of kings; its authority cannot be questioned; its powers are arbitrarily or unjustly administered. Democracy is the "direct" rule of the people and has been repeatedly tried without success. Our Constitutional fathers, familiar with the strength and weakness of both autocracy and democracy, with fixed principles definitely in mind, defined a representative republican form of government. They made a very marked distinction between a republic and a democracy and said repeatedly and emphatically that they had founded a republic.

By order of the Secretary of War: C.P. Summerall, Major General, Chief of Staff. Official: Lutz Wahl, Major General, The Adjutant General.

WHY DEMOCRACIES FAIL

A Democracy cannot exist as a permanent form of Government. It can exist only until the voters discover they can vote themselves largess out of the public treasury. From that moment on the majority always votes for the candidate promising the most benefits from the public treasury with the result that Democracy always collapses over a loose fiscal policy, always to be followed by a Dictatorship.(Written by Professor Alexander Fraser Tytler, nearly two centuries ago while our thirteen original states were still colonies of Great Britain. At the time he was writing of the decline and fall of the Athenian Republic over two thousand years before.)

"Did I say 'republic'? By God, yes, I said 'republic'! Long live the glorious republic of the United States of America. Damn democracy. It is a fraudulent term used, often by ignorant persons but no less often by intellectual fakers, to describe an infamous mixture of socialism, miscegenation, graft, confiscation of property and denial of personal rights to individuals whose virtuous principles make them offensive."

Westbrook Pegler: *New York Journal American*, January 25th and 26th, 1951, under the titles – Upholds Republic of U.S. Against Phony Democracy, Democracy in the U.S. Branded Meaningless.

"This idea that government was beholden to the people, that it had no other source of power is still the newest, most unique idea in all the long history of man's relation to man. This is the issue of this election: Whether we believe in our capacity for self-government or whether we abandon the American Revolution and confess that a little intellectual elite in a far-distant capital can plan our lives for us better than we can plan them ourselves." (Ronald Reagan's Speech at the 1964 National Convention: *A Time for Choosing*).

It would appear that we do indeed have a Democracy and not the Republic, which was guaranteed by the organic Constitution. We, as the collective Sovereign of the United States of America, are responsible for the present day state of affairs. For several generations we were not attentive to those whom we elected to public office. Now is the time in which we, with extreme urgency, must all consolidate our displeasure with events and demand in the strongest terms possible under the Rule of Law that this country be returned to us and taken out of Bankruptcy – that the fiat money scheme of the Federal Reserve be abolished and the country returned to the republican form of government with the constitutional monetary system and common law as is mandated by the Constitution for the United States. If we do not, then history will note our shameful ignorance and deplore our very existence.

All United States Presidents after Andrew Jackson to the present, in my opinion, were supporters of a one-world socialist government. They have answered to their master, the International Bankers and owners of the Federal Reserve, not the American people.

As the citizens of this country continue to suffer unemployment, a result of the NAFTA and GATT treaties; economic weakness, a result of the monetary policy of the Federal Reserve Bank, Inc.; and a deprivation of their personal liberty, a result of the government's alleged war on drugs and terrorism, the ultimate battle for freedom or slavery will soon begin. If it is not fought by our generation, then our children or grandchildren will wage it and it will be more costly than we can imagine for them, but as all of human History reveals, the battle will be fought and fought soon.

If I have induced you into thought about our present circumstance as a nation, then that is all I can ask. I have done my job. Now it is time for you to do yours.

- Melvin Stamper, JD. Sui juris

(Endnotes)

a United States v. Cruikshank, 92 U.S. 588, 540 (1875)

b Enright v. U.S., D.C.N.Y., 437 F.Supp 580, 581

c (Public Law 94-564, Page 5942, U.S. Government Manual 1990-91, pages 480 and 481, 26 U.S.C.A. 7701(a)(II), Treasury Delegation Order No. 150-10),

d (22 U.S.C.A. §286 and 286a)

e (22 U.S.C.A. §611(c)(ii)

f (22 U.S.C.A. §611 (c) (iii)

g (22 U.S.C.A. §611(c)(2))

h (22 U.S.C.A. §263(a), The United States Government Manual, 1990-91, page 385.

i 26 USC 1321(e)(I)(2)

j U.S. Ohio, 324 U.S. 652, 65 S.Ct. 870,880, 89 L.Ed. 1252.

k 182 U.S. 1

l 182 U.S. 244

m 258 U.S. 298

n Tax Commissioner of Ohio, 324 U.S. 652

o 240 U.S. 1.

p 2nd Session, as recorded in the Statutes At Large, December 5, 1859 to March 3, 1863 at Chapter CXX, page 489.

q [Fowler v. Chillingworth, 113 So. 667, 669 (1927)]

r [United States v. Cruikshank, 92 U.S. 588, 540 (1875)]

s [Enright v. U.S., D.C.N.Y., 437 F.Supp 580, 581]

t 26 C.F.R. 1.911-2(g))

u T.D. 2313, 26 C.F.R. 871, and 26 U.S.C. 1461

v 26 C.F.R. 1.911-2(h)

w 26 C.F.R. 871-5, 6 and 12 and 1.932-1

x 26 U.S.C. 911(a)(1)
y 26 C.F.R. 1.932-1(b), IRS Form 2555
z 26 C.F.R. 1.871-71(d)(2)
aa Title 26 U.S.C. 3121(e) (1)
ab Title 26 U.S.C. 7701(a) (9)
ac Omnibus Acts at 86th Congress, 1st Session, Volume 73, 1959, and 2nd Session, Volume 74, 1960, Public Laws 86-70 and 86-624.
ad 22. cf. 1 USCS 1, "Other Provisions"

ae Blacks Law Dictionary, Sixth Edition, page 863

af 28 U.S.C. §1746
ag 6 U.S. 445, 1 Cranch 445, 2 L.Ed 332
ah inclusio unius est exclusio alterius
ai Form 668-A Notice of Levy.
aj 26 U.S.C., § 911(b) and 911(d)(2)
ak IRS Form 2555
al 26 C.F.R. 1.911-2(h)

am 288 F.2d 504 (2nd Circuit, 1961)
an 26 U.S.C. §7421
ao National Foundry Co. of N.Y. v. Director of Int. Rev., 2nd Cir. 1956, 229 F.2d 149, 151.

ap 26 C.F.R. §1.871-8
aq 26 U.S.C. 6020(b)(1)
ar Treasury Decision 2313 and 26 C.F.R. 1.1461-3

Printed in Dunstable, United Kingdom

84078002R00163